NATIVE AMERICAN
College & Career Success

Marsha Fralick ■ Beatrice Zamora ■ Larry Gauthier

Kendall Hunt
publishing company

Book Team

Chairman and Chief Executive Officer   Mark C. Falb
President and Chief Operating Officer   Chad M. Chandlee
Vice President, Higher Education   David L. Tart
Director of Publishing Partnerships   Paul B. Carty
Product/Development Supervisor   Lynne Rogers
Vice President, Operations   Timothy J. Beitzel
Senior Publishing Specialist   Noelle Henneman
Permissions Editor   Caroline Kieler
Cover Designer   Suzanne Millius

Cover art © Rudy Dawahoya, Jr. Back cover headshot of Marsha Fralick used with permission. © Shutterfly, LLC. Back cover headshot of Beatrice Zamora courtesy of Beatrice Zamora. Back cover headshot of Larry Gauthier courtesy of Larry Gauthier.
Rudy is from the Indigenous Nations of the Hopi, Akimel O'Odham, and Tohono O'Odham in Arizona. He is from the Coyote and Snake Clans from the villages of Paaqavi (Hopi) and Schuk Shudag or Blackwater (Akimel.)
"Desert Emotions" reflects the scenery around me and the many colors of the day that present itself. The Velvet Shirt (Navan) Katsina (Hopi) is a beautiful representation of summer for many Nations. The dances and songs for summer rains, Life, the People, and for growth. The squash blossom O'Odham basket design is like strong rays of hope for a good year. The water designs within the desert remind us to stay strong like a river, for even if it is dry, it still has life and will flow again. The changing weather conditions are like an emotional roller coaster, like the deserts where I grew up.

Kendall Hunt
publishing company
www.kendallhunt.com
Send all inquiries to:
4050 Westmark Drive
Dubuque, IA 52004-1840

Copyright © 2012, 2017, 2021 by Kendall Hunt Publishing Company

PAK ISBN: 978-1-7924-7534-4
Text alone ISBN: 978-1-7924-7535-1

Published in the United States of America

CONTENTS

4   **The Moon Will Smile at Your
    Courage: Managing Time and
    Money 103**

Growing up outside Santa Fe, New Mexico, near several Native American reservations, I had the opportunity to learn about Native American culture and attend school with many Native American students. I was one of the few students in my high school who attended college. I have always wondered why this happened. The National Center on Education Statistics reports that only 1% of college students are Native Americans. Only 3% of Native American students will receive a bachelor's degree.

After working for 35 years as a college counselor and professor at Cuyamaca College in El Cajon, California, I came to realize that success in education begins with a positive self-concept. Students need confidence in their abilities and have a vision of what their life can be in the future. For Native students, positive self-concept includes pride in their cultural background. Sadly our educational system has focused on assimilation rather than an appreciation of Native culture, which has resulted in a diminished self-concept for many students and their consequent lack of success in high school and college. It is fortunate that there is a rebirth of the interest in Native culture and appreciation for students of diverse cultural backgrounds.

After many years teaching students to be successful in college and writing a textbook on this topic, *College and Career Success*, I began to think about writing a textbook that incorporated Native and Indigenous cultures. I was encouraged to begin working on this project by the faculty at Navajo Technical College in Crownpoint, New Mexico who were using my textbook, but thought it could be improved by incorporating cultural content. I began to search for Native American coauthors who could share their expertise in this area and add cultural content to college success materials that have been successful with the general population of students across the country.

My two coauthors, Beatrice Zamora from Southwestern Community College in Chula Vista, California, and Larry Gauthier from the Southern Alberta Institute of Technology in Canada have shared their knowledge of Native American and Indigenous cultures for this edition. We have attempted to include materials that would be useful to both Native Americans in the United States and the Indigenous peoples of Canada. In the United States, the terms Native American and Alaskan Native are used. In Canada, Indigenous refers to all Native people of Canada including First Nations, Aboriginal, Metis, and Inuit. Although "Indian" is still used by older tribal members, we are using the more preferred terms above.

The added Native content in this edition includes stories and interviews from the elders, talking circle activities, history, culture, and quotes from famous Native American and Indigenous Chiefs. Chapters include a section titled "Stories from the Elders," which help students to connect universal themes in Native American cultures to learning. Stories from the Elders include contributions from tribes in Canada, the United States, and Mexico. Since various tribal stories are shared, they also bridge commonalities across cultures. The Talking Circle activities provide discussion questions that help students relate their traditional stories to success in college.

Chapter 1, The Spirit Essence of All We Do: Cultural Identity and Success, contains an overview of the history of Native American and Indigenous cultures and educational practices from colonial times to the present day. It helps students to understand their history and increase appreciation for their culture as a foundation for their future success. It provides suggestions for transitioning to college and overcoming obstacles to success.

Native American College and Career Success is the first textbook of its type to include Native American and Indigenous culture as well as college and career success topics. We anticipate future editions of this textbook, which will incorporate additional cultural information along with examples of successful Native American students who can serve as role models for upcoming students. We look forward to your feedback on the effectiveness of this textbook in improving college success for Native American students.

Includes a Native American and Indigenous Cultural Perspective

The book is based on the premise that education for Native American and Indigenous students begins with a positive self-concept. For these students, positive self-concept includes pride in their cultural background.

Chapters contain a section titled "Stories from the Elders" or "Interviews with the Elders," which help students to connect universal themes in Native cultures to college success. Stories from Canada, the United States, and Mexico bridge commonalities across cultures.

Talking circle topics help students to understand traditional culture and how they can build on this knowledge to improve their success in college, careers, and life.

Chapter 1, The Spirit Essence of All We Do: Cultural Identity and Success, contains an overview of Native American and Canadian Indigenous history of higher education from colonization to the present day. It helps students to understand that taking pride in their culture and appreciating diversity is the foundation for learning. It also helps students in transitioning to college and overcoming common obstacles to their success.

Photos of Native American students are used throughout the text.

Famous quotes from Native American Chiefs and other famous sayings have been included in the margins.

New topics have been added including:

- Health and Wellbeing
- Suggestions for Successful Learning from the Native Perspective
- The Native Concept of Time
- Native Ways of Knowing
- Begin Your Journey with Smudging

A new section, Additional Cultural Material, contains added stories and talking circle questions for discussion.

Career Emphasis

A career emphasis helps students to set goals for the future and complete their education in a timely manner.

Online Career Portfolio

Career exploration helps students to create a positive vision of their future career which provides motivation for completing their educational goals. The career material in the online portfolio helps students to make an informed choice of their college major and career. It includes the TruTalent Personality, Multiple Intelligences, Skills, and Learning assessments. The results are linked to the O*Net database of careers for career exploration. It also includes Indeed.com that helps students to find employment while in college or after graduation.

Includes Concepts from Positive Psychology

Concepts from positive psychology are used to help students:

- discover their personal strengths, interests, and multiple intelligences.
- build on their strengths.
- think positively about themselves and their future.
- clarify what happiness means and work toward attaining happiness in life.

Helps Students Assume Responsibility for Their Own Success

Topics include motivation, positive thinking, locus of control, mindset, future mindedness, hope, belief, persistence, emotional intelligence, and learning positive behavior.

Incorporates the Latest Research in Psychology, Education, and Neuroscience

The suggested strategies in this textbook are all based on current research. The latest research in neuroscience is translated into practical strategies for memory and study skills.

Increasing Math Success

Since math is the gateway to high-paying careers and is a challenging requirement for graduation, this edition has expanded material on how to study math, take math notes, deal with math anxiety, and how to be successful on math tests.

Tools for Student Engagement

- Interactive activities within the text help students to practice the material learned.
- Frequent quizzes and answer keys within the chapters help students with reading comprehension and check understanding of key concepts.
- Journal entries help students think critically and apply what they have learned to their personal lives.
- Individual and group exercises are included at the end of each chapter.

Resources for Faculty and Students at College Success 1

The College Success 1 website at www.collegesuccess1.com has additional materials to accompany this textbook. Student resources include key ideas, Internet links related to each chapter, and Word documents for the journal entries. Resources for faculty include the **Instructor Manual** and **Faculty Resources** for teaching college success courses including over 500 pages of classroom exercises, handouts, video suggestions, Internet links to related material, and much more.

ACKNOWLEDGMENTS

The authors would like to extend their sincere thanks to:

- The Elders of the Woodland Cree for sharing their stories,

- The students at First Nations University, Navajo Technical University, and Connor's State College who shared their photos for this textbook,

- Rebecca Clovis of Connor's State College who shared photographs of her students,

- Daniel Vandever and Mike Dubois, the talented photographers who took the photos of students at Navajo Technical University and First Nations University, respectively,

- Dr. Mario Aguilar, Lecturer at the College of Education at San Diego State University, who reviewed content and added his comments and suggestions,

- Carmen Moffett, Director of Indian Education, Gallup, New Mexico, who also reviewed content and added comments and suggestions for student success.

The artwork for the cover of this textbook is titled "Desert Emotions," created by artist Rudy Dawahoya Jr.

"Desert Emotions" reflects the scenery around me and the many colors of the day that present themselves. The Velvet Shirt (Navan) Katsina (Hopi) is a beautiful representation of summer for many Nations: the dances and songs for summer rains, Life, the People, and for growth. The squash blossom O'Odham basket design is like strong rays of hope for a good year. The water designs within the desert remind us to stay strong like a river, for even if it is dry, it still has life and will flow again. The changing weather conditions are like an emotional roller coaster, like the deserts where I grew up.

© Rudy Dawahoya, Jr.

I am from the Hopi, Akimel O'Odham, and Tohono O'Odham Nations of Arizona. I am of the Coyote and Snake-Lizard Clans from the villages of Blackwater (Gila River) and Paaqavi (Hopi), respectively. I enjoy being a part of my community by actively participating as a Recreation Committee Member and also on the State Elections Board. I love being an artist and expressing my talent through art of all mediums. I pursue my creative work as often as I can when not busy with family, work, or my many hobbies. My side hobbies include exercising and cooking traditional foods. Presently, I work as a clerk for the US Postal Service. I have completed my Associates Degree in Fine Arts from Institute of American Indian Arts (IAIA) in Santa Fe, New Mexico. I look forward to completing my Bachelor of Fine Arts degree from Northern Arizona University in the near future. Within the next five years I plan to attend Arizona State University to complete a master's degree in Fine Arts.

ABOUT THE AUTHORS

Used with permission. © Shutterfly, LLC.

Dr. Marsha Fralick is the author of the textbook, *College and Career Success*, which has been used to improve student success and retention across the country since 2000. This specialized edition includes material from this textbook with added Native American and Indigenous cultural content. Dr. Fralick grew up near Santa Fe, New Mexico, and has always been interested in Native American culture and student success. She believes that education is important because it provides a means for accomplishing a person's dreams. She has 53 years of experience working in a variety of roles in education including Spanish teacher, high school counselor, college counselor, college professor, and administrator. Based on her experience, she believes that a positive self-concept is the foundation for success in education. Students need to think positively, believe in themselves, and then take the steps needed to complete their education.

In 1978, Dr. Fralick began working as a college counselor and started teaching college success courses at Cuyamaca College in El Cajon, California where she was one of the founding faculties of the college. She wrote the curriculum, trained faculty, and developed a college success program that increased student success and retention and became part of the culture of the college. Dr. Fralick also published numerous research articles on student success, retention, and career development. Her program was recognized as an Exemplary Program by the California Community College Board of Governors. Upon her retirement in 2007, she was awarded Professor Emeritus status for her contributions to the development of the college and the student success program at Cuyamaca College. She was also recognized by the students of the college with the Golden Rainbow Award for Outstanding Service to the Students of Cuyamaca College.

Since her retirement, Dr. Fralick continues to work as an author and educational consultant working with faculty across the country to improve their student success programs. Based on her work with students and faculty in the development of student success programs, Dr. Fralick was recognized as the 2011 Outstanding First-Year Student Advocate by the National Resource Center for the First-Year Experience and Students in Transition from the University of South Carolina.

She attended the University of New Mexico and Arizona State University where she completed her bachelor's degree in Spanish and English. After working as a high school Spanish teacher for several years, she returned to school to earn a master's degree in counseling from the University of Redlands in California. She later earned her doctorate degree from the University of Southern California.

Introducing Coauthor: Beatrice Zamora

Source: Beatrice Zamora

In traditional Native cultures, education takes place within the family and community in which the elders teach cultural values through example and storytelling. Beatrice Zamora has collected Native American stories and related the lessons to college success. She has been a college educator for nearly 33 years and has just retired as the Dean of Counseling and Student Services at Southwestern Community College in Chula Vista, California. Currently, she has become an award-winning author with her first children's book, *The Spirit of Chicano Park/El Espíritu del Parque Chicano*, published by Tolteca Press in 2020. Additionally, she worked as a college counselor and teacher working with students from low-income, educationally underprepared backgrounds, and those considered under-represented in higher education. She has a passion for creating equity and helping students to reach for their dreams.

Her ethnic background includes roots in Mexico and the Southwestern United States. Her grandparents were from Guanajuato, Mexico and from New Mexico. One of her grandmothers had some Apache heritage, but she never had the pleasure of meeting her as she passed away before Bea was born. Bea has always had a great appreciation for cultural diversity and has explored her own Indigenous heritage through involvement in the oral tradition known as Chichimeca-Aztec Dance of Mexico. Together with her husband, they teach these dances, songs, regalia making, and ceremonial traditions to youth and families in the San Diego community. With over 41 years of involvement in these traditions, they have developed many close relationships with other Northern tribes throughout California, New Mexico, Arizona, Oklahoma, and Colorado. Their dance circle, Danza Mexicayotl, participates in the Inter-Tribal Ceremonial held in Gallup, New Mexico every summer. Here, they have become family with members of the Hopi, Laguna, Zuni, Apache, Comanche, and Navajo tribal communities.

Bea has a deeply rooted love for Native American Indian traditions and belief systems because they are very similar to those of Mexican Indians. They are all cousins of those original peoples who inhabited the Americas; the barrier of the U.S. border is meaningless in terms of cultural linkages. Her 33 years of leadership and service in the California Community Colleges, coupled with her interest and dedication to Native American cultures, and the joy she experiences from reading and writing all come together in writing this textbook. This project is an expression of her deep belief that every student can reach their full potential. She believes that with just a little support, encouragement, and nurturance anything is possible!

Source: Larry Gauthier

Introducing Coauthor: Larry Gauthier

As a member of the Lac La Ronge Indian Band, Larry was raised in the Woodland Cree traditions and incorporates traditional First Nations value and beliefs systems into student support programs. Larry has spent over 20 years working in student support services and at the senior executive level with Southeast College in Saskatchewan. His passion has always been student retention and success.

During his undergraduate years, Larry became a strong advocate in establishing support for Indigenous students. Because institutions failed to lend support to Indigenous students, he was able to provide them support through the learning community of the Native/Indigenous students association. After completing his bachelor's degree he began working as a student advisor at the University of Alberta.

Building on his experiences as a student, he began developing support programs for Native American/Indigenous students. He worked in the student services area for 10 years before joining the SIFC/First Nations University of Canada as an instructor in the Indian Studies department. Teaching provided more direct experience with the struggles Indigenous students face in the world of academia. Larry quickly realized that with appropriate support, Indigenous students can be successful in postsecondary studies. As a result of this belief, he became a passionate advocate for Indigenous student support services. He was instrumental in establishing the National Aboriginal Student Services Association and has published works related to this area. Currently, Larry teaches college and career success skills for Native students at the Southern Alberta Institute of Technology (SAIT).

CHAPTER 1

The Spirit Essence of All We Do: Cultural Identity and Success

Learning Objectives

Read to answer these key questions:

- What is my cultural identity?

- How is success related to my cultural identity?

- What is the history of higher education for Native American and Indigenous students?

- How has education changed since the 1960's?

- What is the role of family and home in your success?

- What are some obstacles to college and career success?

- How can I overcome these obstacles?

- What personal strengths are related to my culture?

- How can I successfully navigate my own culture and the culture of higher education?

- How can I improve my health and wellbeing?

- What are some tips for learning from the Native perspective?

Welcome to college! Whether you are a first-year student just entering college or are returning to college after a break, we hope that the material in this textbook will be useful and valuable. This textbook is designed to help you succeed in college and accomplish your dreams. This new learning environment will give you the tools to expand your knowledge, broaden your perspective, redefine your future, and gain a better understanding of your personal strengths. Topics include college and career success along with Native perspectives.

This textbook is based on the premise that students are more successful if they take pride in their culture and build on their personal strengths. Most Native peoples believe that there is a spirit essence in all things that we do and in all things in nature. Remembering your spirit essence will help you to connect to your past and your present. This focus will allow you to honor your family and community while also honoring your college education.

Many of you come from traditional communities, others come from urban settings, and you may also be one of the first to attend college in your family. We understand that the college environment can be foreign and will challenge you to use your resources to be successful. This book is dedicated to helping you to do just that!

Celebrate Who You Are

There are many names for the Indigenous peoples of North America depending on where you live. In the United States, the terms Native American, American Indian, and Alaskan Native are used, although Native American is becoming the generally accepted term. In Canada, you may use the terms First Nations, Indigenous, Aboriginal, Metis, or Inuit. The term First Nations refers to a specific group of Indigenous peoples, whereas the term "Indigenous" is being used more often to describe all peoples native to the land now called Canada. You may find in this textbook that the terms Indigenous and First Nations are used. They are being used with no disrespect to any peoples that might prefer another term.

In addition, each nation uses their own term in their own language to describe themselves. For example, Cree use the term Nēhiyawi and the Athabascan use the term DEN-ay/Dene. Some older generations use the term "Indian" to describe themselves, but this term is becoming less acceptable to younger tribal members. However, wherever you call home, our goal is to help you to become a successful college/university student.

All men were made by the same Great Spirit Chief. They are all brothers. The Earth is the mother of all people, and all people should have equal rights upon it.

Chief Joseph, Nez Perce

Journal Entry #1

What name do you use to describe yourself? (Native American, American Indian, Alaskan Native, First Nations, Indigenous, Aboriginal, Metis, Inuit, or other) What is your tribal name? Write at least one sentence about being proud of who you are. Remember that you can be empowered by taking pride in yourself and your community. You may be asked to share this information with other students in your class.

Photo courtesy of First Nations University of Canada.

Getting Started

As you engage in the orientation and intake process of your college, one of the first questions you will be asked is, "What are your educational goals and what is your major area of study?" Many of you will be ready to answer these questions because you have considered your future and feel ready to make a commitment; others are still unsure about your future and which field is of most interest to you. This textbook will help you to explore your career options and select the career that matches your personal strengths.

Some of you have parents, aunties and uncles, or friends that have completed a college degree, while others do not know anyone in their community who has attended college. If you or your family has not attended college, it is even more important to ask for help from counselors or advisors at your college. Asking for help is not a weakness; it shows that you want to be successful.

This new world of higher education opens the door to a diverse and complex world, one that may be very different than your community back home. This new world will present challenges along the way and you will need to figure out how to best navigate through college successfully. There is no right or wrong answer. You are about to embark on your own unique journey. Explore and enjoy your process.

Photo courtesy of Navajo Technical University.

College Success

Most students attend college to make a better life for themselves, their families, and their communities. Unfortunately, neither the United States nor Canada can boast about higher education success and completion rates for Native American and First Nations' students. Both the United States and Canada are striving for improvement and have had increases in completion rates over the past 10–15 years, but improvement is still needed. The National Institute for Native Leadership in Higher Education reports that for every 100 Native American students entering high school, only 60 will finish, about 20 will enter college, and only three will receive a bachelor's degree.[1]

The Postsecondary National Policy Institute provides this data for Native American and Alaskan Native students:[2]

- 19% of 18-24-year-old Native American students are enrolled in college compared to 41% of the overall U.S. population in 2018-19.

- Native American students are more likely to attend public institutions over private institutions.

- 89% of all Native American college students attended a Tribal College/University in the fall of 2018.

- 41% of Native American college students who started college in 2012 graduated within 6 years compared to 62% for all college students.
- In 2019, 25% of Native Americans over the age of 25 had an associate degree or higher, compared to 42% of all those over the age of 25.
- In 2015-16, 90% of Native American students received some type of grant aid, compared with 77% of all students.

The data clearly shows that Native American and Alaskan Native students are not graduating from high school, or completing higher level degrees at the rate of the national average, although some improvement is noted. The data also reflects that the Native American and Alaskan Native populations are younger than the national average, and therefore, it is important that we improve educational success for these populations for the betterment of the country and for their communities at large.

According to the Chiefs Assembly on Education, Palais des Congres de Gatineau Quebec, Canada, in 2012[3]:

- First Nations youth are the fastest growing demographic in Canada, with 30% of this population under the age of 30.
- 36% of First Nation students graduate from high school compared to the Canadian graduation rate of 72%
- Aboriginal people have a lower educational attainment than their non-Aboriginal counterparts, with 43.7% not holding a certificate, diploma or degree compared to 23.1% for the Canadian population.
- Poverty and low funding for Aboriginal schools create a serious challenge for 55% of First Nation schools.

Again, we see the parallels for First Nation students with Native American and Alaskan Native students. The school systems in both countries are challenged with improving curriculum and instruction for these younger aged populations.

Journal Entry #2

You have just read about the low completion rates for Native American and Indigenous students. You have made the courageous decision to attend college. What steps can you take to be one of the students who successfully completes his or her education?

The Unfortunate History of Higher Education for Native American and Indigenous Students

Why have Native American/Alaska Natives and First Nation students struggled with formal education? Historically, in both the United States and in Canada, White institutions are not trusted by native peoples for a variety of reasons relating to the colonial period.

Thus, education policy in Australia, Canada, New Zealand, and the United States developed from a racist colonial ideology that positions Indigenous peoples as brutes, wild, and "savage." Education in these countries was used as an instrument of the White settler-state to eliminate Indigenous peoples whether by Christian or secular education. The policies growing out of this ideology explicitly suppressed Indigenous ways of learning, and because of this, higher education for Indigenous peoples in these countries rooted in Indigenous knowledge has only recently developed. Since education

*in general was used as a tool for cultural and linguistic genocide, Indigenous peoples
in all four of these countries have been rightfully suspicious of White settler education,
which may be one reason higher education has been slow to develop."[4]*

In the United States, the boarding schools were often traumatizing institutions to native
communities.

*"[Captain Richard Henry] Pratt opened the Carlisle Indian School in 1879. School offi-
cials closely monitored student behavior and punished students for speaking Native languages and practicing tribal tradition or religions. Pratt's arrogant and paternalistic plans
sought elimination of Native peoples' cultures and identities under the guise of Indian
education. While many boarding schools did not conform entirely to the Carlisle model,
nearly all Native students were subjected to a two-pronged assault on their tribal identities . . . stripped away all outward signs of Indian children's association with tribal life,
(cut hair, changed names) and the . . . school's pedagogy was intended to eliminate the
traditional culture from Native youth and restructure their minds and life ways."[5]*

More recently in Canada, the federal government has recognized, and apologized for the
devastating effects the residential school system has had on First Nations communities.
On June 11, 2008, Canadian Prime Minister Stephen Harper acknowledged, "Two primary
objectives of the residential school system were to remove and isolate children from the
influence of their homes, families, traditions and cultures, and to assimilate them into the
dominant culture. These objectives were based Aboriginal cultures and spiritual beliefs
were inferior and unequal. Indeed, some sought, as it was infamously said, 'to kill the
Indian in the child.' Today, we recognize that this policy of assimilation was wrong, has
caused great harm, and has no place in our country."[6]

Early European colonists not only had the idea that they were masters of nature, but
that they were a superior culture, and Indigenous cultures had to be assimilated into this
superior culture or be exterminated. It included the idea that "Western civilization represented the highest development of humankind . . . where Western Europeans understood
themselves to be at the cutting-edge of history with everybody else requiring instruction
to be brought up to speed."[7] This idea was supported by various Christian denominations
and included a moral mandate to remake other cultures to conform to their world view.
Soon after the arrival of the Spaniards in Mexico, schools were set up to indoctrinate
Indigenous children in Christianity and teach them the ways of Western European culture.
Obviously, these new ideas did not match the world view of Native American populations.

"Injustice anywhere
is a threat to justice
everywhere."
Martin Luther King

© digitalfarmer/Shutterstock.com

Across the Americas the goals of education were assimilation of Native American
cultures. In the United States, compulsory education laws forced Native American children to be removed from their homes and sent to boarding schools. In order for Indian
children to become "productive citizens," they were prohibited from speaking their native

language and often punished if they did so. The purpose of these schools was to erase their culture and to teach them how to live in the White man's world. In effect, they taught Native people how to be White. This often led to cultural disintegration in which Native Americans lost their culture and were still not fully accepted into the dominant White culture resulting in a loss of identity, increased social problems, and the feeling of being misunderstood in both worlds. Because Native American children began to lose their language, communication between children and parents and grandparents became limited, resulting in these children being cut off from their heritage and culture. In the process, these children viewed education as irrelevant, painful, and something to be avoided. This systematic destruction of thousands of years of Native American culture, language, history, and spirituality lead to the self-destructive behaviors of alcoholism, drug addiction, and self-hatred that still haunt Indigenous populations to this day, from the tip of Alaska, to the tip of Tierra del Fuego.

Dillon Platero, director of the Navajo Division of Education, described a typical student named "Kee."

©digitalfarmer/Shutterstock.com

Kee was sent to a boarding school as a child where-as was the practice-he was punished for speaking Navajo. Since he was only allowed to return home during Christmas and summer, he lost contact with his family. Kee withdrew from both the White and Navajo worlds as he grew older because he could not comfortably communicate in either language. He became one of the many Navajo who were non-lingual-a man without a language. By the time he was 16, Kee was an alcoholic, uneducated, and despondent-without identity.[8]

Removing Native children from their parents and community is especially damaging since traditional Native teaching and child rearing comes from parents, grandparents, and extended family members. Examples of the teachings of the Iñupiaq were "knowledge of language, sharing, respect for

© Kendall Hunt Publishing Company

others, cooperation, respect for elders, love for children, hard work, knowledge of family tree, avoidance of conflict, respect for nature, spirituality, humor, family roles, hunter success, domestic skills, humility and responsibility to the tribe."[9] These values would enable Indigenous children to maintain a positive self-identity and to find their place in the world. These children knew who they were and how to live in the world. They accepted the responsibility of becoming a contributing member of society. The accomplishments of the children were viewed as accomplishments of the family.

When Columbus arrived, there were several million Indigenous people living in what is today Canada and the United States. In Mexico alone, there were between 10 and 30 million Indigenous people speaking over 256 distinct languages! In the United States, at the beginning of the 20th century, the numbers decreased to 200,000 because of new diseases introduced since 1492, the introduction of guns that were used in warfare, starvation resulting from the killing of the buffalo and other game, and forced movement of Native Americans to reservations that were on less desirable lands. Alcoholism, drug addiction, diabetes, heart disease, and mental illness have taken a great toll on the Indigenous nations of the Americas. European colonization is often called the "American Indian Holocaust."[10]

The Rebirth of Education and Cultural Identity

It wasn't until the 1960s, during the civil rights era, that there was the realization that Western education was not working neither for Native students nor for society in general. This era was the beginning of education built on the premise of self-determination. Native American groups such as the American Indian Movement (AIM) began to speak up for the First Nations of America. Self-determination and resiliency were stressed as important tools or "weapons" against the mental and spiritual colonization of the Americas. Resiliency is based on the human characteristic of surviving at any cost. Resilient people and communities use their cultural, linguistic, and spiritual heritage to negotiate and overcome the roadblocks that a dominant society puts in front of them. Resiliency comes from within the individual, but it must be fostered from outside: from the extended family that is the community.

> "You must be the change you want to see in the world."
>
> Mahatma Gandhi

In 1973, the Canadian National Indian Brotherhood introduced the concept of "Indian control of Indian education" that tied education to self-determination and self-government. In both the United States and Canada, the policy of self-determination is based on the value of preserving tribal culture and giving tribes the responsibility for self-government and education. Children must feel that they are a part of their family and tribe. Story telling is an important part of Native American and Indigenous education and provides a foundation for cultural identity. Self-determination in education reflects the desire of Native American and Indigenous people to break free from colonization and to determine their own future. It is a continuing challenge to provide education based on an appreciation of diversity and incorporating Native and Indigenous values and culture.

With this unfortunate history in both the United States and in Canada, it is no wonder that Native communities distrust these systems. Over the past 30–40 years, there has been instrumental change in the United States and in Canada's views on Indigenous education, and the role of First Nations involvement in improving these systems has been enhanced by laws. Both countries have embraced tribal colleges and universities, but funding is often inadequate.

It is easy to understand why Native and Indigenous communities are suspicious of these institutions and what influences they may have on their children, who often must leave home to attend. Although many families are supportive and wish for their student's success in the college and university world, they fear that their children will lose part of their heritage. You might also fear this.

The Importance of Family and Home

Many students come to college with a strong tradition of valuing family and home. For most Native students, family and home are important values that provide support, but can create stress for you while in college. Your parents, aunties and uncles, grandparents, and relatives may be very excited about your college attendance. They may be so excited because they may think you are the "one" who made it. Your success is important to your family. And even though it is great to have this kind of support and hope for your future, this can create stress for you. College does create stress for everyone and you may have times that you doubt your capability and your ability to succeed. The pressure of not wanting to disappoint your family can be great at times. It is important to discuss these feelings with your family or college counselor or adviser.

©LeshaBu/Shutterstock.com

Conversely, if you are one of the first to attend college in your family, your family does not always understand what you are encountering and how these encounters may impact the person you are. Family sometimes fear the "new person" you will become. Perhaps, they think you will not want to come home, be close to your culture, or that you will become "White" in your thinking and in your actions. Again, this can present a source of stress for you as you learn to walk in the world of higher education and your world at home.

Many Native and Indigenous students, especially those whose college is some distance from home, miss home. You miss the food, the family, the friends, the community, and the ceremonial life of home. Being mindful that college and university study does come to an end, and knowing that you will be home again can be helpful to remember. Knowing that your institution is most likely based on Eurocentric values, missing class to attend to family and community events can be challenging. Attending a ceremonial event that goes far into the night and makes you late for class, may not be understood by your professors. It is these types of experiences that can create more stress for you as you progress through higher education.

©aceshot1/Shutterstock.com

Journal Entry #3

Take a moment to reflect on home. What does home mean to you? Is home the house you live(d) in or is it the community you grew up in? Does your family understand your goals and support you in attending college?

As described earlier, Native American and Indigenous students have cultural values based on community and cooperation, and not so much on the individual. Many students feel as though their college degree will allow them to return to their communities and "Give back to the community." Others feel that by becoming educated they may be able to make societal change that will benefit their family and tribal communities. Others may just want to improve their career prospects and create a better life for themselves and their families. For many students it is important to define why you are in college. What is your reason for wanting to earn a college degree?

Overcoming Obstacles

There are many types of obstacles that you may face as you begin your college education. It is important to be aware of them and to develop successful coping strategies.

Cultural Differences

The college/university setting can present many challenging situations for students coming from Native and Indigenous cultures because the institutional value system is often based on Eurocentric curriculum, culture and climate, quite the opposite of your own families' value system. For instance, higher education is based on the individual. It is an environment that focuses upon the success of the individual, the goals of the individual, and the needs of the individual, and therefore creates a competitive environment. This is often an alien concept for many students who come from traditions that value the family and community foremost, before the individual.[11] It is the difference between cooperation and competition, two opposite modes of thinking.

©Barna Tanko/Shutterstock.com

Beliefs and definitions of what time represents can be another area of cultural conflict. The institution is built upon the concept of time management, planning an exact schedule for your weekly study routine, and planning each semester's course selection to help you reach a timely goal of completion and graduation. Native and Indigenous communities often joke about "Indian Time," but in reality it is a part of the social structure of Native life. Things begin when all have gathered and it ends when all is done. The Native belief that things will happen as they should is often in conflict with the institutions' definition of time.

Native students are often attending institutions with very few other Native students enrolled and feelings of alienation occur. This feeling of "I don't belong here or I haven't seen anyone else who looks like me in days" can create feelings of loneliness and estrangement. For those students coming from traditional communities, life away from home can be lonely, and if the institution does not provide a way for you to connect with a support network, conflict can arise.[12]

Another example of cultural conflict has to do with communication styles. As stated, the institution is a community based on individualism and competition. Therefore, in White society, a strong value is placed upon the individual who makes direct eye contact, questions, and contributes in class with assertiveness, and is comfortable challenging others' opinions that may differ from their own. For many Native and Indigenous students, this just doesn't fit within their own cultural norms based on cooperation, kindness, and acceptance.

©Paul Rich Studio/Shutterstock.com

Academic and Financial Issues

Another source of challenge for many Native students is the need for academic preparation and for added financial support to get through college. You are not alone. Students of all cultures and backgrounds are often disappointed to see that they are required to take lower level coursework before taking college level English and math courses. There are placement exams and state standards you are asked to meet, many of which are not culturally sensitive and do place burden on you to take prerequisite preparatory courses. And college is expensive. It's expensive because it takes your time and energy to be successful. It takes time from your ability to work and supplement your education, and it takes a great deal of stamina to stay the course, one that we want to help you to complete. You will need motivation and stamina to complete any required courses and to apply for financial aid. Once you have received your financial aid, you will need to learn to manage your money so that you can stay in college. Keep your goals in mind and take the steps needed to accomplish them. Remember to ask for help along the way.

The challenges presented here are meant to help you to understand some of the experiences you might encounter. We believe that you can overcome these obstacles and challenges and in the next section we will share with you some theories that just might help you along the way.

Personal Empowerment through Culture

Taking pride in your culture is important because it serves as a foundation for learning. You are more likely to be successful if you approach learning with an understanding of yourself, which includes a sense of belonging to your family and tribe, and an understanding and appreciation of your culture and history. Since colonial times, the story of the Native American experience has been a sad one in which the colonizers attempted to destroy Native culture, language, and religious practices and assimilate Native Americans into the dominant culture. Fortunately, there is a cultural renaissance beginning to take place in Native American societies today.

> "You already possess everything necessary to become great."
>
> Crow

Photo courtesy of Navajo Technical University.

Teaching has always been an important part of Native American culture, but was done in a different way than in our schools today. Children were taught by experiential or "hands-on" learning, storytelling, and examples from the elders. Children were taught values and beliefs through stories and practical skills were learned first by observation and then by practice. Teaching was the primary responsibility of the women and the elders, but the extended family and whole community took part in teaching children. Extended family included blood and ceremonial family. Children represented the future of the Tribe or Nation. Children learned the skills that they needed to survive in the natural environment and also how to become contributing and respectful member of the community. Today, our modern society expects parents (many times single mothers) and teachers (sometimes good, sometimes bad), and law enforcement to rear our children.

> "Out of the Indian approach to life there came a great freedom, an intense and absorbing respect for life, enriching faith in a Supreme Power, and principles of truth, honesty, generosity, equity, and brotherhood as a guide to mundane relations."
>
> Mourning Dove Salish

The world changed when Christopher Columbus first set foot in what he thought to be India. This set in motion a series of events over the past 500 years that would challenge the survival of Native American culture and populations. It is interesting to read about his first encounters with Native populations. In 1492, when Christopher Columbus first arrived in the Americas, he commented on the goodness of the Taino Indians in the Caribbean Islands. He stated that the Indians were "very gentle and without knowledge of what is evil nor do they murder or steal. They love their neighbors as themselves."[13]

When the colonialists arrived, they found that the Indigenous population had a good understanding of their natural world and a unifying set of beliefs governing the world and the relationship of all things in it. They had a system of knowledge that included morality, ecology, spirituality, and philosophy. They possessed accurate knowledge about the plants and animals in their environment. They also had knowledge of astronomy and complex astronomical cycles. They had ceremonies, stories, and customs based on the constellations and the rhythmic cycle of nature.

For example, the value systems of nations such as the plains Cree, Dokota, Blackfoot, and Ojibwa include respect, obedience, and humility. These three teachings are represented by the three center poles of their home, more contemporarily known as the

> "I am going to venture that the man who sat on the ground in his tipi meditating on life and its meaning, accepting the kinship of all creatures, and acknowledging unity with the universe of things, was infusing into his being the true essence of civilization."
>
> Chief Luther Standing Bear, Lakota Sioux

"teepee." The three center poles lean on and support each other to create a strong foundation for the home. The remaining poles and cover are all supported by those three foundation poles. The first pole represents Respect, which means giving honor; they give honor to their elders and to strangers who visit their community. They honor the basic rights of all others as they honor all life, especially mother Earth. The second pole represents Obedience, which relates to right and wrong. It means that they listen; they listen to their fellow students, their teachers, their parents, and to their traditional stories. Obedience means they listen so they can accept wisdom and guidance from others. The third pole represents Humility, which means they are humbled when they understand their relationship with creation. They are not above or beneath others and this understanding of their harmonious relationship helps them to value all life. All life is equal.

©Petr Podrouzek/Shutterstock.com

Spirituality is based on the connectedness of all living and nonliving things and the relationship of humans to each other, to plants and animals and to the air, water and land. Duwamish Chief Seattle stated: "We are all related . . . whatever befalls the earth, befalls man."[14] Because of the interrelatedness of all things, there are rules for moral behavior since the actions of one person affects all others. Moral behavior includes respecting the environment and acting responsibly and respectfully. Respect for the elders, those persons who have survived the difficult course of life and have earned their wisdom, is a cornerstone of Indigenous cultural and spiritual tradition. Animals and plants are considered part of the family and treated with understanding and respect. If an animal is killed for food, it is necessary to respect the animal. They recognize that resources were limited and must be available for future generations. Indigenous people throughout the American continent are instructed to learn about the natural environment and respect it; they were the first ecologists.

Indigenous spirituality is very different from Western religion, which was introduced during the colonial period. In Western religion, it is believed that human beings were given mastery of the world in the Garden of Eden. Human beings are seen as the only creatures "created in God's image." They viewed nature as resources to be developed and used. Respect and care for the natural world is alien to Christianity because the world is seen as inherently evil, and will be destroyed on Judgment Day. On the other hand, Indigenous people see humankind and all other living things as created equally.

Another difference in the world view of Indigenous people is the concept of what is "alive." In Western thought, animals and plants are the only things that are alive and humans are the only living things that are imbued with a "soul" or "spirit." But in Indigenous spirituality, trees, rivers, rocks, mountains, animals, water, and fire, all have a spirit. Thus, they too deserve to be respected, and taken into consideration. In many Indigenous languages there are no gender differences; the differences are animate and inanimate. Onondaga elder, Oren Lyons says, "We don't call a tree a resource, we don't call fish a resource. We don't call a bison a resource. We call them our relatives. But the general population uses the term resources, so you want to be careful of that term—resources for just you?"[15] Since animals and plants were created before humans, they were considered relatives or elders deserving of respect.

Part of self-determination is the recognition of the value of all tribes and working together to improve education and opportunities for all Indigenous people. When Hernán Cortés conquered the great Aztec capitol, Tenochtitlán, he had only a few hundred soldiers. He was able to conquer this great nation by forming alliances with different tribes and then getting them to fight among each other. It is important for Native Americans and Indigenous people to work together to accomplish mutual goals. In education today, this idea includes respecting fellow students, the learning community, and members of different tribes.

One of the key tenets of the Declaration of Independence of 1776 is "that all men are created equal, that they are endowed by their Creator with certain unalienable Rights that among these are Life, Liberty, and the pursuit of Happiness." However, these rights were only for White men with property and excluded women and people of color. The history of the United States documents these groups and their quest for equal rights, self-determination, and empowerment. Indigenous people are empowered when education is built upon a foundation of appreciating diversity and the unique contributions of tribal cultures. As we move forward to realizing democracy for all groups, it is helpful to remember Martin Luther King's famous quote in 1963, "Injustice anywhere is a threat to justice everywhere."

Across the Americas, Indigenous populations are striving toward equal rights and rebuilding their identity based on their cultures and communities. As they take pride in their heritage, they not only become more successful, but they are in a position to contribute to the greater good of society. Lakota Chief Luther Standing Bear asked, "Why not a school of Indian thought, built on the Indian pattern and conducted by Indian instructors? Why not a school of tribal art? Why should not America be cognizant of itself and aware of its identity? In short, why should not America be preserved? . . . In denying the Indian his ancestral rights and heritages the White race is but robbing itself. But American culture can be revived and rejuvenated by recognizing and appreciating a Native American school of thought. The Indian can save America."[16]

> "With all things and in all things, we are relatives."
> Sioux

> "All men were made by the same Great Spirit Chief. They are all brothers. The Earth is the mother of all people, and all people should have equal rights upon it."
> Chief Joseph, Nez Perce

©Pecold/Shutterstock.com

Perhaps one of the greatest contributions of Indigenous people is a respect for the environment and an understanding of the place of human beings in the ecosystem. There is a famous Cree prophecy, which goes like this: "When all the trees have been cut down, when all the animals have been hunted, when all the waters are polluted, when all the air is unsafe to breathe, only then will you discover that you can't eat money." Do we deplete our resources or try to maintain the quality of living for future generations? Will technology be used to destroy the planet or to improve the human condition? We can benefit by combining the insights of both cultures.

Lakota Chief Sitting Bull has suggested that "Native people should take what is good from the White man's culture and reject what is bad. For this to happen, Native American people should understand their history and be grounded in their own communities and cultures."[17] Luther Standing Bear, a leader for the Lakota tribe, has suggested that "education of the future must incorporate what was valuable in the old ways while becoming members of modern American society. The new generation of Native Americans can maintain the sense of family and community in order to bring stability and success to their communities."[18]

Photo courtesy of William Bright of Connors State College.

For Native American people to reclaim their identity and place in society, it is important to transcend the culture shock and harmful effects of Euro-centric colonization. The future is self-determination; it is the preservation of tribal life and culture. It is taking control of your own future for the sake of future generations in your tribe. It is important to maintain the positive in the traditional ways in which there was a sense of confidence based on knowledge of one's culture that allowed people to treat each other with respect and civility. It is also critical to acknowledge the traditions that once served an important function in your community, but in today's world, may be counter-productive to your tribe's future. Education that includes tribal knowledge and traditions is the force behind self-determination.

Education of the future must incorporate what was valuable in the traditional ways while becoming members of modern American society. "When we leave the culture shock behind, we will be masters of our own fate again and able to determine for ourselves what kind of lives we will lead."[19] The new generation of Native Americans who are grounded in their knowledge of history and tribal culture can achieve success and become role models for their communities. To achieve this goal, they must understand who they are and their unique place in their family, community, and the world. It is a process of self-discovery.

Journal Entry #4

Think about the obstacles you might face while attending college. What steps can you take to overcome these obstacles?

What are some of the strengths of your culture? How can your culture empower you to complete your education?

Cultural Traditionalism

Cultural Traditionalism is a concept that describes how closely one adheres to traditional culture. Native students living on reservation lands or within First Nation reserves would probably have a greater degree of cultural traditionalism, living daily life among their communities and participating in cultural events regularly. While those Native students living in urban settings, away from their traditional community, may be somewhat more assimilated to the greater society and not feel as culturally traditional. In a study conducted by Terry Huffman, he found that "culturally traditional students used their strong sense of ethnicity to form a firm social-psychological anchor."[20]

Even though the cultural traditional students were more aware of the cultural conflict they encountered in higher education, they had a solid sense of cultural identity and stronger confidence and were able to negotiate the conflict successfully. Thus, they were overall more successful college students.[21]

According to Huffman, ". . . successful performance in college requires dual operation at an American Indian cultural level and a college mainstream level." The transcultured students are able to function across two cultures and have the ability to successfully navigate both worlds without diminishing their own cultural affiliation.[22]

Family as a support network and maintaining home involvement is very important to traditionally cultured students. It makes sense that Native and Indigenous students derive much of the strength of their identity and confidence from maintaining a support network at home with family and community. It is sort of like going back to well for nurturance, especially during those challenging times when cultural conflicts arise. Your task will be to find ways to include your family in your college experience, explaining to them the experiences and challenges you face as you move through college.

Finding a Safe Place

We have now seen that successful Native and Indigenous students are those who are able to navigate the terrain of two distinct worlds as they bridge the gap between their own culture and that of the college/university setting. We also know that those students with confidence in self and strong feelings of culture have an anchor from which they can draw strength.

According to Dr. Mario E. Aguilar, in a research study he conducted called *The Ritual of Kindness*, he suggests that a healthy aspect of this transculturation is to learn to create your own unique Third Space, a safe space. He explains that the First Space is where you live or where you have come from, and the Second Space is where you must learn to negotiate [college].[23] Learning to adapt as needed within the two realms can be challenging, but with practice and introspection, you can develop a healthy place that he calls the Third Space.

Give some thought to how you will create your own safe place between your own culture and that of the university environment. Once you learn to trust in your culture and gain strength from knowing who you are in this world and why you are in college, you will be invigorated and increase your chances of success.

Health and Well-Being

Native Americans, Alaska Natives, and First Nations communities of the U.S. and Canada have a rich and long history of strength and resiliency. After all the destruction from invaders that these communities have endured, they are still here and, in many instances, still thriving.

Good health has four components: the spiritual, the emotional, the physical, and the mental. All these elements must be in balance for good health and learning.

Living a natural lifestyle is challenging in modern days. Traditional living styles that promote well-being and health are often no longer practiced. Traditional lifestyles promoted an active and healthy lifestyle, with a diet rich in natural and healthy foods. Those traditional practices allowed for physical exercise as a part of providing food and nutrition in the home, i.e., farming, fishing, hunting, and food gathering, all of which called for physical activity.

Creating health for oneself is also part of student success. Taking responsibility for your own well-being is a skill that will help you throughout your life. Some practices are what you already know about healthy living, and others relate to your community practices and spiritual rituals, while still others come from science and learning about how to maintain good health. They can all work together to increase your feelings of well-being: mental health, spiritual health, and physical health. Included among these are factors to help build motivation in college and set lifelong goals.

Native Americans and Alaskan Natives are about 1.7 percent of the U.S. population, and include 5.6 million people. Native Americans are challenged by conditions that prevent them from receiving quality healthcare, including cultural barriers, geographic isolation, inadequate sewage disposal, lack of running water, and low income. Native Americans, like many other groups in the U.S., are afflicted with several health issues.[24]

- The leading diseases include heart disease, cancer, unintentional injuries (accidents), diabetes, and stroke.
- Other areas of high risk include mental health and suicide, obesity, substance use, sudden infant death syndrome, teenage pregnancy, diabetes, liver disease, and hepatitis.
- Sexual abuse continues to have a high prevalence in many communities.

One of the most important health issues facing Native communities is the worldwide pandemic created by the COVID-19 crisis. Unfortunately, many have suffered tremendous loss from this dangerous virus. Due to inadequately funded health care systems and political dynamics, many have not received the services and care needed, while others did not believe the virus to be dangerous. Using masks, social distancing, and washing hands have been a problem for traditional communities that rely heavily on communal ties and suffer from not having running water and other community resources. These health challenges need to be addressed to ensure the good health of Native communities.

According to The National Center for Chronic Disease and Prevention and Health Promotion:[25]

- many Natives are affected by poverty, discrimination, unemployment, and poor housing.
- these factors contribute to higher rates of disease and premature death.

These steps are suggested to promote wellness:

- Connect cultural teachings to health and wellness.
- Support seasonal cultural practices that support health and wellness.
- Develop social and cultural activities that promote community wellness.
- Establish and maintain collaborations that strengthen well-being.
- Support intergenerational learning about well-being and resilience.
- Promote traditional healthy foods and traditional and contemporary physical activities.

The Tribal Practices for Wellness in Indian Country (TPWIC) suggests that tribal practices that increase resilience and connections to community, family, and culture, are having a positive impact on wellbeing.[26] This includes:

health promotion including increased traditional physical activity, traditional foods, and overall healthy living practices.

- **cultural practices** including increased knowledge and sharing of tribal history and cultural practices.
- **social and emotional well-being** including an increased sense of belonging to tribe, sense of connection to culture, and intergenerational interactions.

Every Native community has their own cultural practices for well-being. Some include community celebrations that bring people together for a common love of culture, and some include spiritual healing practices like the sweat lodge, the Tepee Ceremony, traditional dance, the Medicine Wheel, and many others. Participating in these rituals can keep you connected to your community and help you to build motivation to learn and practice a healthy lifestyle that can enrich your life and the lives of community members.

Suggestions for Successful Learning from the Native Perspective

While acknowledging that we are all unique individuals and learn in different ways, here are some suggestions to consider for increasing learning success. The ultimate goal of learning is the well-being of self, family, community, the land, and the spirits. Education is a gift that increases your opportunities.

- One of the best ways to learn is to engage all the senses, including visual, auditory, touch, movement, smell, and taste. Chapter 6 contains many examples of using all the senses to improve study skills.
- Each chapter includes a section titled "Stories from the Elders." What can you learn about success from these stories?
- Build on your experience. How does the material you are learning relate to your personal experience? How is it connected to what you already know? How is it different from your experience?
- The talking circle is used for discussion in each chapter. Everyone in the circle learns to listen and respect the views of others.
- Part of learning is the concept of teaching a person's heart. This refers to learning that occurs inside a person and includes the realization that all people need significance, competence, power, and virtue. The elders often say, "Think with your heart."
- For good mental health, it is important to maintain the sense of belonging to your family, friends, community, and tribe.
- Every human being has a desire to succeed. Invest your time in learning and build on your success.
- Adapting to two different worlds with different views of time can be challenging. Think about how you can use the benefits of both the traditional and modern world.

Journal Entry #5

Using some of the ideas from the above sections on personal empowerment, health and wellbeing, and suggestions for learning, write five intention statements about your success in college, careers, and life. I intend to . . .

Stories from the Elders

You have just read about the challenges faced by Native American and Indigenous students as they begin college. As you read this story about Wesakechak and Crane, think about the obstacles that Wesakechak faced as he traveled to the Moon and how he used his ingenuity to come up with creative solutions that allowed him to travel to the Moon and back.

Wesakechak and Crane

This story is written by Larry Gauthier, as told to him by Colin "Buster" Sanderson, an elder of the Canadian Woodland Cree, and Larry's grandfather.

Kiyas maga, (long time ago), in the days of our ancestors, when man could talk with animals and learned from them, Wesakechak was lying in the grass looking up at Moon. He was thinking how nice it would be if he could ride Moon; he would be able to see the whole world. He began to think how he could get up there. He was thinking of all kinds of ways to get to Moon. First he thought he could walk. He began to walk . . . and walk . . . and walk. After hours of walking Moon did not appear any closer. As he walked, he began to think that maybe he needed to try a different way to reach Moon. Finally he came upon Crane. He saw Crane's big wings and began thinking. "Crane," he asked, "can you take me to the moon?" When Crane did not look up, Wesakechak added, "I will give you a great gift." "Ok," said Crane, "hold on to my legs and I will fly you to the moon." Wesakechak held on for dear life as Crane flew higher and higher. They flew and flew and after a while Wesakechak felt his arms beginning to hurt. It was taking so long

he thought they would never get there. Finally just when Wesakechak was about to let go, they crashed into Moon and fell asleep because they were so tired.

Having done all the work, Crane was still asleep when Wesakechak woke up. Wesakechak looked around and noticed Cranes legs had stretched so far, they did not go back to their original length. It was then that Crane awoke and asked, "Where is my gift, Wesakechak?" Wesakechak replied, "Look at your legs, Crane. With those legs you can walk deeper in the water to forge for food. You will never be hungry." Crane was very happy and flew back to the earth eager to try her new legs.

Wesakechak was so in awe of the great beauty of Mother Earth and stars that he wanted to stay on the Moon forever. But soon Moon began shrinking. Wesakechak began to wonder how he was going to get down. He tried calling Crane, but she was too far away from Moon and no one could hear him. Moon soon fixed the problem for Wesakechak. Moon shrank so much she disappeared. Wesakechak tumbled toward the earth. Wesakechak got scared and looked for a nice soft place to land. He spotted a lake and called out to the lake to catch him. He landed softly in the water but sank down to the mud. Even though he was all covered in mud, he thanked Lake for saving his life. Lake replied that water always gives life . . .

The Woodland Cree

The Cree nation stretches from the East side of the Hudson River and James Bay, to central and south Manitoba, Saskatchewan and Central Alberta, and parts of Montana and Wyoming. The Cree have slowly integrated into Western society and become involved with various industries in joint or full ownership ventures. Traditionally Cree men were hunters and gatherers while the women were nurturers and caregivers. Women had responsibility for the home. The Elders were the repositories of knowledge; they held the nation's histories and passed on this knowledge to the children. Thus, children represented the future of the tribe. Today approximately 65% of Cree are moving from reserve lands to urban centers in Canada. In the far north, many of those still living on the reserves continue to maintain a strong connection to the land. While many modern Cree have incorporated Catholic and Anglican religions, many still observe traditional ceremonial practices. Native American / First Nation spiritual and cultural practices were outlawed by the federal government and these practices had to go underground to survive. Today a spiritual and cultural rebirth is occurring, where many young people are learning the language, culture, and spiritual practices. The Cree are considered the most populous nations of Native Americans and cover the largest geographic area in North America.

Talking Circle

Use these questions for discussion in a talking circle or consider at least one of these questions as you respond in a journal entry:

1. Wesakechak had a need to explore and get to the Moon. He contracted the help of Crane to accomplish his goal. Who are some people on campus and in your community that you can ask for help when needed? Who are the people in your college world that can help you to create your safe space?

2. Crane provides a service to Wesakechak and in return is paid with the gift of long legs. These long legs helped Crane to walk about the water and provide for his sustenance in life. What will be the pay-off be for you as you complete your educational and career goals? What impact will this have on your family and your community? How can you create "long legs" or greater resiliency in your life?

3. The story ends with the concept that "water always gives life." Giving thanks to the Earth and all creation for life is an important value to most Native and Indigenous peoples. This is a universal theme among many cultures of the word. Consider your own beliefs and values as they relate to these concepts. How will your beliefs and cultural values impact your ability to reach your educational and career goals?

Notes

1. Wendy Burton, "Programs in Place to Boost Native American Graduation Rates," December 19, 2010 retrieved from http://muskogeephoenix.com/local/x1707770120/Programs-in-place-to-boost-Native-American-graduation-rates.

2. "Native American Students in Higher Education," Postsecondary National Policy Institute (PNPI,) November 17, 2020, https://pnpi.org/native-american-students/.

3. Palais des Congres de Gatineau, "A Portrait of First Nations and Education," Chiefs Assembly on Education (2012): 1–3.

4. Roger Geertz Gonzalez and Patricia Colangelo, "The Development of Indigenous Higher Education: A Comparative Historical Analysis between Australia, Canada, New Zealand, and the U.S., 1880–2005," *Journal of American Indian Education*, Vol. 49, No. 3 (2010): 5.

5. Executive Office of the President, "2014 Native Youth Report," White House special report (2014): 8.

6. Steven Harper, "Statement of Apology to former students of Indian Residential Schools," June 11, 2008, accessed from https://www.aadnc-aandc.gc.ca/eng/1100100015644/1100100015649.

7. Vine Deloria, Jr., and Daniel R. Wildcat, *Power and Place in American Education* (Golden, Colorado: Fulcrum, 2001), 37–38.

8. Jon Reyner and Jeanne Eder, *American Indian Education: A History* (Norman, Oklahoma: University of Oklahoma Press, 2004), 5.

9. Ibid., 7.

10. Ibid., 3.

11. Stephanie J. Waterman, "A Complex Path to Haudenosaunee Degree Completion," *Journal of American Indian Education*, Vol. 46, No. 1 (2007): 27.

12. Terry Huffman, "Resistance Theory and the Transculturation Hypothesis as Explanations of College Attrition and Persistence among Culturally Traditional American Indian Students," *Journal of American Indian Education*, Vol. 40, No. 3 (2001): 6–8.

13. Deloria and Wildcat, *Power and Place*, p. 142.

14. Ibid., 14.

15. Ibid., 94.

16. K. Tsianina Lomawaima and Teresa L. McCarty, *To Remain an Indian, Lessons in Democracy for a Century of Native American Education* (New York: Teachers College Press, 2006), 170–171.

17. Deloria and Wildcat, *Power and Place*, p. 82.

18. Margaret Connell Szasz, *Indian Education in the American Colonies, 1607–1783* (Lincoln: University of Nebraska Press, 1988), 170–171.

19. Deloria and Wildcat, *Power and Place*, p. 133.

20. Terry Huffman, "Resistance Theory and the Transculturation Hypothesis as Explanations of College Attrition and Persistence among Culturally Traditional American Indian Students," p. 11–15.

21. Terry Huffman and Ron Ferguson, "Evaluation of the College Experience among American Indian Upperclassmen," *Great Plains Research*, Vol. 17, No. 1 (Spring, 2007): 62.

22. Terry Huffman, "Resistance Theory and the Transculturation Hypothesis as Explanations of College Attrition and Persistence among Culturally Traditional American Indian Students," *Journal of American Indian Education*, Vol. 40, No. 3 (2001): 6–8.

23. Mario E. Aguilar, "The Rituals of Kindness," Claremont Graduate University and San Diego State University, 2009: 166–183.

24. "Profile: American Indian/Alaska Native," U.S. Department of Health and Human Services, Office of Minority Health, www.minorityhealth.hhs.gov

25. Centers for Disease Control and Prevention, www.cdc.gov

26. "Tribal Practices for Wellness in Indian Country (TPWIC)," June 23, 2020, www.cdc.gov/healthytribes/tribalpractices.htm

27. Several reviewers added comments and ideas for this section including Larry Gauthier, Director of Student Success Services at the First Nations University of Canada; Mario Aguilar, Lecturer at the College of Education at San Diego State University; and Carmen Moffett, Director of Indian Education, Gallup, New Mexico.

CHAPTER 2

Dreams Bring Knowledge: Understanding Motivation

Learning Objectives

Read to answer these key questions:

- What do I want from college?

- What is the value of a college education?

- How do I choose my major and career?

- How can I motivate myself to be successful?

- How can I begin habits that lead to success?

- How can I be persistent in achieving my goal of a college education?

M
ost students attend college with dreams of earning a college degree and improving their lives. Some students are there to explore interests and possibilities while others have more defined career goals. Although college students enter college with good intentions, about half of them (or less) graduate within 6 years. Here are the graduation rates within 6 years for various types of colleges:[1]

- 50% of four-year public college students
- 60% of four-year private college students
- 26% of public two-year college students

Being successful in college and attaining your dreams begins with motivation. It provides the energy or drive to find your direction and reach your goals. It is easier to be motivated if you have chosen a major and career that matches your interests and personal strengths. Motivation can also be increased by having a positive mindset and exploring strategies to increase perseverance. Use the tools in this chapter to become one of the successful college students. ⌊We are taught by the elders that our dreams bring us messages from the spirit world, from our ancestors. Building an awareness of who you are and what you will do can be strengthened by your resting dreams as well as your career and college dreams.⌋

What Do I Want from College?

Succeeding in college requires time and effort. You will have to give up some of your time spent on leisure activities and working. You will give up some time spent with your friends and families. Making sacrifices and working hard are easier if you know what you want to achieve through your efforts. One of the first steps in motivating yourself to be successful in college is to have a clear and specific understanding of your reasons for attending college. Are you attending college as a way to obtain a satisfying career? Is financial security one of your goals? Will you feel more satisfied if you are living up to your potential? What are your hopes and dreams, and how will college help you to achieve your goals?

When you are having difficulties or doubts about your ability to finish your college education, remember your hopes and dreams and your plans for the future. It is a good idea to write these ideas down, think about them, and revise them from time to time.

What Is the Value of a College Education?

Many college students say that getting a satisfying job that pays well and achieving financial security are important motivators for attending college. As a result of the rising cost of higher education, students have started to question whether a college education is still a good investment. Recent analyses by the Federal Reserve Bank have shown that the benefits still outweigh the cost for both an associate's and a bachelor's degree. These degrees have a 15% return, which is considered a good investment.[2] By getting a degree, you can get a job that pays more per hour, work fewer hours to earn a living, and have more time for leisure activities. In addition, you can spend your time at work doing something that you enjoy. A report issued by the Bureau of Labor Statistics in 2019 listed the following education and income statistics for all races and both genders throughout the United States.[3] Lifetime income assumes that a person works 30 years before retirement.

Average Earnings Based on Education Level

Education	Yearly Income	Lifetime Income
High school graduate	38,792	1,163,760
Some college, no degree	43,316	1,299,480
Associate degree	46,124	1,383,720
Bachelor's degree	64,896	1,946,880
Professional degree	96,772	2,903,160

© sergign/Shutterstock.com

Notice that income rises with educational level. Over a lifetime, a person with a bachelor's degree earns about 60% more than a high school graduate. Of course, these are average figures across the nation and some individuals earn higher or lower salaries. People fantasize about winning the lottery, but the reality is that the probability of winning the lottery is very low. In the long run, you have a better chance of increasing your income by going to college.

Let's do some further comparisons. A high-school graduate earns an average of $1,163,760 over a lifetime. A college graduate with a bachelor's degree earns $1,946,880 over a lifetime. A college graduate earns $783,120 more than a high-school graduate does over a lifetime. So how much is a college degree worth? It is worth $783,120 over a lifetime. Would you go to college and finish your degree if someone offered to pay you $783,120? Here are some more interesting figures we can derive from the above table:

Completing one college course is worth $19,578.
($783,120 divided by 40 courses in a bachelor's degree)

Going to class for one hour is worth $408.
($19,578 divided by 48 hours in a semester class)

Would you take a college course if someone offered you $19,578? Would you go to class today for one hour if someone offered you $408? Of course, if this sounds too good to be true, remember that you will receive these payments over a working lifetime of 30 years.

While college graduation does not guarantee employment, it increases your chances of finding a job. College graduates have lower unemployment rates as compared to high school graduates. Increase your chances of finding employment by continuing your education.

Employment and earnings are only some of the values of going to college. College helps develop your potential and increase your confidence, self-esteem, self-respect, and happiness. It increases your understanding of the world and prepares you to be an informed citizen.

Journal Entry #1

What are your dreams for the future? Write at least a five sentence paragraph about what you hope to accomplish by going to college.

Choosing a Major and Career

© iQoncept/Shutterstock.com

Having a definite major and career choice is a good motivation for completing your college education. It is difficult to put in the work necessary to be successful if you do not have a clear picture of your future career; however, three out of four college students are undecided about their major. For students who have chosen a major, 30 to 75 percent of a graduating class will change that major two or more times.[4] Unclear or indefinite career goals are some of the most significant factors that identify students at risk of dropping out of college.[5] Choosing an appropriate college major is one of the most difficult and important decisions that college students can make.

How can you choose the major that is best for you? The best way is to first understand yourself: become aware of your personality traits, interests, preferred lifestyle, values, gifts, and talents. The next step is to do career research to determine the career that best matches your personal characteristics. Then, plan your education to prepare for your career. By following these steps, you can find the major that is best for you and minimize the time you spend in college. This textbook helps you to move through the process of self-understanding and find the major and career that is the best match for you.

How to Be Motivated

There are many ways to be motivated to be successful in college and in your future career. Set the stage with a positive mindset, increase your perseverance, think positively about the future, and find something interesting in your studies. Apply some concepts from psychology including intrinsic motivation, locus of control, affiliation, achievement, and simply using a reward. We will examine each of these concepts in more detail. As you read through them, think about how you can apply them to your personal life.

Your Mindset Makes a Difference

Did you know that your mindset has a powerful effect on learning and college success? Mindset is related to your self-image as a learner. It affects the effort you put into your studies and how you deal with challenges and setbacks. A positive mindset can even make you smarter as you learn new material and exercise your brain. Scientists have identified a **growth mindset** that leads to success.[6] It includes the belief that

- Intelligence is increased as you learn new knowledge.
- Through practice and effort, skills can be improved.
- Learning and self-improvement continue over a lifetime.
- Challenges are a way to be tested and improve performance.
- Failure is an opportunity to learn.

© Aliwak/Shutterstock.com

- Constructive criticism improves performance.
- The success of others is an inspiration.

In contrast, the **fixed mindset** is an obstacle to success. It includes these beliefs:

- Intelligence is fixed at birth.
- Increased effort does not lead to success.
- There is a limit to what we can accomplish.
- Roadblocks or obstacles are an excuse to be absent.
- It is best to take on only easy tasks in which success is guaranteed.
- Constructive criticism is a personal attack.
- The success of others makes me look bad.
- Hard work is unpleasant.
- The amount of work needed to be successful is underestimated.

The good news is that you can learn to identify and change your mindset so that you can be successful in college, in your career, and in your personal life. If you believe that effort can produce rewards, you are on your way to success.

Activity: What Is Your Mindset?

Circle the number that best describes your mindset.

	Strongly Agree	Agree	Disagree	Strongly Disagree
People are born with a certain amount of intelligence that cannot be changed.	0	1	2	(3)
I appreciate feedback on my performance and use it to improve my skills.	(3)	2	1	0
I avoid challenges and prefer to complete school work that is easy.	0	(1)	2	3
The more you learn, the more intelligent you become.	3	2	1	0
Completing challenging work is worth the effort because it gives me a sense of accomplishment.	3	2	1	0
When the work is difficult, I feel like I am not very smart.	0	1	2	3
When I receive a failing grade, I feel discouraged and feel like giving up.	0	1	2	3
When I receive a failing grade, I look at what I did wrong and try to do better next time.	3	2	1	0
I get angry when teachers or coaches tell me how to improve my performance.	0	1	2	3
The more work you put into learning a new skill, the better you will get at doing it.	3	2	1	0

Write your total points here: _____

25–30	You have a growth mindset that will help you to be successful in college.
20–24	You have many qualities of a positive mindset, but could benefit from thinking more positively about learning.
15–19	You have some qualities of a growth mindset, but would benefit from re-reading the information about growth mindset and thinking about how you can use this material to increase your success.
14 or less	Re-read the material on growth mindset and think about how you can apply it to improve your success in college.

Grit: A Powerful Tool for Student Success

Psychologists have found that one of the most important factors related to success in college is grit. What is grit? Grit is defined as a combination of perseverance and passion. Psychologist Angela Duckworth studied students who were successful at the United States Military Academy at West Point, one of the most selective colleges in the country.[7] Even though only the top students are admitted, 20% of these students drop out before graduation. Most of the dropouts leave during the first two months of college. What is the difference between those who are successful and those who drop out? **Those who are successful have a "never give up" attitude, or grit**. They are constantly tested with tasks that challenge their skills and are successful because they have grit, and not because of superior academic or athletic ability. The successful students can keep going through challenges and even failure.

Grit includes the element of passion, or the drive to constantly improve. Successful students have a goal or vision of the future and they strive to achieve it. Their goals are achievable because they match their interests and personal strengths. For this reason, having goals that match your personal strengths and interests is essential to your success. These goals give you the motivation and grit to continue when the going gets tough. Some of you have clear goals for the future while others are re-evaluating or beginning to work on them. The material in the following chapters helps you to think about your interests and personal strengths to set goals for the future and increase the motivation to complete your education.

What is more important, talent or grit? We have traditionally assumed that talent or intelligence is the key to success. In fact, there is a bias in society in which people assume that success is the result of talent. We look at successful people, admire their talent, and assume that their unusual talent made them successful. However, "our talent is one thing. What we do with it is quite another."[8] The most talented individuals are not always the most successful. The great philosopher Nietzsche proposed that we think of gifted individuals as people who worked hard to become geniuses.

How do famous people achieve excellence? Psychologists have studied famous musicians, athletes, scientists, and others to find out what makes them successful. Rather than talent, the characteristic connected to success is **effortful training.** Effortful training involves identifying a goal that challenges your skills, finding your weaknesses, and working to improve them one small step at a time. Life is easier if you can establish a habit or daily ritual of effortful practice. For example, you can make it a habit of exercising first thing in the morning. You can make a habit of studying at a certain time and place each day. If you are in the habit of doing something, you don't have to think about it; you just do it.

It is estimated that it takes about 10,000 hours to learn a complex skill.[9] The practice is often difficult and boring, but motivated individuals persist by keeping in mind what they want to accomplish. Here are some examples of effortful practice:

- Do you want to become an NBA superstar? Superstars such as Lebron James, Giannis Antetokounmpo, Luca Doncic, and Stephen Curry spend at least five hours a day for seven days a week practicing.[10]
- Do you want to be an all pro football player? Tom Brady spends 16 hours a day practicing, viewing films, and preparing for meetings before a Super Bowl game.[11]
- Do you want to become an Olympic gold medalist gymnast? Simone Biles practices 32 hours a week, 6 days a week.[12]
- Do you want to become a world-famous violinist? Itzhak Perlman suggests that students spend from four to five hours of effortful practicing each day.[13]

These successful musicians and athletes have true grit and practice until their performance becomes a habit. The key idea is that learning complex skills is challenging, takes time, and is accomplished through effortful practice one small step at a time.

© Castleski/Shutterstock.com

How does grit apply to college students? To be successful in college, it is important to spend a significant amount of time on your studies. A common rule is to spend two hours a week for each unit enrolled. For example, a three-unit course would require three hours a week in class and six hours outside of class reading and studying. Of course, the time required varies with the difficulty of the subject and your prior knowledge. In math courses, students may need to spend 10 hours per week studying and practicing problems to be successful. Start spending time studying from the very beginning. Remember that most dropouts happen early in the semester as students quickly realize that they are too behind to catch up.

Most importantly, don't give up! It is important to understand that college is challenging and requires a great deal of effort to be successful. Because college is difficult, there may be times that you may struggle or even receive a failing grade. Maintain a positive attitude, spend more time on the subject, and ask for help. Seek out tutoring or see your college professor during office hours if you need extra help. Asking for help is not a sign of weakness. College professors generally respect students who are interested enough in their field of expertise to ask for help. Colleges set up programs such as tutoring to help students be successful.

Are there times when it is better to give up? Don't give up your important goals just because you think they are difficult. However, if you realize that the goals you have set for yourself do not match your interests, it is better to set new goals and follow a different path. Prioritize how you spend your time so that you are spending it on what is most important. If you realize that the time spent on your current goal is a distraction to accomplishing more important goals, then it is better to change directions. There may be times when you must take courses that you don't consider interesting to complete your long-term goal of a college degree. In this case, it is best to think about your long-term goal of graduating from college, be gritty, and persevere.

How can you develop grit? The good news is that grit is related to the growth mindset and can be learned. Here are three steps for learning grit:

1. The first step in learning grit is finding interest. Become aware of what you enjoy doing and follow your interests. Chapter 3 in this textbook helps you to explore your interests and values.

2. Invest your time in practice. Find your weaknesses and strive to improve them. Practice frequently and work one small step at a time.

3. Find your purpose. One of the most difficult questions you may ask yourself is, "What is my purpose in life?" To answer this important question, ask yourself why your work is important and how it will help others. Knowing about your purpose helps you to maintain interest, invest your time in practice, and become passionate about your work.[14]

Activity: How Gritty Are You?

	Strongly Agree	Agree	Disagree	Strongly Disagree
I have a "never give up" attitude.	3	(2)	1	0
I spend a significant amount of time studying each week.	3	2	1	(0)
A failing grade shows a lack of intelligence.	(0)	1	2	3
Failure is an opportunity to figure out what went wrong and fix it.	(3)	2	1	0
I believe that the most talented and intelligent people will become the most successful.	0	(1)	2	3
When work is challenging, I tend to get discouraged and lose interest.	(0)	1	2	3
I have a good awareness of my interests and what I enjoy doing.	3	(2)	1	0
I can write a statement about what is my purpose in life.	3	2	(1)	0
I have goals in life and spend my time on what is most important.	3	2	(1)	0
I would describe myself as a person who has grit.	3	2	(0)	0

Write your total points here: __11__

25–30	Your grittiness will help you to be successful in college, careers, and life.
20–24	You have many qualities of a gritty person, but could benefit from thinking more about how to increase your grit.
15–19	You have some qualities of a gritty person, but would benefit from re-reading the information about grit and thinking about how you can use this material to increase your success.
14 or less	Re-read the material on grit and think about how you can apply it to improve your success in college.

Journal Entry #2

In how many units are you enrolled this term? Approximately how many hours per week will you have to study to be successful? Write five intention statements about improving your mindset and grit.

I am enrolled in ___ units. I will need to study approximately ___ hours per week to be successful. To improve my mindset and grit, I intend to . . .

Thinking Positively about the Future

Developing a growth mindset and grit both depend on positive thinking. You can motivate yourself to complete your education by thinking positively about the future. If you believe that your chances of graduating from college are good, you can be motivated to take the steps necessary to achieve your goals. Conversely, if you think that your chances of graduating are poor, it is difficult to motivate yourself to continue. The degree of optimism that you possess is greatly influenced by past experiences. For example, if you were a good student

Photo courtesy of Navajo Technical University

in the past, you are likely to be optimistic about the future. If you struggled with your education, you may have some negative experiences that you will need to overcome. Negative thoughts can often become a self-fulfilling prophecy: what we think becomes true.

How can you train yourself to think more optimistically? First, become aware of your thought patterns. Are they mostly negative or positive? If they are negative, make a conscious decision to change them to positive thoughts. Here is an example.

Pessimism

I failed the test. I guess I am just not college material. I feel really stupid. I just can't do this. College is too hard for me. My (teacher, father, mother, friend, boss) told me I would never make it. Maybe I should just drop out of college and do something else.

Optimism

I failed the test. Let's take a look at what went wrong, so I can do better next time. Did I study enough? Did I study the right material? Maybe I should take this a little slower. How can I get help so that I can understand? I plan to do better next time.

Can a person be too optimistic? In some circumstances, this is true. There is a difference between optimism and wishful thinking, for example. Wishful thinking does not include plans for accomplishing goals and can be a distraction from achieving them. Working toward unattainable goals can be exhausting and demoralizing, especially when the resources for attaining them are lacking. Goals must be realistic and achievable. Psychologists recommend that "people should be optimistic when the future can be changed by positive thinking, but not otherwise."[15] Using optimism requires some judgment about possible outcomes in the future.

There are some good reasons to think more positively. Psychologists have done long-term studies showing that people who use positive thinking have many benefits over a lifetime, including good health, longevity, happiness, perseverance, improved problem solving, and enhanced ability to learn. Optimism is also related to goal achievement. If you are optimistic and believe a goal is achievable, you are more likely to take the steps necessary to accomplish the goal. If you do not believe that a goal is achievable, you are likely to give up trying to achieve it. Being optimistic is closely related to being hopeful about the future. If you are hopeful about the future, you are likely to be more determined to reach your goals and to make plans for reaching them. Be optimistic about graduating from college, find the resources necessary to accomplish your goal, and start taking the steps to create your success.

> "Life is very interesting. In the end, some of your greatest pains become your greatest strengths."
> Drew Barrymore

> "There is nothing good or bad, but thinking makes it so."
> Shakespeare's Hamlet

Are you generally an optimist or pessimist about the future? Read the following items and rate your level of agreement or disagreement:

Rate the following items using this scale:

5   I definitely agree
4   I agree
3   I neither agree or disagree (neutral)
2   I disagree
1   I strongly disagree

_____   My chances of graduating from college are good.

_____   I am confident that I can overcome any obstacles to my success.

_____   Things generally turn out well for me.

_____   I believe that positive results will eventually come from most problem situations.

_____   If I work hard enough, I will eventually achieve my goals.

_____   Although I have faced some problems in the past, the future will be better.

_____   I expect that most things will go as planned.

_____   Good things will happen to me in the future.

_____   I am generally persistent in reaching my goals.

_____   I am good at finding solutions to the problems I face in life.

Add up your total points and multiply by two. My total points (× 2) are _____.

90–100   You are an excellent positive thinker.
80–89   You are a good positive thinker.
70–79   Sometimes you think positively, and sometimes not. Can you re-evaluate your thinking?
60 and below   Work on positive thinking.

Journal Entry #3

Write five positive statements about your college education and your future.

"No pessimist ever discovered the secrets of the stars, or sailed to an uncharted land, or opened a new doorway for the human spirit."
Helen Keller

Find Something Interesting in Your Studies

Finding something interesting in your studies helps you to maintain a growth mindset and improve grit. If you can think positively about what you are studying, it makes the job easier and more satisfying. Begin your studies by finding something interesting in the course and your textbook. Contrast these two ideas:

I have to take economics. It is going to be difficult and boring. What do I need economics for anyway? I'll just need to get through it so I can get my degree.

I have to take economics. I wonder about the course content. I often hear about it on the news. How can I use this information in my future? What can I find that is interesting?

Make sure to attend the first class meeting. Remember that the professor is very knowledgeable about the subject and finds the content interesting and exciting. At the first class meeting, the professor will give you an overview of the course and should provide some motivation for studying the material in the course. Look at the course syllabus to find what the course is about and to begin to look for something that could be interesting or useful to you.

Skimming a textbook before you begin a course is a good way to find something interesting and to prepare for learning. Skimming will give you an organized preview of what's ahead. Here are the steps to skimming a new text:

1. **Quickly read the preface or introduction.** Read as if you were having a conversation with the author of the text. In the preface or introduction, you will find out how the author has organized the material, the key ideas, and his or her purpose in writing the text.

2. **Look at the major topics in the table of contents.** You can use the table of contents as a window into the book. It gives a quick outline of every topic in the text. As you read the table of contents, look for topics of special interest to you.

3. **Spend five to 15 minutes quickly looking over the book.** Turn the pages quickly, noticing boldfaced topics, pictures, and anything else that catches your attention. Again, look for important or interesting topics. Do not spend too much time on this step. If your textbook is online, skim through the website.

4. **What resources are included?** Is there an index, glossary of terms, answers to quiz questions, or solutions to math problems? These sections will be of use to you as you read. If your book is online, explore the website to find useful features and content.

Skimming a text or website before you begin to read has several important benefits. The first benefit is that it gets you started in the learning process. It is an easy and quick step that can help you avoid procrastination. It increases motivation by helping you notice items that have appeal to you. Previewing the content will help you to relax as you study and remember the information. Early in the course, this step will help you verify that you have chosen the correct course and that you have the prerequisites to be successful in the class.

Avoid Multi-Tasking

Multi-tasking is trying to study while talking on the cell phone, checking social media, and thinking about something else. It is difficult to focus and be motivated if you are multi-tasking. It is a common myth that the brain can multi-task and pay attention to several inputs at once.

However, the brain cannot multi-task; it pays attention to one input at a time. Research shows the following:[16]

- A person who is interrupted takes 50% longer to complete a task.
- The interruptions results in 50% more errors.

A good example of the problems with multi-tasking is driving while talking on the phone. The brain constantly switches between paying attention to the phone and driving. If you are talking on a cell phone, you are half a second slower in stepping on the brake. At 70 mph, the car travels 51 feet in half a second. In addition, drivers miss 50% of the visual clues noticed by drivers who are not trying to multi-task. Driving while using a cell phone is like driving drunk.[17] While studying, cell phones and other distractions reduce productivity and increase the chance for errors. Focusing on one task at a time saves time, improves the quality of work, and improves motivation.

"A pessimist se[e]
the difficulty in [
opportunity; an[
sees the oppor[
every difficulty.'
Winst[o

© Arson0618/Shutterstock.com

Intrinsic or Extrinsic Motivation

Intrinsic motivation comes from within. It means that you do an activity because you enjoy it or find personal meaning in it. With intrinsic motivation, the nature of the activity itself or the consequences of the activity motivate you. For example, let's say that I am interested in learning to play the piano. I am motivated to practice playing the piano because I like the sound of the piano and feel very satisfied when I can play music that I enjoy. I practice because I like to practice, not because I have to practice. When I get tired or frustrated, I work through it or put it aside and come back to it because I want to learn to play the piano well.

You can be intrinsically motivated to continue in college because you enjoy learning and find the college experience satisfying. Look for ways to enjoy college and to find some personal satisfaction in it. If you enjoy college, it becomes easier to do the work required to be successful. Think about what you say to yourself about college. If you are saying negative things such as "I don't want to be here," it will be difficult to continue.

Extrinsic motivation comes as a result of an external reward from someone else. Examples of extrinsic rewards are certificates, bonuses, money, praise, and recognition. Taking the piano example again, let's say that I want my child to play the piano. The child does not know if he or she would like to play the piano. I give the child a reward for practicing the piano. I could pay the child for practicing or give praise for doing a good job. There are two possible outcomes of the extrinsic reward. After a while, the child may gain skills and confidence and come to enjoy playing the piano. The extrinsic reward is no longer necessary because the child is now intrinsically motivated. Or the child may decide that he or she does not like to play the piano. The extrinsic reward is no longer effective in motivating the child to play the piano.

You can use extrinsic rewards to motivate yourself to be successful in college. Remind yourself of the payoff for getting a college degree: earning more money, having a satisfying career, being able to purchase a car and a house. Extrinsic rewards can be a first step in motivating yourself to attend college. With experience and achievement, you may come to like going to college and may become intrinsically motivated to continue your college education.

If you use intrinsic motivation to achieve your goal, you will be happier and more successful. If you do something like playing the piano because you enjoy it, you are more likely to spend the time necessary to practice to achieve your goal. If you view college as something that you enjoy and as valuable to you, it is easier to spend the time to do the required studying. When you get tired or frustrated, tell yourself that you are doing a good job (praise yourself) and think of the positive reasons that you want to get a college education.

Locus of Control

Being aware of the concept of locus of control is another way of understanding motivation. The word **locus** means place. The locus of control is where you place the responsibility for control over your life. In other words, who is in charge? If you place the responsibility on yourself and believe that you have control over your life, you have an internal locus of control. If you place the responsibility on others and think that luck or fate determines your future, you have an external locus of control. Some people use the internal and external locus of control in combination or favor one type in certain situations. If you favor an internal locus of control, you believe that to a great extent your actions determine your future. **Studies have shown that students who use an internal locus of control are likely to have higher achievement in college.**[18] The characteristics of students with internal and external locus of control are listed below.

Students with an internal locus of control:

- Believe that they are in control of their lives.
- Understand that grades are directly related to the amount of study invested.
- Are self-motivated.
- Learn from their mistakes by figuring out what went wrong and how to fix the problem.
- Think positively and try to make the best of each situation.
- Rely on themselves to find something interesting in the class and learn the material.

Students with an external locus of control:

- Believe that their lives are largely a result of luck, fate, or chance.
- Think that teachers give grades rather than students earning grades.
- Rely on external motivation from teachers or others.
- Look for someone to blame when they make a mistake.
- Think negatively and believe they are victims of circumstance.
- Rely on the teacher to make the class interesting and to teach the material.

> "Ability is what you're capable of doing. Motivation determines what you do. Attitude determines how well you do it."
> Lou Holtz

ACTIVITY

Internal or External Locus of Control

Decide whether the statement represents an internal or external locus of control and put a checkmark in the appropriate column.

Internal	External	
_____	_____	1. Much of what happens to us is due to fate, chance, or luck.
_____	_____	2. Grades depend on how much work you put into it.
_____	_____	3. If I do badly on the test, it is usually because the teacher is unfair.
_____	_____	4. If I do badly on the test, it is because I didn't study or didn't understand the material.
_____	_____	5. I often get blamed for things that are not my fault.
_____	_____	6. I try to make the best of the situation.
_____	_____	7. It is impossible to get a good grade if you have a bad instructor.
_____	_____	8. I can be successful through hard work.

(Continued)

Internal	External	
_____	_____	9. If the teacher is not there telling me what to do, I have a hard time doing my work.
_____	_____	10. I can motivate myself to study.
_____	_____	11. If the teacher is boring, I probably won't do well in class.
_____	_____	12. I can find something interesting about each class.
_____	_____	13. When bad things are going to happen, there is not much you can do about it.
_____	_____	14. I create my own destiny.
_____	_____	15. Teachers should motivate the students to study.
_____	_____	16. I have a lot of choice about what happens in my life.

As you probably noticed, the even-numbered statements represent internal locus of control. The odd-numbered statements represent external locus of control. Remember that students with an internal locus of control have a greater chance of success in college. It is important to see yourself as responsible for your own success and achievement and to believe that with effort you can achieve your goals.

"I am a great believer in luck, and I find that the harder I work, the more I have of it."
Thomas Jefferson

Other Ways to Improve Motivation

Here are some additional ideas for improving your motivation and success:

- Participate in extra-curricular activities. When you join a club, participate in athletics, or involve yourself in student government, you gain new friends and develop a sense of belonging. You also get to explore some of your interests and gain future employment skills.

- Some students are achievement motivated, especially students interested in business, sales, law, engineering, or architecture. Strive to be the best that you can be so that you can be proud of your accomplishments.

- If a behavior is followed by a reward, it is likely to be increased. Do your studying first and follow it with a reward such as watching TV, playing your favorite video game, using social media, participating in athletics, or enjoying your favorite music. Just remember to do the work first and then follow it by a reward. If you have the reward first, you will not get around to studying.

Photo courtesy of Navajo Technical University

Motivation, Part I

1. The following statement is an example of grit:

   a. I have a "never give up" attitude.
   b. I believe that the most talented people are the most successful in life.
   c. I think that a failing grade shows a lack of intelligence

2. You can increase your motivation for studying by

   a. taking the required courses.
   b. reminding yourself that you have to do it.
   c. finding something interesting in your studies.

3. Intrinsic motivation

   a. comes from within.
   b. is the result of an external reward.
   c. involves higher pay or recognition for a job well done.

4. To be successful in college, it is best to use

   a. an external locus of control.
   b. extrinsic motivation.
   c. intrinsic motivation.

5. A person who is multitasking:

   a. Uses time efficiently.
   b. Takes 50% longer to complete a task.
   c. Minimizes errors.

How did you do on the quiz? Check your answers: 1. a, 2. c, 3. a, 4. c, 5. b

Journal Entry #4

Make a list of five ideas you can use to improve motivation. Include any of these ideas: mindset, grit, positive thinking, finding interest, concentration, attention, intrinsic motivation, locus of control, affiliation, achievement, and using rewards.

Success Is a Habit

We establish habits by taking small actions each day. Through repetition, these individual actions become habits. I once visited the Golden Gate Bridge in San Francisco and saw a cross section of the cable used to support the bridge. It was made of small metal strands twisted with other strands; then those cables were twisted together to make a stronger cable. Habits are a lot like cables. We start with one small action, and each successive action makes the habit stronger. Have you ever stopped to think that success can be a habit? We all have learned patterns of behavior that either help us to be successful or interfere with our success. With some effort and some basic understanding of behavior modification, you can choose to establish some new behaviors that lead to success or to get rid of behaviors that interfere with it.

Eight Steps to Change a Habit

You can establish new habits that lead to your success. Once a habit is established, it can become a pattern of behavior that you do not need to think about very much. For example, new students often need to get into the habit of studying. Following is an outline of steps that can be helpful to establish new behaviors.

1. **State the problem.** What new habit would you like to start? What are your roadblocks or obstacles? What bad habit would you like to change? Be truthful about it. This is sometimes the most difficult step. Here are two different examples:

   • I need to study to be successful in college. I am not in the habit of studying. I easily get distracted by work, family, friends, and other things I need to do. At the end of the day, I am too tired to study.

   • I need to improve my diet. I eat too much fast food and am not careful about what I eat. I have no time for exercise.

2. **Change one small behavior at a time.** If you think about climbing a mountain, the task can seem overwhelming. However, you can take the first step. If you can change one small behavior, you can gain the confidence to change another. For example:

   • I plan to study at least two hours each day on Mondays through Fridays.

   • I plan to eat more fruits and vegetables each day.

State the behavior you would like to change. Make it small.

3. **State in a positive way the behavior you wish to establish.** For example, instead of the negative statements "I will not waste my time" or "I will not eat junk food," say, "I plan to study each day" or "I plan to eat fruits and vegetables each day."

4. **Count the behavior.** How often do you do this behavior? If you are trying to establish a pattern of studying, write down how much time you spend studying each day. If you are trying to improve your diet, write down everything that you eat each day. Sometimes just getting an awareness of your habit is enough to begin to make some changes.

5. **Picture in your mind the actions you might take.** For example:

   • I picture myself finding time to study in the library. I see myself walking to the library. I can see myself in the library studying.

   • I see myself in the grocery store buying fruits and vegetables. I see myself packing these fruits and vegetables in my lunch. I see myself putting these foods in a place where I will notice them.

6. **Practice the behavior for 10 days.** In 10 days, you can get started on a new pattern of behavior. Once you have started, keep practicing the behavior for about a month to firmly establish your new pattern of behavior. The first three days are the most difficult.

If you fail, don't give up. Just realize that you are human and keep trying for 10 days. Think positively that you can be successful. Write a journal entry or note on your calendar about what you have accomplished each day.

7. **Find a reward for your behavior.** Remember that we tend to repeat behaviors that are rewarded. Find rewards that do not involve too many calories, don't cost too much money, and don't involve alcohol or drugs. Also, rewards are most effective if they directly follow the behavior you wish to reinforce.

8. **Ask yourself,** "What am I going to do to maintain the change?" In the long run, the new behavior has to become part of your lifestyle.

Ten Habits of Successful College Students

Starting your college education will require you to establish some new habits to be successful.

1. Attend class.

College lectures supplement the material in the text, so it is important to attend class. Many college instructors will drop you if you miss three hours of class. After three absences, most students do not return to class. If your class is online, log in frequently.

2. Read the textbook.

Start early and read a little at a time. If you have a text with 400 pages, read 25 pages a week rather than trying to read it all at once.

3. Have an educational plan.

Counselors or advisors can assist you in making an educational plan so that you take the right classes and accomplish your educational goal as soon as possible.

4. Use college services.

Colleges offer valuable free services that help you to be successful. Take advantage of tutoring, counseling, health services, financial aid, the learning resources center (library) and many other services.

5. Get to know the faculty.

You can get to know the faculty by asking questions in class or meeting with your instructors during office hours. Your instructors can provide extra assistance and write letters of recommendation for scholarships, future employment, or graduate school.

6. Don't work too much.

Research has shown that full-time students should have no more than 20 hours of outside employment a week to be successful in college. If you have to work more than 20 hours a week, reduce your college load. If you are working 40 hours a week or more, take only one or two classes.

7. Take one step at a time.

If you are anxious about going to college, remember that each class you attend takes you another step toward your goal. If you take too many classes, especially in the beginning, you may become overwhelmed.

8. Have a goal for the future.

Know why you are in college and what you hope to accomplish. What career will you have in the future? Imagine your future lifestyle.

9. Visualize your success.

See yourself walking across the stage and receiving your college diploma. See yourself working at a job you enjoy.

10. Ask questions if you don't understand.

Asking questions not only helps you to find the answers, but it shows you are motivated to be successful.

Motivation, Part II

1. When you participate in student activities in campus such as athletics, student government, or a club, you will be

   a. distracted from your studies.
   b. using affiliation motivation.
   c. decreasing your chances of success in college.

2. If the behavior is followed by a reward

   a. it is likely to be increased.
   b. it is likely to be decreased.
   c. there will probably be no effect.

3. For rewards to be effective, they must occur

   a. before the behavior.
   b. immediately after the behavior.
   c. either before or after the behavior.

4. If you plan to increase time spent studying, the following statement is most likely to help you to achieve your goal.

   a. I will increase the time I spend studying.
   b. I plan to study for at least two hours each day on Mondays through Fridays.
   c. I will study for five hours on Monday to prepare for the test on Tuesday.

5. To change a habit,

   a. set high goals.
   b. focus on negative behavior.
   c. begin with a concrete behavior that can be counted.

How did you do on the quiz? Check your answers: 1. b, 2. a, 3. b, 4. b, 5. c

---

KEYS TO SUCCESS

Persistence

There is an old saying that persistence will get you almost anything eventually. This saying applies to your success in life as well as in college. The first two to six weeks of college are a critical time in which many students drop out. Realize that college is a new experience and that you will face new challenges and growth experiences. Make plans to persist, especially in the first few weeks. Get to know a college counselor or advisor. These professionals can help you to get started in the right classes and answer any questions you might have. It is important to make a connection with a counselor or faculty member so that you feel comfortable in college and have the resources to obtain needed help. Plan to enroll on time so that you do not have to register late. It is crucial to attend the first class. In the first class, the professor explains the class requirements and expectations and sets the tone for the class. You may even get dropped from the class if you are not there on the first day. Get into the habit of studying right away. Make studying a habit that you start immediately at the beginning of the semester or quarter. If you can make it through the first six weeks, it is likely that you can finish the semester and complete your college education.

It has been said that 90 percent of success is just showing up. Any faculty member will tell you that the number one reason for students dropping out of college is lack of attendance. They know that when students miss three classes in a row, they are not likely to return. Even very capable students who miss class may find that they are lost when they come back. Many students are simply afraid to return. Classes such as math and foreign languages are sequential, and it is very difficult to make up work after an absence. One of the most important ways you can be successful is to make a habit of consistently showing up for class.

You will also need commitment to be successful. Commitment is a promise to yourself to follow through with something. In athletics, it is not necessarily the one with the best physical skills who makes the best athlete. Commitment and practice make a great athlete. Commitment means doing whatever is necessary to succeed. Like the good athlete, make a commitment to accomplishing your goals. Spend the time necessary to be successful in your studies.

When you face difficulties, persistence and commitment are especially important. History is full of famous people who contributed to society through persistence and commitment. Consider the following facts about Abraham Lincoln, for example.

- Failed in business at age 21.
- Was defeated in a legislative race at age 22.
- Failed again in business at age 24.
- Overcame the death of his sweetheart at age 26.
- Had a nervous breakdown at age 27.
- Lost a congressional race at age 34.
- Lost a congressional race at age 36.
- Lost a senatorial race at age 45.
- Failed in an effort to become vice president at age 47.
- Lost a senatorial race at age 49.
- Was elected president of the United States at age 52.[19]

© Gustavo Frazao/Shutterstock.com

The goal of getting a college education may seem like a mountain that is difficult to climb. Break it into smaller steps that you can accomplish. See your college counselor or advisor, register for classes, attend the first class, read the first chapter, do the first assignment, and you will be on the road to your success. Then continue to break tasks into small, achievable steps and continue from one step to the next. And remember, persistence will get you almost anything eventually.

Journal Entry #5

What will you do if you are tempted to drop out of college? What steps can you take to be persistent in achieving your college goals? Are there times when it is best to change goals rather than to be persistent if your efforts are not working? Write a paragraph about how you will be persistent in reaching your college goals.

Interviews and Stories from the Elders

This chapter has focused upon several important principles that can either improve or hinder your ability to stay the course and reach your goals. You have been asked to consider, "Why am I in college?" and "What's involved with choosing a major?" or "What are my interests and my values?" Once you begin to answer these questions you will need to consider, "How do I maintain my locus of control and stay motivated, focused, and responsible for my success?"

This is an exciting time in your life. You have the ability to choose to become a stronger, more focused individual. You may believe that your success is part of a larger success—one that impacts your family and your community. You may be the first in your family to attend college, or you might feel community pressure to become an educational role model and an example for others to follow. These types of expectations can create greater motivation for success as long as you remain true to your own self-assessment of your interests and your values.

To bring forth a new perspective on learning strategies and techniques for college success, we have provided traditional Native stories or interviews at the end of each chapter. Interviews of the elders provide examples of how they successfully navigated higher education and preserved their cultural values. The oral tradition of storytelling is an ancient practice that all indigenous cultures embrace. Some stories focus upon creation and the spiritual beliefs of the tribe, while others teach a moral lesson. Stories can be historical, can depict a special and sacred geographic characteristic, or impart important cultural knowledge and history to its people. Stories are entertaining and sometimes comical, but all will usually promote a beneficial change in attitude toward a basic value or responsibility as members of that community. Some stories teach about relationships with other living creatures including people, animals, and elements like the wind, water, and the universe. All stories are intergenerational and intra-familial in that stories are passed down from grandfather to child and so on.

Some tribes are willing to share their stories for the good of all and some nations are quite protective and believe that stories can only be shared with others when given as gifts. One of the co-authors of this textbook, Larry Gauthier, is a Woodland Cree and he has asked the elders for permission to use their stories. One of the elders "took the tobacco and prayed that their students and those who use the text will find value and meaning in the stories." The stories take on a spirit of their own and, in a way, define a shared cultural experience and belief system of a community. With that in mind, we share with you a collection of interviews and stories.

Interview from the Elder: Juanita Edaakie

The following interview is from Juanita Edaakie, a Zuni elder from New Mexico. She continues her cultural heritage through the dance group, The Zuni Olla Maidens. She is also a graduate of the University of New Mexico. She encourages students to find their hidden talents and provides some tips for college success.

Interviews from the Elders

Juanita Edaakie, Zuni, New Mexico
Retired Educator and Zuni Olla Maiden, Dance Group Leader and Singer
Interviewed by Beatrice Zamora March 11, 2021

Juanita Edaakie is a retired schoolteacher and leader of the dance group known as The Zuni Olla Maidens of Zuni, New Mexico. Juanita graduated from the University of New Mexico and became a teacher in her Pueblo of Zuni. When she was a child she was sent to Utah, where she attended a Mormon elementary school and lived with Mormon foster parents. Her story is very interesting, and she has learned much along the way.

Juanita learned the traditional dance from her mother, Cornelia Bowannie, who learned from her mother Chrystal. Juanita and her sister Loretta are the current leaders of this famous dance group who have traveled the world sharing the Zuni traditional dance that honors the women who brought water into the pueblo by holding a filled olla on their heads as they made several trips a day to care for their families. The ollas are a beautiful representation of the culture, and the dance allows the women dancers to pay homage to their ancestral women. Juanita is happy to share these traditions and the Zuni Pueblo is proud of The Zuni Olla Maidens' accomplishments.

Group Photo of the Zuni Olla Maidens. From left to right: Kimberly Dewa, Juanita Edaakie, Loretta Beyuka, Breanna Yamutewa, Joy Edaakie

Juanita says the dance tradition has taught her a great deal about being a Zuni Woman and credits her mother for teaching her to be gracious and kind, and to learn how to talk to others outside of their culture. The leadership role includes many responsibilities, such as public speaking, negotiating contracts, preparing biographies of the members, learning the music and songs created by the Zuni men, sewing, creating the dance regalia, and practice, practice, practice of song and dance. Being part of this traditional dance group requires a great deal of commitment and self-discipline.

Juanita says her Zuni pueblo celebrates life with dance. They celebrate Harvest dance, Rain dance, religious dances, and giving thanks to their women, as they are a matrilineal society. She says "Women are the backbone of our society, and even though we are encouraged to marry and carry on the lineage, some women chose other paths. I have been a single mother for 30 years, and I raised a wonderful son who is a good man, is kind, and respects women, and respects me, too," (she chuckles).

Juanita says that being a member of this group has allowed her to travel to places she would never have imagined. She says "Imagine me, a small Zuni woman, walking down Wall Street in New York, dressed in my traditional regalia, stopping along the way and chatting with complete strangers who were interested in my traditions! Who would have ever thought that about me?" She says she never saw herself as a dance leader or public singer, but she says, **"You might be surprised at your hidden talents. If you try something new, you might be surprised at what you can do."**

Juanita says when she was a young girl, her mother decided it would be best if the children attended schools in Utah and lived with host families. Her mother was concerned and wanted her children to have a good education. Juanita says it was challenging and somewhat of a culture shock, but that her overall experience was incredibly positive. Some of her siblings did not enjoy Utah, and came back home after a short while. One of her brothers, who had beautiful long hair, came back home to Zuni after the host family cut his hair without his permission. Juanita says she was lucky to be placed with a host family who was very respectful of her culture, and for that reason she stayed and attended junior high and high school there. As she got a little older, the Mormons began to share more about their religion, and Juanita realized there were clashes with her own Zuni religious beliefs, so she decided to leave that religion. She had many experiences that opened the world to her and enjoyed the time she spent there, but eventually came back home to Zuni.

One thing she learned in Utah was to love school. "I learned that I was an artist while in junior high school. In high school, I also did well, except for the religious classes. I realized that I really believed in my Zuni religion." Juanita's mom finished eighth grade, but Juanita and some of her siblings completed their college education.

Juanita says, **"Once you learn and identify with your culture, the education helps you to solidify what you believe in. Especially if the school balances the instructional unit that includes cultural ties. There can be a balance of the White teachings with your own cultural teachings. That's what I always did with my students in my classes**.

"I had great mentors along the way, and that's how I became a good teacher. And I taught children to value knowledge and to not always stay in the classroom, but go to the outside world and learn from nature," she says.

Juanita is an artist in music, dance, art, and sewing. This is a good way to learn discipline. How does your creativity feed your spirit?

"My sister Loretta always says to me that I never ask for much, but that I give a lot to others. You painted our pottery, you sew our dresses, you create our banners, you learn the new songs and teach us," Juanita says. **"I feel that I have gifts from my mom and dad, who were very talented. When I am creating, it is a spiritual experience. I'm at peace when I am drawing or sewing. I'm at peace."**

"People always ask us, 'Do you break pottery?' And we always say, not intentionally. That's a hard thing and sometimes things break and there is always a reason. For instance, my niece had dropped some, and we feel devastated when a piece of pottery breaks. **But we know one of the reasons why we drop it may be that it wasn't blessed before we used it, or the pottery becomes such a part of you, that you forget it is on your head, and take a sip of water and tilt your head, and boom. We try to collect all the pieces and take them home to be reused in the next olla that is created because these pieces of pottery come from our home.**

"I am happy and blessed that I have come from an artistic family of silversmiths, pottery makers, dancers, singers, and so much more."

Native American students come to college and they learn about time management, deadlines, test taking, and competition with other students. How can you help them cope? What are some of the challenges you experienced? How can Native American students maintain who they are and use that as a strength in their education?

Juanita says:

- "One of the things I learned when I was in college was not to procrastinate. We get teased about being on Indian Time, but that's not a good way to be successful. I started out as a procrastinator, but I learned to create timelines for myself to stay on track. I had my sister and brother who taught me a lot. It's important to have support, especially within your family."

- "If you aren't understanding the content or the vocabulary of the college text, you need extra help. Do not be afraid to ask for help. Ask friends to help you or get a tutor. Ask for extra help."

- "If you are into partying and stuff, that's not going to help you. You can socialize and have fun, but remember why you are there. Make the most of your time, especially when you are on scholarship; don't waste the time or the resource."

- "You have to have a plan. It makes a big difference. Make phone calls and meet your paperwork deadlines. Get to college early and check to see that financial aid and everything is in place. It will help a lot if you can take a family member with you to all the offices. The university is huge. Try and get a good roommate in college or get your own room if you can."

- "Study like crazy! Do not think one hour of study will get you through. I had to learn to take tests, so learn new strategies. The tests in college are different from high school. Isolate yourself, plan for a lot of study hours, study with a friend, and you can balance being cultural wherever you are."

One tip that Juanita shared is **"For instance, when we travel as a dance group, we offer some of our food to the ancestors whenever we sit down to eat at a restaurant. If you are at a university that does not understand your culture, you can create that space for yourself. If there are no offering bowls at the table, you can put some food on a napkin and offer to the spirits. Or if you use cornmeal to say your morning prayers, make sure your friends understand it, so they don't misuse the corn meal. You can balance what your beliefs are when you are away at school. To be a successful student, you need to prioritize your time and balance your beliefs."**

Some students fear that college will change them, but Juanita says that **"going to school in Utah did not change me. I know who I am, and it has never been repressed. If you are strong in your cultural beliefs and present yourself with confidence in your identity, and you show respect for yourself and for others, then there is nothing to be afraid of. With humility, you can be the best you can be. You have to do that. Part of the journey of becoming an adult is learning to do things for yourself. If you make a mistake, that's fine. Learn how to fix it. That's how we learn to become what we will be in life. Don't be embarrassed to ask for help."**

"Take things with you to college that remind you of who you are. That will help you to stay strong and resolute. Knowing you can learn different and new ways, but you don't have to give up who you are. It doesn't mean you have to turn yourself into them."

Juanita also said, **"Be strong in who you are and be proud of who you are. You can learn to walk in your traditional world and the college world, you can walk with intentionality."**

Create a safe environment for yourself. Juanita shared hard lesson she had to learn while at college: "Not everyone is going to treat you well; you have to trust your instincts, so you don't get hurt. Be aware of your surroundings."

Juanita is an artist, learned to love school, practices her cultural dances, and attended college. She says "When we perform, I always tell the audience that we have more in common than we have differences. We should look for those commonalities. We have family, we have culture, we celebrate occasions with our family, we all die, and we all go on to where we think we come from. So, what we have learned throughout our travels, we might encounter people who are racists or who don't care for us, but if you think about it, we all come from the same place. So, we like to end with a friendship dance; it brings us together in a sacred circle.

"All things in life are a cycle, a circle, the passing of energy of love and spirit. All of our experiences guide our paths. It's always good to learn and to stay involved in the world."

Talking Circle

Use these questions for discussion in a talking circle or consider at least one of these questions as you respond in a journal entry.

1. What motivation techniques did Juanita use to become successful in her personal life and in college?

2. What were the lessons Juanita learned about being a Zuni woman? Have you ever had a similar experience?

3. What is the role and importance of dance in Native culture?

4. How did Juanita deal with being sent to Utah for her education? How did she maintain her culture and religion in a different cultural environment? Are there things you can do at your college or university to hold on to your cultural roots?

5. Juanita provides several suggestions for success in college. From your point of view, which piece of advice is most powerful or meaningful to you?

6. Juanita comments on the journey to becoming an adult.

   "Part of the journey of becoming an adult is learning to do things for yourself. If you make a mistake, that's fine. Learn how to fix it. That's how we learn to become what we will be in life. Don't be embarrassed to ask for help."

   How do you define this process of becoming an adult for yourself? Can you think of some ways to apply these ideas to your success?

7. What is the most important thing that Juanita learned from her travels? She encountered some racism along the way. How did she deal with it?

© Lyudmyla Kharlamova/
Shutterstock.com

College Success 1

The College Success 1 website is continually updated with supplementary material for each chapter including Word documents of the journal entries, classroom activities, handouts, videos, links to related materials, and much more. See http://www.collegesuccess1.com/.

Notes

1. Moneybox: A Blog about Business and Economics, "America's Awful College Dropout Rates, in Four Charts," retrieved from http://www.slate.com/blogs/moneybox/2014/11/19/u_s_college_dropouts_rates_explained_in_4_charts.html, July 2017.

2. Federal Reserve Bank of New York, "Do the Benefits of College Still Outweigh the Costs?," *Current Issues in Economics and Finance* 20, no. 3, 2014. Available at www.newyorkfed.org/research/current-issues

3. U.S Census Bureau, "Earnings and Unemployment by Educational Attainment 2019," retrieved from https://www.bls.gov/emp/tables/unemployment-earnings-education.htm, last modified September 1, 2020.

4. W. Lewallen, "The Impact of Being Undecided on College Persistence," *Journal of College Student Development* 34 (1993): 103–112.

5. Marsha Fralick, "College Success: A Study of Positive and Negative Attrition," *Community College Review* 20 (1993): 29–36.

6. Terry Doyle and Todd Zakrajsek, The New Science of Learning (Sterling, Virginia: Stylus), 85–87.

7. Angela Duckworth, *Grit: The Power of Passion and Perseverance* (New York: Simon & Schuster, 2016).

8. Ibid., 14.

9. Ibid., 29.

10. Retrieved from https://www.quora.com/How-many-hours-a-week-does-an-NBA-player-work-during-the-season, July 2017.

11. Retrieved http://patriotswire.usatoday.com/2017/02/02/behind-tom-bradys-preparation-for-super-bowl-li/, July 2017.

12. Retrieved from https://www.popsugar.com/fitness/Simone-Biles-Ellen-DeGeneres-Show-March-2016-40475107, January 2021.

13. Retrieved from http://www.thestrad.com/violinist-itzhak-perlman-talks-about-practice/, July 2017.

14. Duckworth, p. 91.

15. Christopher Peterson, *A Primer in Positive Psychology* (New York: Oxford University Press, 2006), 127.

16. John Medina, Brain Rules (Seattle: Pear Press, 2008), 87.

17. Ibid., 87.

18. M.J. Findley and H.M. Cooper, "Locus of Control and Academic Achievement: A Literature Review," *Journal of Personality and Social Psychology* 44 (1983): 419–427.

19. Anthony Robbins, Unlimited Power (New York: Ballantine Books, 1986), 73.

Begin with Self-Assessment

Name _____ Date _____

A good way to begin your success in college is to assess your present skills to determine your strengths and areas that need improvement. Complete the following assessment to get an overview of the topics presented in the textbook and to measure your present skills.

Measure Your Success

The following statements represent major topics included in the textbook. Read the following statements and rate how true they are for you at the present time. At the end of the course, you will have the opportunity to complete this assessment again to measure your progress.

5 Definitely true
4 Mostly true
3 Somewhat true
2 Seldom true
1 Never true

© Kenishirotie/Shutterstock.com

_____ I am motivated to be successful in college.

_____ I know the value of a college education.

_____ I know how to establish successful patterns of behavior.

_____ I avoid multi-tasking while studying.

_____ I am attending college to accomplish my own personal goals.

_____ I believe to a great extent that my actions determine my future.

_____ I am persistent in achieving my goals.

_____ **Total points for Motivation**

_____ I understand the steps in making a good decision about a major and career.

_____ I can describe my personality type and matching careers.

_____ I can describe my personal strengths and matching careers.

_____ I can list my vocational interests and matching careers.

_____ I can list my five most important values and tell how they are useful in deciding on a career.

_____ I understand career outlook and what careers will be in demand in the future.

_____ **Total Points for Choosing a Major**

_____ I have a list or mental picture of my lifetime goals.

_____ I know what I would like to accomplish in the next four years.

_____ I spend my time on activities that help me accomplish my lifetime goals.

_____ I effectively use priorities in managing my time.

_____ I can balance study, work, recreation, and time spent on technology.

_____ I generally avoid procrastination on important tasks.

_____ I am good at managing my money.

_____ **Total points for Managing Time and Money**

_____ I understand the difference between short-term and long-term memory.

_____ I use effective study techniques for storing information in long-term memory.

_____ I can apply memory techniques to remember what I am studying.

_____ I know how to minimize forgetting.

_____ I know how to use mnemonics and other memory tricks.

_____ I know how to keep my brain healthy throughout life.

_____ I use positive thinking to be successful in my studies.

_____ **Total points for Brain Science and Memory**

_____ I understand the latest findings in brain science and can apply them to studying.

_____ I use a reading study system based on memory strategies.

_____ I am familiar with e-learning strategies for reading and learning online.

_____ I know how to effectively mark my textbook.

_____ I understand how math is different from studying other subjects.

_____ I have the math study skills needed to be successful in my math courses.

_____ I take responsibility for my own success in college and in life.

_____ **Total points for Brain Science and Study Skills**

_____ I know how to listen for the main points in a college lecture.

_____ I am familiar with note-taking systems for college lectures.

_____ I know how to review my lecture notes.

_____ I feel comfortable with writing.

_____ I know the steps in writing a college term paper.

_____ I know how to prepare a speech.

_____ I am comfortable with public speaking.

_____ **Total points for Taking Notes, Writing, and Speaking**

_____ I know how to adequately prepare for a test.

_____ I can predict the questions that are likely to be on the test.

_____ I know how to deal with test anxiety.

_____ I am successful on math exams.

_____ I know how to make a reasonable guess if I am uncertain about the answer.

_____ I am confident of my ability to take objective tests.

_____ I can write a good essay answer.

_____ **Total points for Test Taking**

_____ I expect good things to happen in the future and work to make them happen.

_____ Despite challenges, I always remain hopeful about the future.

_____ I have self-confidence.

_____ I use positive self-talk and affirmations.

_____ I have a visual picture of my future success.

_____ I have a clear idea of what happiness means to me.

_____ I usually practice positive thinking.

_____ **Total points for Future**

_____ I am confident of my ability to succeed in college.

_____ I am confident that my choice of a major is the best one for me.

_____ **Total additional points**

Total your points:

_____ Motivation

_____ Personality and Major

_____ Managing Time and Money

_____ Brain Science and Memory

_____ Brain Science and Study Skills

_____ Taking Notes, Writing, and Speaking

_____ Test Taking

_____ Future

_____ Additional Points

_____ **Grand total points**

If you scored

290–261 You are very confident of your skills for success in college. Maybe you do not need this class?

260–232 You have good skills for success in college. You can always improve.

231–203 You have average skills for success in college. You will definitely benefit from taking this course.

Below 202 You need some help to survive in college. You are in the right place to begin.

Use these scores to complete the Success Wheel that follows this assessment. Note that the additional points are not used in the chart.

Success Wheel

Use your scores from the Measure Your Success assessment to complete the following Success Wheel. Use different colored markers to shade in each section of the wheel.

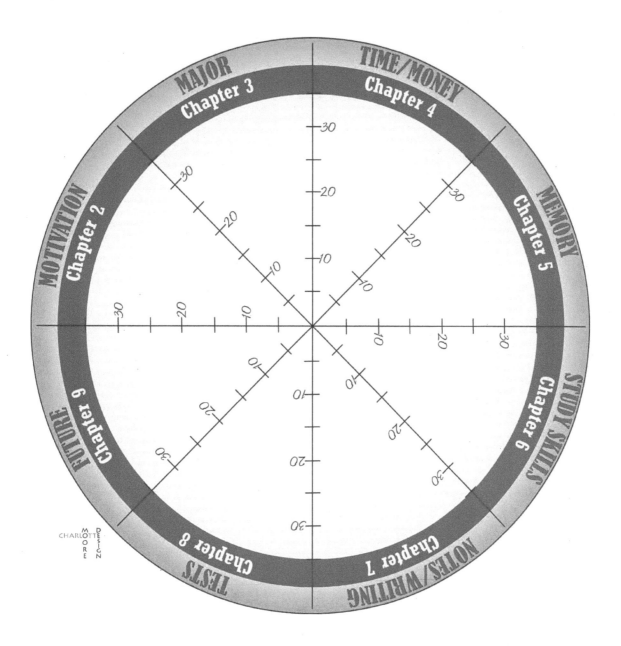

Courtesy of Charlotte Moore. © Kendall Hunt Publishing Company.

1. What are your best areas?

2. What are areas that need improvement?

What Do I Want from College?

Name _____ Date _____

Read the following list and place checkmarks next to your reasons for attending college. Think about why you are attending college and add your own personal reasons to the list.

_____ 1. To have financial security

_____ 2. To find a satisfying career

_____ 3. To explore possibilities provided by college

_____ 4. To expand my options

_____ 5. To become an educated person

_____ 6. To figure out what I want to do with my life

_____ 7. To develop my potential

_____ 8. To become a role model for my children

_____ 9. To make my parents happy

_____ 10. To respect myself

_____ 11. To feel good about myself

_____ 12. To see if I can do it

_____ 13. To meet interesting people

_____ 14. To have something to do and prevent boredom

_____ 15. To become the best I can be

_____ 16. To have better job opportunities

_____ 17. To have no regrets later on

_____ 18. To prepare for a good job or profession

_____ 19. To have job security

_____ 20. To gain confidence in myself

_____ 21. To get a degree

_____ 22. To gain a greater understanding of the world

_____ 23. To have fun

_____ **24.** To understand myself

_____ **25.** To learn how to think

_____ **26.** To enjoy what I do for a living

_____ **27.** To reach my potential

_____ **28.** Because my parents want me to get a degree

_____ **29.** For my own personal satisfaction

_____ **30.** To make a difference in other people's lives

_____ **31.** To have a position of power

_____ **32.** To have respect

_____ **33.** To have prestige

_____ **34.** To have time and money for travel

_____ **35.** To acquire knowledge

_____ **36.** _____

_____ **37.** _____

What are your top six reasons for attending college? You may include reasons not listed above. If you are tempted to give up on your college education, read this list and think about the reasons you have listed below.

1. _____   **4.** _____

2. _____   **5.** _____

3. _____   **6.** _____

Roadblocks and Pathways to Success

Name _____   Date _____

© IQoncept/Shutterstock.com

Students come to college with a dream of making a better future for themselves. What is your dream? Your instructor may have you share your ideas with other students in the course.

Place a checkmark next to any item that could be a roadblock to your success in college.

_____ Too much work   _____ Family obligations   _____ Lack of study skills

_____ Financial difficulties _____ Social life   _____ Using time wisely

_____ Lack of confidence   _____ Computer games   _____ Speaking in class

_____ Difficulty with reading _____ Social media   _____ Negative thinking

_____ Difficulty with writing _____ Phone use and texting   _____ Lack of motivation

_____ Difficulty with math   _____ Lack of career goals   _____ Learning disabilities

_____ Difficulty with tests   _____ Dislike of homework   _____ Lack of persistence

_____ Difficulty with memory _____ Dislike of school   _____ Health problems

List any other roadblocks in addition to the items checked above:

What are your top three roadblocks?

1. _____

2. _____

3. _____

Spend 5 minutes skimming through the table of contents in your textbook and looking quickly through the chapters to find ideas that will help you overcome any roadblocks to your success. List 5 topics from the textbook that can help you to be successful in college.

1. _____

2. _____

3. _____

4. _____

5. _____

What are other resources that can help you to overcome your roadblocks? (tutoring, financial aid, advising, family support, self-motivation)

Your instructor will help the class brainstorm ideas for overcoming roadblocks. What is your plan for overcoming the roadblocks to achieve your hopes and dreams for the future?

Textbook Skimming

Name _____ Date _____

Use this text or any new text to answer the following questions. Challenge yourself to do this exercise quickly. Remember that a textbook survey should take no longer than five to 15 minutes. Try to complete this exercise in 15 minutes to allow time for writing. Notice the time when you start and finish.

1. Write two key ideas found in the introduction or preface to the book.

2. Looking at the table of contents, list the first five main ideas covered in the text.

3. Write down five interesting topics that you found in the book.

4. What did you find at the back of the book (e.g., index, glossary, appendixes)?

5. How long did it take you to do this exercise? _____

6. Briefly, what did you think of this textbook skimming exercise?

CHAPTER 3

Walk with Nature as One: Choosing Your Major

Learning Objectives

Read to answer these key questions:

- What are the steps in choosing a major?

- What is my personality type and know how is it related to choosing a major and career?

- What is my preferred work environment?

- What are my personal strengths or multiple intelligences?

- What are my vocational interests?

- What are some careers that match my personality type, personal strengths, and interests?

- What are my values and how do they influence career decision making?

- How can I find a career with good employment opportunities and pay?

- What careers will be in demand in the future?

To assure your success in college, it is important to choose the major that is best for you. If you choose a major and career that matches your personal strengths, interests, and values, you will enjoy your studies, complete your education, and excel in your work. It was Picasso who said that you know you enjoy your work when you do not notice the time passing by. If you can become interested in your work and studies, you are on your way to developing passion and joy in your life. If you can get up each morning and enjoy the work that you do (at least on most days) you will surely have one of the keys to happiness.

Most students attend college to make a better life for themselves. Choosing your major is choosing a path that leads to this better life. Education is our buffalo. In the past buffalos provided everything we needed for survival, including tools. clothing, shelter, threads, and heat from the buffalo chips. Education is our new buffalo. It provides us with everything we need to be good providers for our families.

Learning to Walk with Nature as One is to understand that you are part of this living world, just as the trees and the birds and the fish are. We all carry a spirit force within and learning to live in harmony in this way will help you to be true to yourself, your personality, and your talents.

Making a Career Decision

Knowing how to make a good decision about your career and important life events is very important to your future, as this short poem by J. Wooden sums up:

© Anastasia vish/Shutterstock.com

There is a choice you have to make, In everything you do

And you must always keep in mind, The choice you make, makes you.[1]

Sometimes people end up in a career because they simply seized an opportunity for employment. A good job becomes available and they happen to be in the right place at the right time. Sometimes people end up in a career because it is familiar to them, because it is a job held by a member of the family or a friend in the community. Sometimes people end up in a career because of economic necessity. The job pays well and they need the money. These careers are the result of chance circumstances. Sometimes they turn out well, and sometimes they turn out miserably.

Whatever your gender or marital status, you will spend a great deal of your life working. By doing some careful thinking and planning about your career, you can improve your chances of success and happiness. Use the following steps to do some careful decision making about your career. Although you are the person who needs to make the decision about a career, you can get help from your college career center or your college counselor or advisor.

Steps in Making a Career Decision

1. **Begin with self-assessment.**
   - What is your personality type?
   - What are your interests?
   - What are your talents, gifts, and strengths?
   - What are your values?

2. **Explore your options.**
   - What careers match your personal characteristics?

3. **Research your career options.**
   - Read the job description.
   - Investigate the career outlook.
   - What is the salary?
   - What training and education is required?
   - Speak with an advisor, counselor, or person involved in the career that interests you.
   - Choose a career or general career area that matches your personal characteristics.

4. **Plan your education to match your career goal.**
   - Try out courses in your area of interest.
   - Start your general education if you need more time to decide on a major.
   - Try an internship or part-time job in your area of interest.

5. **Make a commitment to take action and follow through with your plan.**

6. **Evaluate.**
   - Do you like the courses you are taking?
   - Are you doing well in the courses?
   - Continue research if necessary.

7. **Refine your plan.**
   - Make your plan more specific to aim for a particular career.
   - Select the college major that is best for you.

8. **Change your plan if it is not working.**
   - Go back to the self-assessment step.

> "Find a job you like and add five days to every week."
>
> H. Jackson Browne

Choose a Major That Matches Your Gifts and Talents

The first step in choosing the major that is right for you is to understand your personality type. Psychologists have developed useful theories of personality that can help you understand how personality type relates to the choice of major and career. The personality theory used in this textbook is derived from the work of Swiss psychologist Carl Jung (1875–1961). Jung believed that we are born with a predisposition for certain personality preferences and that healthy development is based on the lifelong nurturing of inborn preferences rather than trying to change a person to become something different. Each personality type has gifts and talents that can be nurtured over a lifetime.

> "To be what we are, and to become what we are capable of becoming, is the only end of life."
>
> Robert Louis Stevenson

While assessments are not exact predictors of your future major and career, they provide useful information that will get you started on the path of career exploration and finding the college major that is best suited to you. Knowledge of your personality and the personalities of others is not only valuable in understanding yourself, but also in appreciating how others are different. This understanding of self and others will empower you to communicate and work effectively with others. Knowledge of your multiple intelligences will help you match your personal strengths with careers.

Photo courtesy of Navajo Technical University

This textbook includes an online career portfolio to help in choosing your major. See the directions located on the inside front cover of your text to set up your portfolio and complete the career assessments. Complete the TruTalent Personality and Multiple Intelligences assessments before you begin this chapter.

Understanding Personality Types

Just as no two fingerprints or snowflakes are exactly alike, each person is a different and unique individual. Even with this uniqueness, however, we can make some general statements about personality. When we make generalizations, we are talking about averages. These averages can provide useful information about ourselves and other people, but it is important to remember that no individual is exactly described by the average. As you read through the following descriptions of personality types, keep in mind that we are talking about generalizations or beginning points for discussion and thoughtful analysis.

As you read through your personality description from the AchieveWORKS Personality assessment and the information in this text, **focus on your personal strengths and talents**. Building on these personal strengths has several important benefits. It increases self-esteem and self-confidence, which contribute to your success and enjoyment of life. Building on your strengths provides the energy and motivation required to put in the effort needed to accomplish any worthwhile task. The assessment also identifies some of your possible weaknesses or "blind spots." Just be aware of these blind spots so that they do not interfere with your success. Being aware of your blind spots can even be used to your advantage. For example, some personality types thrive by working with people. A career that involves much public contact is a good match for this personality type, whereas choosing a career where public contact is limited can lead to job dissatisfaction. Knowing about your personality type can help you make the right decisions to maximize your potential.

Personality type has four dimensions:

1. Extraversion or Introversion
2. Sensing or Intuition
3. Thinking or Feeling
4. Judging or Perceiving

These dimensions of personality will be defined and examined in more depth in the sections that follow.

Extraversion or Introversion

The dimension of extraversion or introversion defines how we interact with the world and how our energy flows. In the general school population, 75 percent of students are usually extraverts and 25 percent are introverts.

> *Extraverts (E) focus their energy on the world outside themselves. They enjoy interaction with others and get to know a lot of different people. They enjoy and are usually good at communication. They are energized by social interaction and prefer being active. These types are often described as talkative and social.*
>
> *Introverts (I) focus their energy on the world inside of themselves. They enjoy spending time alone to think about the world in order to understand it. Introverts prefer more limited social contacts, choosing smaller groups or one-on-one relationships. These types are often described as quiet or reserved.*

We all use the introvert and extravert modes while functioning in our daily lives. Whether a person is an extravert or an introvert is a matter of preference, like being left- or right-handed. We can use our nondominant hand, but it is not as comfortable as using our dominant hand. We are usually more skillful in using the dominant hand. For example, introverts can learn to function well in social situations, but later may need some peace and quiet to recharge. On the other hand, social contact energizes the extravert.

One personality type is not better than the other: it is just different. Being an extravert is not better than being an introvert. Each type has unique gifts and talents that can be used in different occupations. An extravert might enjoy working in an occupation with lots of public contact, such as being a receptionist or handling public relations. An introvert might enjoy being an accountant or writer. However, as with all of the personality dimensions, a person may have traits of both types.

ACTIVITY

Introverts and Extraverts

The list below describes some qualities of introverts and extraverts. **For each pair of items,** quickly choose the phrase that describes you best and highlight or place a checkmark next to it. Remember that one type is not better than another. You may also find that you are a combination type and act like an introvert in some situations and an extravert in others. Each type has gifts and talents that can be used in choosing the best major and career for you. To get an estimate of your preference, notice which column has the most checkmarks.

Introvert (I)	Extravert (E)
_____ Energized by having quiet time alone	_____ Energized by social interaction
_____ Tend to think first and talk later	_____ Tend to talk first and think later
_____ Tend to think things through quietly	_____ Tend to think out loud
_____ Tend to respond slowly, after thinking	_____ Tend to respond quickly, before thinking
_____ Avoid being the center of attention	_____ Like to be the center of attention
_____ Difficult to get to know, private	_____ Easy to get to know, outgoing
_____ Have a few close friends	_____ Have many friends, know lots of people
_____ Prefer quiet for concentration	_____ Can read or talk with background noise
_____ Listen more than talk	_____ Talk more than listen
_____ View telephone calls as a distraction	_____ View telephone calls as a welcome break
_____ Talk to a few people at parties	_____ Talk to many different people at parties
_____ Share special occasions with one or a few people	_____ Share special occasions with large groups
_____ Prefer to study alone	_____ Prefer to study with others in a group
_____ Prefer the library to be quiet	_____ Talk with others in the library
_____ Described as quiet or reserved	_____ Described as talkative or friendly
_____ Work systematically	_____ Work through trial and error

(Continued)

Here are some qualities that describe the ideal work environment. Again, as you **read through each pair of items**, place a checkmark next to the work environment that you prefer.

Introvert (I)

_____ Work alone or with individuals

_____ Quiet for concentration

_____ Communication one-on-one

_____ Work in small groups

_____ Focus on one project until complete

_____ Work without interruption

_____ **Total** (from both charts above)

Extravert (E)

_____ Much public contact

_____ High-energy environment

_____ Present ideas to a group

_____ Work as part of a team

_____ Variety and action

_____ Talk to others

_____ **Total** (from both charts above)

Do these results agree with your TruTalent Personality assessment? If your results are the same, this is a good indication that your results are useful and accurate. Are there some differences with the results obtained from your personality assessment? If your results are different, this provides an opportunity for further reflection about your personality type. Here are a couple of reasons why your results may be different.

1. You may be a combination type with varying degrees of preference for each type.

2. You may have chosen your personality type on the TruTalent Personality assessment based on what you think is best rather than what you truly are. Students sometimes do this because of the myth that there are good and bad personality types. It is important to remember that each personality type has strengths and weaknesses. By identifying strengths, you can build on them by choosing the right major and career. By being aware of weaknesses, you can come up with strategies to compensate for them to be successful.

Look at the total number of checkmarks for extravert and introvert on the two above charts. Do you lean toward being an introvert or an extravert? Remember that one type is not better than the other and each has unique gifts and talents. On the chart below, place an X on the line to indicate how much you prefer introversion or extraversion. If you selected most of the introvert traits, place your X somewhere on the left side. If you selected most of the extravert traits, place your X somewhere on the right side. If you are equally introverted and extraverted, place your X in the middle.

Introvert _____|_____ Extravert

Do you generally prefer introversion or extraversion? In the box below, write **I** for introversion or **E** for extraversion. If there is a tie between **E** and **I**, write **I**.

Notice that it is possible to be a combination type. At times you might prefer to act like an introvert, and at other times you might prefer to act like an extravert. It is beneficial to be able to balance these traits. However, for combination types, it is more difficult to select specific occupations that match this type

Sensing or Intuition

The dimension of sensing or intuition describes how we take in information. In the general school population, 70 percent of students are usually sensing types and 30 percent are intuitive types.

Sensing (S) persons prefer to use the senses to take in information (what they see, hear, taste, touch, smell). They focus on "what is" and trust information that is concrete and observable. They learn through experience.

Intuitive (N) persons rely on instincts and focus on "what could be." While we all use our five senses to perceive the world, intuitive people are interested in relationships, possibilities, meanings, and implications. They value inspiration and trust their "sixth sense" or hunches. (Intuitive is designated as N so it is not confused with I for Introvert.)

We all use both of these modes in our daily lives, but we usually have a preference for one mode or the other. Again, there is no best preference. Each type has special skills that can be applied to the job market. For example, you would probably want your tax preparer to be a sensing type who focuses on concrete information and fills out your tax form correctly. An inventor or artist would probably be an intuitive type.

ACTIVITY

Sensing and Intuitive

Here are some qualities of sensing and intuitive persons. As you **read through each pair of items**, quickly highlight or place a checkmark next to the item that usually describes yourself.

Sensing (S)	INtuitive (N)
_____ Trust what is certain and concrete	_____ Trust inspiration and inference
_____ Prefer specific answers to questions	_____ Prefer general answers that leave room for interpretation
_____ Like new ideas if they have practical applications (if you can use them)	_____ Like new ideas for their own sake (you don't need a practical use for them)
_____ Value realism and common sense	_____ Value imagination and innovation
_____ Think about things one at a time and step by step	_____ Think about many ideas at once as they come to you

(Continued)

Sensing (S)	INtuitive (N)
_____ Like to improve and use skills learned before	_____ Like to learn new skills and get bored using the same skills
_____ More focused on the present	_____ More focused on the future
_____ Concentrate on what you are doing	_____ Wonder what is next
_____ Do something	_____ Think about doing something
_____ See tangible results	_____ Focus on possibilities
_____ If it isn't broken, don't fix it	_____ There is always a better way to do it
_____ Prefer working with facts and figures	_____ Prefer working with ideas and theories
_____ Focus on reality	_____ Use fantasy
_____ Seeing is believing	_____ Anything is possible
_____ Tend to be specific and literal (say what you mean)	_____ Tend to be general and figurative (use comparisons and analogies)
_____ See what is here and now	_____ See the big picture

Here are some qualities that describe the ideal work environment. Again, as you **read through each pair of items**, place a checkmark next to the work environment that you prefer.

Sensing (S)	INtuitive (N)
_____ Use and practice skills	_____ Learn new skills
_____ Work with known facts	_____ Explore new ideas and approaches
_____ See measurable results	_____ Work with theories
_____ Focus on practical benefits	_____ Use imagination and be original
_____ Learn through experience	_____ Freedom to follow your inspiration
_____ Pleasant environment	_____ Challenging environment
_____ Use standard procedures	_____ Invent new products and procedures
_____ Work step-by-step	_____ Work in bursts of energy
_____ Do accurate work	_____ Find creative solutions
_____ **Total** (from both charts above)	_____ **Total** (from both charts above)

Look at the two charts above and see whether you tend to be more sensing or intuitive. One preference is not better than another: it is just different. On the chart below, place an X on the line to indicate your preference for sensing or intuitive. Again, notice that it is possible to be a combination type with both sensing and intuitive preferences.

Sensing _____|_____Intuitive

Do you generally prefer sensing or intuition? In the box below, write **S** for sensing or **N** for intuitive. If there is a tie between **S** and **N**, write **N**.

Thinking or Feeling

The dimension of thinking or feeling defines how we prefer to make decisions. In the general school population, 60 percent of males are thinking types and 40 percent are feeling types. For females, 60 percent are feeling types and 40 percent are thinking types.

Thinking (T) individuals make decisions based on logic. They are objective and analytical. They look at all the evidence and reach an impersonal conclusion. They are concerned with what they think is right.

Feeling (F) individuals make decisions based on what is important to them and matches their personal values. They are concerned about what they feel is right.

We all use logic and have feelings and emotions that play a part in decision making. However, the thinking person prefers to make decisions based on logic, and the feeling person prefers to make decisions according to what is important to self and others. This is one category in which men and women often differ. Most women are feeling types, and most men are logical types. When men and women are arguing, you might hear the following:

Man: "I think that . . ."

Woman: "I feel that . . ."

By understanding these differences, it is possible to improve communication and understanding. Be careful with generalizations, since 40 percent of men and women would not fit this pattern.

When thinking about careers, a thinking type would make a good judge or computer programmer. A feeling type would probably make a good social worker or kindergarten teacher.

ACTIVITY

Thinking and Feeling

The following chart shows some qualities of thinking and feeling types. As you **read through each pair of items**, quickly highlight or place a checkmark next to the items that usually describe yourself.

Thinking (T)	Feeling (F)
_____ Apply impersonal analysis to problems	_____ Consider the effect on others
_____ Value logic and justice	_____ Value empathy and harmony
_____ Fairness is important	_____ There are exceptions to every rule
_____ Truth is more important than tact	_____ Tact is more important than truth
_____ Motivated by achievement and accomplishment	_____ Motivated by being appreciated by others

(Continued)

Thinking (T)

_____ Feelings are valid if they are logical

_____ Good decisions are logical

_____ Described as cool, calm, and objective

_____ Love can be analyzed

_____ Firm-minded

_____ More important to be right

_____ Remember numbers and figures

_____ Prefer clarity

_____ Find flaws and critique

_____ Prefer firmness

Feeling (F)

_____ Feelings are valid whether they make sense or not

_____ Good decisions take others' feelings into account

_____ Described as caring and emotional

_____ Love cannot be analyzed

_____ Gentle-hearted

_____ More important to be liked

_____ Remember faces and names

_____ Prefer harmony

_____ Look for the good and compliment

_____ Prefer persuasion

Here are some qualities that describe the ideal work environment. As you **read through each pair of items**, place a checkmark next to the items that usually describe the work environment that you prefer.

Thinking (T)

_____ Maintain business environment

_____ Work with people I respect

_____ Be treated fairly

_____ Fair evaluations

_____ Solve problems

_____ Challenging work

_____ Use logic and analysis

_____ **Total** (from both charts above)

Feeling (F)

_____ Maintain close personal relationships

_____ Work in a friendly, relaxed environment

_____ Be able to express personal values

_____ Appreciation for good work

_____ Make a personal contribution

_____ Harmonious work situation

_____ Help others

_____ **Total** (from both charts above)

While we all use thinking and feeling, what is your preferred type? Look at the charts above and notice whether you are more the thinking or feeling type. One is not better than the other. On the chart below, place an X on the line to indicate how much you prefer thinking or feeling.

Thinking _____|_____ Feeling

Do you generally prefer thinking or feeling? In the box below, write **T** for thinking or **F** for feeling. If there is a tie between **T** and **F**, write **F**.

Journal Entry #3

Look at the results from the TruTalent Personality assessment and your own self-assessment above. Are you a thinking, feeling, or combination type? Can you give examples of how it affects your social life, school, or work? Write a paragraph about this preference.

Judging or Perceiving

The dimension of judging or perceiving refers to how we deal with the external world. In other words, do we prefer the world to be structured or unstructured? In the general school population, the percentage of each of these types is approximately equal.

*Judging (J) types like to live in a structured, orderly, and planned way. They are happy when their lives are structured and matters are settled. They like to have control over their lives. **Judging does not mean to judge others.** Think of this type as being orderly and organized.*

*Perceptive (P) types like to live in a spontaneous and flexible way. They are happy when their lives are open to possibilities. They try to understand life rather than control it. **Think of this type as spontaneous and flexible.***

Since these types have very opposite ways of looking at the world, there is a great deal of potential for conflict between them unless there is an appreciation for the gifts and talents of both. In any situation, we can benefit from people who represent these very different points of view. For example, in a business situation, the judging type would be good at managing the money, while the perceptive type would be good at helping the business to adapt to a changing marketplace. It is good to be open to all the possibilities and to be flexible, as well as to have some structure and organization.

ACTIVITY

Judging and Perceptive

As you **read through each pair of items**, quickly highlight or place a checkmark next to the items that generally describe yourself.

Judging (J)	Perceptive (P)
_____ Happy when the decisions are made and finished	_____ Happy when the options are left open; something better may come along
_____ Work first, play later	_____ Play first, do the work later
_____ It is important to be on time	_____ Time is relative
_____ Time flies	_____ Time is elastic
_____ Feel comfortable with routine	_____ Dislike routine
_____ Generally keep things in order	_____ Prefer creative disorder
_____ Set goals and work toward them	_____ Change goals as new opportunities arise
_____ Emphasize completing the task	_____ Emphasize how the task is done
_____ Like to finish projects	_____ Like to start projects
_____ Meet deadlines	_____ What deadline?
_____ Like to know what I am getting into	_____ Like new possibilities and situations
_____ Relax when things are organized	_____ Relax when necessary
_____ Follow a routine	_____ Explore the unknown
_____ Focused	_____ Easily distracted
_____ Work steadily	_____ Work in spurts of energy

(Continued)

Here are some qualities that describe the ideal work environment. Again, as you **read through each pair of items**, place a checkmark next to the work environment that you prefer.

Judging (J)	Perceptive (P)
_____ Follow a schedule	_____ Be spontaneous
_____ Clear directions	_____ Minimal rules and structure
_____ Organized work	_____ Flexibility
_____ Logical order	_____ Many changes
_____ Control my job	_____ Respond to emergencies
_____ Stability and security	_____ Take risks and be adventurous
_____ Work on one project until done	_____ Juggle many projects
_____ Steady work	_____ Variety and action
_____ Satisfying work	_____ Fun and excitement
_____ Like having high responsibility	_____ Like having interesting work
_____ Accomplish goals on time	_____ Work at my own pace
_____ Clear and concrete assignments	_____ Minimal supervision
_____ **Total** (from both charts above)	_____ **Total** (from both charts above)

Look at the charts above and notice whether you are more the judging type (orderly and organized) or the perceptive type (spontaneous and flexible). We need the qualities of both types to be successful and deal with the rapid changes in today's world. On the chart below, place an X on the line to indicate how much you prefer judging or perceiving.

Judging _____|_____Perceptive

Do you generally have judging or perceptive traits? In the box below, write **J** for judging or **P** for perceptive. If there is a tie between **J** and **P**, write **P**.

Journal Entry #4

Look at the results from the TruTalent Personality assessment and your own self-assessment above. Are you a judging, perceptive, or combination type? Can you give examples of how it affects your social life, school, or work? Write a paragraph about this preference.

"Knowing thyself is the height of wisdom."
Socrates

Summarize Your Results

Look at your results above and summarize them on this composite chart. Notice that we are all unique, according to where the Xs fall on the scale.

Extravert (E) _____|_____ Introvert (I)

Sensing (S) _____|_____ Intuitive (N)

Thinking (T) _____|_____ Feeling (F)

Judging (J) _____|_____ Perceptive (P)

Write the letters representing each of your preferences.

The above letters represent your estimated personality type based on your understanding and knowledge of self. It is a good idea to confirm that this type is correct for you by completing the online TruTalent Personality assessment.

© Gustavo Frazao/Shutterstock.com

Personality Types

Test what you have learned by selecting the correct answer to the following questions.

1. A person who is energized by social interaction is a/an:

   a. introvert
   b. extravert
   c. feeling type

2. A person who is quiet and reserved is a/an:

   a. introvert
   b. extravert
   c. perceptive type

3. A person who relies on experience and trusts information that is concrete and observable is a/an:

   a. judging type
   b. sensing type
   c. perceptive type

4. A person who focuses on "what could be" is a/an:

   a. perceptive type
   b. thinking type
   c. intuitive type

5. A person who makes decisions based on logic is a/an:

   a. thinker
   b. perceiver
   c. sensor

6. A person who makes decisions based on personal values is a/an:

   a. feeling type
   b. thinking type
   c. judging type

7. The perceptive type:

   a. has extrasensory perception
   b. likes to live life in a spontaneous and flexible way
   c. always considers feelings before making a decision

8. The judging type likes to:

   a. judge others
   b. use logic
   c. live in a structured and orderly way

9. Personality assessments are an exact predictor of your best major and career.

   a. true
   b. false

10. Some personality types are better than others.

    a. true
    b. false

How did you do on the quiz? Check your answers: 1. b, 2. a, 3. b, 4. c, 5. a, 6. a, 7. b, 8. c, 9. b, 10. b

"Choose a job you love, and you will never have to work a day in your life."
Confucius

Personality and Career Choice

While it is not possible to predict exactly your career and college major by knowing your personality type, it can help provide opportunities for exploration. The TruTalent Personality assessment links your personality type with suggested matching careers in the O*Net career database continually updated by the U.S. Department of Labor. You can find additional information at the College Success 1 website: http://www.collegesuccess1.com/careers.html. This page includes a description of each type, general occupations to consider, specific job titles, and suggested college majors.

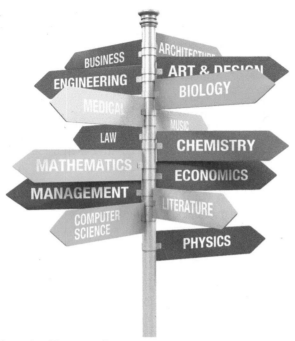

© Nerthuz/Shutterstock.com

Personality and Preferred Work Environment

Knowing your personality type will help you to understand your preferred work environment and provide some insights into selecting the major and career that you would enjoy. Selecting the work environment that matches your personal preferences helps you to be energized on the job and to minimize stress. Understanding other types will help you to work effectively with coworkers. As you read this section, think about your ideal work environment and how others are different.

Extroverts are career generalists who use their skills in a variety of ways. Extroverts

- like variety and social interaction.
- communicate well and meet people easily.
- learn new tasks by talking with others and trying out new ideas.
- are energized by working as part of a team.

Introverts are career specialists who develop in-depth skills. Introverts

- prefer to focus on a task until it is complete.
- choose to work alone or with one other person.
- prefer written communication.
- are energized when they can work in a quiet environment with few interruptions.

Sensing types are realistic and practical and like to develop standard ways of doing the job. Sensing types

- are observant and interested in facts and finding the truth.
- use common sense and learn from experience.
- keep track of details, do precise work, and like to follow routines.
- are energized when they are doing practical work with tangible outcomes.

© cristovao/Shutterstock.com

Intuitive types like to work on challenging and complex problems where they can follow their inspirations to find creative solutions. Intuitive types

- focus on the whole picture rather than the details.
- enjoy change and finding new ways of doing the job.
- are initiators, promoters, and inventors of ideas.
- are energized by working in an environment where they can use creative insight, imagination, originality, and individual initiative.

Thinking types like to use logical analysis in making decisions. Thinking types

- expect logical reasons before accepting new ideas.
- are objective and rational and treat others fairly.
- enjoy working with others who are competent and efficient.
- are energized when they are respected for their expertise and recognized for a job well done.

Feeling types like harmony and the support of coworkers. Feeling types

- know their personal values and apply them consistently.
- are personal, enjoy warm relationships, and relate well to most people.
- enjoy doing work that provides a service to people and contributes to humanity.
- are energized when they work in a friendly, congenial, and supportive work environment.

Judging types like a work environment that is structured, settled, and organized. Judging types

- make lists and get the job done on time.
- prefer work assignments that are clear and definite.
- excel at purposeful and exacting work.
- are energized by working in a predictable and orderly environment with clear responsibilities and deadlines.

Perceptive types like to be spontaneous and go with the flow. Perceptive types

- feel restricted by structures and schedules.
- are comfortable in handling the unplanned or unexpected work environment.
- can adapt and deal with change.
- are energized in a flexible work environment where they can relax and control their own time.

"True greatness is starting where you are, using what you have, and doing what you can."

Arthur Ashe

Photo courtesy of First Nations University, Canada.

Exploring Your Personal Strengths

Another way to explore your personal strengths is by understanding your multiple intelligences. **Multiple intelligences are defined as the human ability to solve problems or design or compose something valued in at least one culture**. A key idea in this theory is that most people can develop all of their intelligences and become relatively competent in each area. Another key idea is that these intelligences work together in complex ways to make us unique. Take the TruTalent Intelligences assessment which is included in your online portfolio to see how your personal strengths can be connected to careers. Below is a summary of multiple intelligences. As you read through this list, think about your results on the TruTalent Intelligences assessment. Think about your strong areas as well as areas that may need improvement to accomplish your goals.

© Aquir/Shutterstock.com

- **Musical intelligence** involves hearing and remembering musical patterns and manipulating patterns in music. Related careers include musician, performer, composer, and music critic.

- **Interpersonal intelligence** is defined as understanding people. Related careers involve working with people and helping them, as in education or health care.

- **Logical-mathematical intelligence** involves understanding abstract principles and manipulating numbers, quantities, and operations. Related careers include mathematician, tax accountant, scientist, and computer programmer.

- **Spatial intelligence** involves the ability to manipulate objects in space. For example, a baseball player uses spatial intelligence to hit a ball. Related occupations include pilot, painter, sculptor, architect, inventor, and surgeon. This intelligence is often used in athletics, the arts, and the sciences.

- **Bodily-kinesthetic intelligence** is defined as being able to use your body to solve problems. People with this intelligence make or invent objects or perform. Related occupations include athlete, performer (dancer, actor), craftsperson, sculptor, mechanic, and surgeon.

- **Linguistic intelligence** describes people who are good with language and words. They have good reading, writing, and speaking skills. Linguistic intelligence is an asset in any occupation. Specific related careers include writing, education, and politics.

- **Intrapersonal intelligence** is the ability to understand yourself and how to best use your natural talents and abilities. Related careers include novelist, psychologist, or being self-employed.

- **Naturalist intelligence** includes people who are able to recognize, classify, and analyze plants, animals, and cultural artifacts. Related occupations include botanist, horticulturist, biologist, archeologist and environmental occupations.

- **Existential intelligence** is the capacity to ask profound questions about the meaning of life and death. This intelligence is the cornerstone of art, religion, and philosophy. Related occupations include philosopher, psychologist, and artist.

Build on Your Strengths

Consider your personal strengths when deciding on a career. People in each of the multiple intelligence areas have different strengths:

- Musical strengths include listening to music, singing, playing a musical instrument, keeping a beat, and recognizing musical patterns. People with this intelligence are "musical smart."

- Interpersonal strengths include communication skills, social skills, helping others, understanding other's feelings, and the ability to resolve conflicts. People with this intelligence are "people smart."
- Logical-mathematical strengths include math aptitude, interest in science, problem-solving skills, and logical thinking. People with this intelligence are "number/reasoning smart."
- Spatial strengths include visualization, understanding puzzles, navigation, visual arts, reading, and writing. People with this intelligence are "picture smart."

ACTIVITY

© iQoncept/Shutterstock.com

Some Careers and Multiple Intelligences

Circle any careers that seem interesting to you		
Musical	**Interpersonal**	**Logical–Mathematical**
disc jockey	cruise director	engineer
music teacher	mediator	accountant
music retailer	human resources	computer analyst
music therapist	dental hygienist	physician
recording engineer	nurse	detective
singer	psychologist	researcher
song writer	social worker	scientist
speech pathologist	administrator	computer programmer
music librarian	marketer	database designer
choir director	religious leader	physicist
music critic	teacher	auditor
music lawyer	counselor	economist
Spatial	**Bodily-Kinesthetic**	**Linguistic**
architect	athlete	journalist
artist	carpenter	writer
film animator	craftsperson	editor
mechanic	mechanic	attorney
pilot	jeweler	curator
webmaster	computer game designer	newscaster
interior decorator	firefighter	politician
graphic artist	forest ranger	speech pathologist
sculptor	physical therapist	translator
surveyor	personal trainer	comedian
urban planner	surgeon	historian
photographer	recreation specialist	librarian
		marketing consultant

Intrapersonal	Naturalist	Existential
career counselor	park ranger	counselor
wellness counselor	dog trainer	psychologist
therapist	landscaper	psychiatrist
criminologist	meteorologist	social worker
intelligence officer	veterinarian	minister
entrepreneur	animal health technician	philosopher
psychologist	ecologist	artist
researcher	nature photographer	scientist
actor	wilderness guide	researcher
artist	anthropologist	motivational speaker
philosopher	environmental lawyer	human resources
writer	water conservationist	writer

- Bodily-kinesthetic strengths include hand and eye coordination, athletics, dance, drama, cooking, sculpting, and learning by doing. People with this intelligence are "body smart."

- Linguistic strengths include good reading, writing, vocabulary, and spelling skills; good communication skills; being a good listener; having a good memory; and learning new languages easily. People with this intelligence are "word smart."

- Intrapersonal strengths include good self-awareness. They are aware of their feelings and emotions and are often independent and self-motivated to achieve. People with this intelligence are "self-smart."

- Naturalist strengths include exploring and preserving the environment and are very aware of natural surroundings. People with this intelligence are "nature smart."

- Existential strengths include reflecting on important questions about the universe, the purpose of life, and religious beliefs. People with this intelligence are "curiosity smart."

Using Emotional Intelligence in Your Personal Life and Career

Emotional intelligence is related to interpersonal and intrapersonal intelligences. It is the ability to recognize, control, and evaluate your own emotions while realizing how they affect people around you. Emotional intelligence affects career and personal success because it is related to the ability to build good relationships, communicate, work as part of a team, concentrate, remember, make decisions, deal with stress, overcome challenges, deal with conflict, and empathize with others. Research has shown emotional intelligence can predict career success and that workers with high emotional intelligence are more likely to end up in leadership positions in which workers are happy with their jobs.

The premise of emotional intelligence is that you can be more successful if you are aware of your own emotions as well as the emotions of others. There are two aspects of emotional intelligence:

- Understanding yourself, your goals, intentions, responses, and behavior.
- Understanding others and their feelings.

Daniel Goleman has identified the five most important characteristics of emotional intelligence:[2]

1. **Self-Awareness**

   People with high emotional intelligence are aware of their emotions including strengths and weaknesses.

2. **Self-Regulation**

   This involves the ability to control emotions and impulses. Being impulsive can lead to careless decisions like attending a party the night before a final exam. Characteristics of self-regulation include comfort with change, integrity, and the ability to say no.

3. **Motivation**

   People with high emotional intelligence can defer immediate results for long-term success. For example, investing your time in education can lead to future career opportunities and income.

4. **Empathy**

   Empathy is the ability to understand the needs and viewpoints of others around you and avoiding stereotypes. It involves good listening skills that enhance personal relationships.

5. **Social Skills**

   People with good social skills are good team players and willing to help others to be successful.

You can enhance your personal and career success by developing your emotional intelligence. Here are some tips for developing good relationships in your personal life and on the job.

- Be empathetic when working with others by trying to put yourself in their place to understand different perspectives and points of view. Don't be quick to jump to conclusions or stereotype others.
- Think about how your actions affect others. Always treat others as you would like to be treated.
- Be open-minded and intellectually curious. Consider the opinions of others in a positive manner. Be willing to examine and change your mind-set.
- Give others credit for accomplishments in their personal life and in the workplace. When speaking about your own accomplishments, confidently state what you accomplished without trying to seek too much attention.
- Evaluate your own strengths and weaknesses. Focus on your strengths, but be aware of the weaknesses and work to improve them. The personality assessment in the previous chapter helps you to understand your personal strengths and weaknesses.
- Work on stress management by finding some stress reduction techniques that work for you. In stressful situations, it is helpful to remain calm and in control. Seek workable solutions without blaming others. Your college health services office often provides workshops on stress management. There is also additional material in this textbook on stress management.

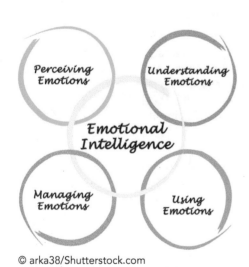

- Take a college course to improve verbal as well as nonverbal communication. When talking with others, focus on what they are saying rather than what you are going to say next. Learn how to make "I statements" that effectively communicate your thoughts without blaming others. Become aware of nonverbal communication which adds a significant dimension to communication.

- Use humor to help you deal with challenges. Humor helps you to keep things in perspective, deal with differences, relax, and come up with creative solutions.

- Deal with conflicts in a way that builds trust. Focus on win-win solutions that allow both parties to have their needs met.

Photo courtesy of William Bright of Connors State College.

- Take responsibility for your actions. Admit when you make mistakes and work to improve the situation in the future.

- Use critical thinking to analyze the pros and cons of the situation.

- Be goal oriented and focus on the task and the steps needed to achieve your goals.

- Be optimistic. Optimism leads to greater opportunities and results in better personal relationships.

Exploring Your Interests

Interests are simply what a person likes to do. As interests are developed, they can become a passion. Research shows that students who choose a major that matches their interests are more likely to earn high grades and finish their degrees.[3] It's is difficult to be gritty if you are not interested in what you are doing. After college, people are more satisfied with their jobs if it matches their interests. If you like your job, both your job performance and life satisfaction increase.

How do you learn about your interests? Interests are a result of many factors, including personality, family life, values, and interaction with the environment. Part of developing an interest is trying new things and sticking with them for a while to find out if they match your interests. Participating in extracurricular activities, volunteering, internships, and working part time while in college can help you to explore your interests. One barrier to discovering your interests is unrealistic expectations. Often students are expecting the perfect job, however, every job has enjoyable aspects and aspects you don't like.

Another way to explore your interests is through vocational interest assessments. By studying people who are satisfied with their careers, psychologists can help people choose careers based on their interests. The U.S. Department of Labor has developed the O*Net Interest Profiler, which helps to identify your career interests.[4] The O*Net Interest Profiler is compatible with Holland's Theory of Vocational Personality. This is one of the most widely accepted approaches to vocational choice. According to the theory, there are six vocational personality types. These six types and their accompanying definitions are presented below. As you read through each description, think about your own interests.

> "Choose a job you love, and you will never have to work a day in your life."
> Confucius

Realistic

People with **realistic** interests like work activities that include practical, hands-on problems and solutions. They enjoy dealing with plants, animals, and real-world materials like wood, tools, and machinery. They enjoy outside work. Often people with realistic interests do not like occupations that mainly involve doing paperwork or working closely with others.

Investigative

People with **investigative** interests like work activities that have to do with ideas and thinking more than with physical activity. They like to search for facts and figure out problems mentally rather than to persuade or lead people.

Artistic

People with **artistic** interests like work activities that deal with the artistic side of things, such as forms, designs, and patterns. They like self-expression in their work. They prefer settings where work can be done without following a clear set of rules.

Social

People with **social** interests like work activities that assist others and promote learning and personal development. They prefer to communicate more than to work with objects, machines, or data. They like to teach, give advice, help, or otherwise be of service to people.

Enterprising

People with **enterprising** interests like work activities that have to do with starting up and carrying out projects, especially business ventures. They like persuading and leading people and making decisions. They like taking risks for profit. These people prefer action rather than thought.

Conventional

People with **conventional** interests like work activities that follow set procedures and routines. They prefer working with data and detail rather than with ideas. They prefer work in which there are precise standards rather than work in which you have to judge things by yourself. These people like working where the lines of authority are clear.

According to Holland, most individuals can be described by one or more of these six personality types, frequently summarized as R-I-A-S-E-C (the first letter of each personality type). Additionally, the theory proposes that there are six corresponding work environments (or occupational groups), and that people seek out work environments that match their personality types. The better the match individuals make, the more satisfied they will be with their jobs.5

Holland arranged these interests on a hexagon that shows the relationship of the interests to one another. He notes that most people are not just one type, but rather a combination of types. Types that are close to each other on the hexagon are likely to have interests in common. For example, a person who is social is likely to have some artistic interests and some enterprising interests. Interests on opposite points of the hexagon are very different. For example, artistic and conventional types are opposites. Artistic types prefer freedom to be creative; conventional types prefer structure and order. The figure that follows illustrates the relationship between interest areas.6

Photo courtesy of William Bright of Connors State College.

> "The only way to do great work is to love what you do."
>
> Steve Jobs

> "Even if you're on the right track, you'll get run over if you just sit there."
>
> Will Rogers

> "Real success is finding your life work in work that you love."
>
> David McCullough

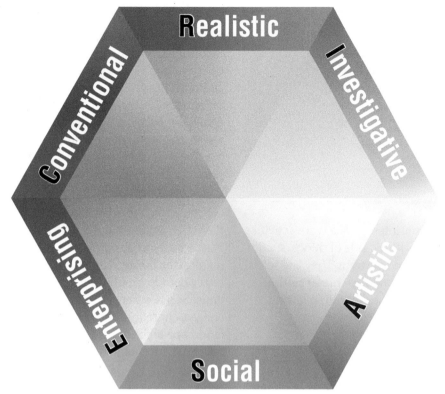

Figure 3.1 Relationships between interest areas.
© Kendall Hunt Publishing Company

Exploring Your Interests

Read the definition of these interests and circle any jobs that seem interesting to you.

Vocational Interest	Matching Jobs
Realistic People with realistic interests like work activities that include practical, hands-on problems and solutions. They enjoy dealing with plants, animals, and real-world materials like wood, tools, and machinery. They enjoy outside work. Often people with realistic interests do not like occupations that mainly involve doing paperwork or working closely with others.	Construction worker, building contractor, cook, landscaper, housekeeper, janitor, firefighter, hazardous materials removal worker, security guard, truck driver, automotive mechanic, cardiovascular technologist, civil engineer, commercial pilot, computer support specialist, plumber, police officer, chemical engineer, fish and game warden, surveyor, archaeologist, athletic trainer, dentist, veterinarian

(Continued)

Investigative People with investigative interests like work activities that have to do with ideas and thinking more than with physical activity. They like to search for facts and figure out problems mentally rather than to persuade or lead people.	Electronic engineering technician, emergency medical technician, fire investigator, paralegal, police detective, engineer (aerospace, biomedical, chemical, electrical, computer, environmental, or industrial), chemist, computer systems analyst, geoscientist, market research analyst, anesthesiologist, biochemist, biophysicist, clinical psychologist, dietician, physician, microbiologist, pharmacist, psychiatrist, surgeon, veterinarian, science teacher, college professor
Artistic People with artistic interests like work activities that deal with the artistic side of things, such as forms, designs, and patterns. They like self-expression in their work. They prefer settings where work can be done without following a clear set of rules.	Model, actor, fine artist, floral designer, singer, tile setter, architectural drafter, architect, dancer, fashion designer, film and video editor, hairdresser, makeup artist, museum technician, music composer, photographer, self-enrichment education teacher, art director, broadcast news analyst, choreographer, editor, graphic designer, landscape architect, creative writer, public relations specialist, teacher (of art, drama, or music)
Social People with social interests like work activities that assist others and promote learning and personal development. They prefer to communicate more than to work with objects, machines, or data. They like to teach, give advice, help, or otherwise be of service to people.	Host, hostess, bartender, lifeguard, food server, child care worker, home health aide, occupational therapist, personal and home care aide, physical therapist, veterinary assistant, dental hygienist, fitness trainer, medical assistant, nanny, teacher, registered nurse, respiratory therapist, self-enrichment education teacher, tour guide, mediator, educational administrator, health director, park naturalist, probation officer, recreation worker, chiropractor, clergy, counseling psychologist, social worker, substance abuse counselor, physician assistant, speech and language pathologist
Enterprising People with enterprising interests like work activities that have to do with starting up and carrying out projects, especially business ventures. The like persuading and leading people and making decisions. The like taking risks for profit. These people prefer action rather than thought.	Cashier, food worker, customer service representative, sales worker, supervisor, inspector, retail sales clerk, chef, food service manager, operations manager, real estate broker, realtor, sheriff, buyer, advertiser, appraiser, construction manager, criminal investigator, financial manager, insurance sales agent, meeting and convention planner, personal financial advisor, judge, lawyer, business or political science teacher, educational administrator, librarian, medical health manager, treasurer, controller

Conventional	Cashier, cook, janitor, landscaping worker,
People with conventional interests like work activities that follow set procedures and routines. They prefer working with data and detail rather than with ideas. They prefer work in which there are precise standards rather than work in which you judge things by yourself. These people like working where the lines of authority are clear.	resort desk clerk, medical records technician, bookkeeping and accounting clerk, dental assistant, drafter, loan officer, paralegal, pharmacy technician, accountant, auditor, city and regional planner, computer security specialist, cost estimator, credit analyst, database administrator, environmental compliance inspector, financial analyst, librarian, proofreader, computer science teacher, pharmacist, statistician, treasurer

Journal Entry #5

You can learn about your vocational interests and matching careers by taking the Interest Profiler at https://www.mynextmove.org/explore/ip. After taking this assessment, complete the following steps:

1. Click on your highest interest and briefly describe it.
2. Click on your second-highest interest and briefly describe it.
3. Click on your third-highest interest and briefly describe it.
4. Click on the Job Zone button and select your future level of education. Click on Careers and list three careers that match your vocational interests.
5. Click on one career and write one sentence about what you found interesting about this career.

Using Values to Make Important Life Decisions

Values are what we think is important and what we feel is right and good. Our values tell the world who we are. They help us to determine which goals are more valuable than others and to spend time on what is most important. Our values make us different and unique individuals. We often take pride in our values by displaying them on bumper stickers, tee shirts, and tattoos.

Values come from many sources, including our parents, friends, the media, our religious background, our culture, society, and the historical time in which we live. Knowing our values helps to make good decisions about work and life. For example, consider a situation in which a person is offered a high-paying job that involves a high degree of responsibility and stress. If the person values challenge and excitement and views stress as a motivator, the chances are that it would be a good decision to take the job. If the person values peace of mind and has a difficult time coping with stress, it might be better to forgo the higher income and maintain quality of life. Making decisions consistent with our values is one of the keys to happiness and success.

Researchers studied values in 70 different countries around the world and found 10 values rated as important around the world.[7] As you read the list, think about your own personal values.

"Try not to be a man of success, but rather to become a man of value."
Albert Einstein

The 10 Most Important Values around the World

- **Achievement**: personal success
- **Benevolence**: concern about the welfare of others
- **Conformity**: acting within social norms
- **Hedonism**: personal gratification and pleasure
- **Power**: status and prestige
- **Security**: safety, harmony, law, and order
- **Self-direction**: independent thought and action
- **Stimulation**: excitement, novelty, and challenge
- **Tradition**: respect for cultural or religious customs
- **Universalism**: understanding and appreciating all people and nature

ACTIVITY

Values Checklist

Assessing Your Personal Values

Use the following checklist to begin to think about what values are important to you.
Place a checkmark next to any value that is important to you. There are no right or wrong answers. If you think of other values that are important to you, add them to the bottom of the list.

✓ Having financial security   ✓ Having good family relationships

✓ Making a contribution to humankind   ✓ Preserving the environment

✓ Being a good parent   ✓ Having the respect of others

✓ Being honest   _____ Becoming famous

✓ Acquiring wealth   ✓ Happiness

✓ Being a wise person   ✓ Freedom and independence

✓ Becoming an educated person   ✓ Common sense

_____ Believing in a higher power (God)   ✓ Having pride in my culture

✓ Preserving civil rights   ✓ Doing community service

✓ Never being bored   ✓ Achieving my goals in life

✓ Enjoying life and having fun   ✓ Having adventures

✓ Making something out of my life   ✓ Having leisure time

✓ Being an ethical person   ✓ Having good health

✓ Feeling safe and secure   ✓ Being loyal

✓ Having a good marriage   ✓ Having a sense of accomplishment

_____ Having good friends	_____ Participating in church activities
_____ Having social status	_____ Being physically fit
_____ Being patriotic	_____ Helping others
_____ Having power	_____ Being a good person
_____ Having good morals	_____ Having time to myself
_____ Being creative	_____ Loving and being loved
_____ Having control over my life	_____ Being physically attractive
_____ Growing and developing	_____ Achieving something important
_____ Feeling competent	_____ Accepting who I am
_____ Feeling relaxed	_____ Appreciating natural beauty
_____ Having prestige	_____ Using my artistic talents
_____ Improving society	_____ Feeling good about myself
_____ Having good mental health	_____ Making a difference
_____ Being a good athlete	_____ Other: _____
_____ Enjoying the present moment	_____ Other: _____
_____ Maintaining peace of mind	_____ Other: _____

What is your most important value? Why is it important to you?

Work Skills for the Twenty-First Century

Rapid changes in technology make it difficult to plan your future. Developing your job skills can prepare you for whatever lies ahead. The TruTalent Skills Assessment helps you to identify your highest skills and connect them to majors and careers. This assessment also has suggestions for improving your skills. Skills include critical thinking, conscientiousness, leadership, social-emotional factors, and creativity.

Another way to prepare for careers in the future is to develop strong foundational skills in reading, writing, basic arithmetic, higher-level mathematics, listening, and speaking. These skills help you to be a successful employee, regardless of your major.

Career Trends 2019–2029

The following are some trends to watch that may affect your future career. As you read about each trend, think about how it could affect your future. For specific information about career trends and your major, search the US Bureau of Labor Statistics site at https://www.bls.gov/.

Working from Home

As a result of the pandemic of 2020, more people are working at home. Currently, approximately 58 percent of the workforce is working from home. A hybrid model of working from home and attending office meetings will allow for greater productivity, collaboration, and socialization.

Flexibility

Another result of the pandemic of 2020, as well as increased use of technology, is the trend toward greater work flexibility. Current research suggests that future employees will "find importance in work/life balance, team focus, empowerment, support, flexibility, involvement, creativity, innovation and a global working atmosphere. They are also characterized by multiple jobs, lifelong learning, multiple careers and entrepreneurship."[8]

Diversity at Work

Most employers (78 percent) believe in the value of increased diversity in the workplace. Productivity and profits are increased when diverse people feel appreciated and can work collaboratively to come up with creative solutions. Successful employees will have the skills to function in this diverse work environment.[9]

© Rawpixel.com/Shutterstock.com

Preference for Soft Skills

Soft skills include empathy, emotional intelligence, creativity, and communication skills. In a survey by LinkedIn, 92 percent of human resources managers considered soft skills more important than other skills required for the job.[10]

© Trueffelpix/Shutterstock.com

Green Jobs

Green jobs are occupations dealing with the efficient use of energy, finding renewable sources of energy, and preserving the environment. Jobs in this field include engineers who design new technology, consultants who audit energy needs, and technicians who install and maintain systems. Here are some green job titles: environmental lawyer, environmental engineer, sustainability consultant, green architect, green building project manager, marine biologist, environmental technician, energy efficiency specialist, organic farmer, compliance manager, product engineer, wind energy engineer, solar engineer, and solar installer.

Finance and Business

Money management has become increasingly complex and important requiring professionals who understand finance, investments, and taxes. Today's business managers need to understand increased competition, the global economy, and must stay up to date with the latest forms of communication and social media. Businesses will increasingly rely on virtual collaboration. The median salaries in this category range from $70,000 to $80,000 and beyond making this occupation a good choice for those interested in higher incomes. Jobs with fast growth include market research analysts, marketing specialists, personal financial advisors, and health care managers.

© zhang kan/Shutterstock.com

Entrepreneurship and Small Business

Small businesses that can find innovative ways of meeting customer needs will be in demand for the future. A growing number of entrepreneurs operate their small businesses from home, taking advantage of telecommunication and the Internet to communicate with customers. While there is increased risk involved, the benefits include flexible scheduling, being your own boss, taking charge of your destiny, and greater potential income.

Higher Earnings in STEM Occupations

The median annual wage for science, technology, engineering, and math (STEM) occupations in 2019 was $86,980 as compared to $38,160 for non-STEM occupations. The job outlook in this area remains high. Develop your skills in these areas to improve your employment prospects.[11]

> "One child, one teacher, one book, one pen can change the world."
> Malala Yousafzai

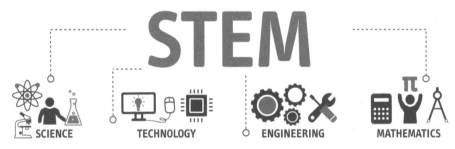

© Trueffelpix/Shutterstock.com

Increased Need for Education

Constant change in society and innovation in technology will require lifelong learning on the job. Education will take place in a variety of forms: community college courses, training on the job, online learning, and learning on your own. Those who do not keep up with new technology will quickly find their job skills becoming obsolete. Higher education is linked to greater earnings and increased employment opportunities.

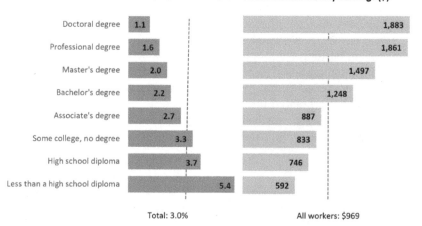

Unemployment rates and earnings by educational attainment, 2019

	Unemployment rate (%)	Median usual weekly earnings ($)
Doctoral degree	1.1	1,883
Professional degree	1.6	1,861
Master's degree	2.0	1,497
Bachelor's degree	2.2	1,248
Associate's degree	2.7	887
Some college, no degree	3.3	833
High school diploma	3.7	746
Less than a high school diploma	5.4	592

Total: 3.0%   All workers: $969

Note: Data are for persons age 25 and over. Earnings are for full-time wage and salary workers.
Source: U.S. Bureau of Labor Statistics, Current Population Survey.

Source: US Bureau of Labor Statistics, "Unemployment Rates and Earnings by Educational Attainment," last modified September 4, 2019, https://www.bls.gov/emp/chart-unemployment-earnings-education.htm.

Increasing Opportunities in Healthcare, Social Service, Computer, and Mathematical Occupations

Careers include mental health workers, nurse practitioners, occupational therapy assistants, physician assistants, computer security, software developers, and information security.

6 of the 10 Fastest Growing Occupations are Related to Healthcare

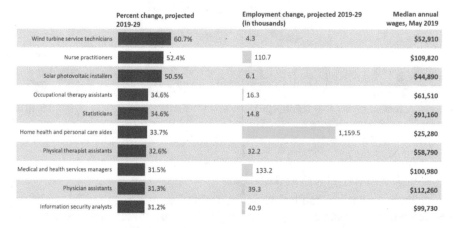

	Percent change, projected 2019-29	Employment change, projected 2019-29 (in thousands)	Median annual wages, May 2019
Wind turbine service technicians	60.7%	4.3	$52,910
Nurse practitioners	52.4%	110.7	$109,820
Solar photovoltaic installers	50.5%	6.1	$44,890
Occupational therapy assistants	34.6%	16.3	$61,510
Statisticians	34.6%	14.8	$91,160
Home health and personal care aides	33.7%	1,159.5	$25,280
Physical therapist assistants	32.6%	32.2	$58,790
Medical and health services managers	31.5%	133.2	$100,980
Physician assistants	31.3%	39.3	$112,260
Information security analysts	31.2%	40.9	$99,730

Source: US Bureau of Labor Statistics, "6 of the 10 Fastest Growing Occupations Are Related to Healthcare," https://www.bls.gov/emp/images/growing_occupations.png.

Projected Percent Change, by Selected Occupational Groups, 2019-29

Percent employment growth, projected 2019-2029

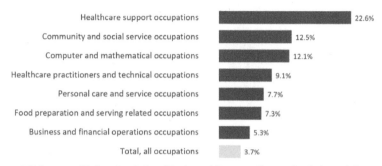

Source: US Bureau of Labor Statistics, "Projected Percent Change by Selected Occupational Groups, 2019–29," https://www.bls.gov/emp/images/percent_change.png.

Technological Advancement

Advances in technology will lead to increased employment in professional, business, and scientific services. Careers include computer systems design and consulting services related to management, scientific, and technical consulting. New developments in artificial intelligence will increasingly be used in robots and smart machines.[12]

Declining Careers in Manufacturing, Retail Trade, Sales, and Administrative Support

Increased automation, robotics, international competition, and the rise in e-commerce will cause declines in these careers. Manufacturing will lose more jobs than any other sector.[13]

Career Outlook

Career outlook includes pay and the availability of employment. Some students are disappointed after graduation when they find there are few job opportunities in their chosen career. Sometimes students graduate and cannot find jobs with the salary they had hoped to earn. It is important to think about the opportunities you will have in the future. If you have several options for a career you would enjoy, you may want to consider the career that has the best outlook.

According to the Bureau of Labor Statistics, fields with the best outlook include health care, computers, and the new "green" jobs related to preserving the environment. The top-paying careers all require math skills and include the science, engineering, computer science, health care, and business fields. Only 4% of college graduates choose the engineering and computer science fields. Since there are fewer students in these majors, the salaries and employment opportunities are higher. If you have a talent or interest in math, you can develop this skill and use it in high paying careers.

© Maryna Pleshkun/Shutterstock.com

Some Majors with the Highest Earnings for Bachelor's Degrees, 2020*[14]

Notice that the majors with the highest earnings require math, science, and/or business.

College Major	Beginning Median Salary	Mid-Career Median Salary
Petroleum Engineering	92,300	182,000
Electrical Engineering and Computer Science	101,200	152,300
Applied Economics and Management	60,900	139,600
Public Accounting	60,000	138,800
Chemical Engineering and Materials Science	74,500	137,800
Aeronautics and Astronautics	74,000	133,100
Actuarial Mathematics	61,900	130,500
Information and Computer Science	70,300	127,600
Economics and Mathematics	65,000	121,400
Bioengineering	67,400	115,000
Statistics	63,7000	114,400
Physics	62,300	113,800
Physician's Assistant	92,900	112,200
Environmental Health and Safety	58,300	104,200

*Includes bachelor's degrees only. Excludes medicine, law, and careers requiring advanced degrees.

Other Common Majors and Earnings[15]

College Major	Beginning Median Salary	Mid-Career Median Salary
Business Finance	54,600	99,800
Accounting and Auditing	55,400	95,700
Entrepreneurship	52,300	95,600
Advertising Design	49,300	89,700
Biological Sciences	46,200	89,200
Political Science/Public Law	43,900	88,900
Marketing and Communications	46,600	88,700
Architecture	48,300	87,800
Construction Technology	55,500	85,300
Film Studies	42,500	82,300
Nursing	63,700	80,900
History	45,300	80,300
Literature	44,400	79,500
Foreign Languages	47,800	78,300
Web Development	54,100	78,300
Speech Communication	43,900	76,800
Forestry	44,700	75,400
English Language	42,100	74,500
Liberal Arts	42,500	73,000
Exercise Physiology	41,600	71,701
Criminal Justice	43,700	71,600
Art History	44,400	71,200
Psychology	42,000	70,700
Secondary Education	42,700	68,500
Art	40,600	63,000

Most Meaningful College Majors[16]

Money is often not the most important consideration in choosing a major. These careers were determined to be the most meaningful, with the potential for changing the world.

College Major	Beginning Median Salary	Mid-Career Median Salary
Occupational Therapy	55,100	89,200
Physical Therapy	53,500	93,900
Special Education	27,600	39,100
Pastoral Ministry	37,300	55,600
Veterinary Technology	30,600	41,000
Respiratory Therapy	48,200	63,000
Mental Health	28,100	38,500
Fire Technology	42,500	72,700
Early Childhood Education	34,100	43,300
Social Work	36,600	51,600
Radiology	49,000	63,400
Athletic Training	39,700	57,000
Elementary Teaching	34,400	50,700
Child Development	35,500	49,100
Health	41,900	66,400
Exercise Science	38,900	61,300
Foods and Nutrition	45,000	64,400

Every career counselor can tell stories about students who ask, "What is the career that makes the most money? That's the career I want!" However, if you choose a career based on money alone, you might find it difficult and uninteresting for a lifetime of work. You might even find yourself retraining later in life for a job that you really enjoy. Remember that the first step is to figure out who you are and what you like. Then look at career outlook and opportunity. If you find your passion in a career that is in demand and pays well, you will probably be very happy with your career choice. If you find your passion in a career that offers few jobs and does not pay well, you will have to use your ingenuity to find a job and make a living. Many students happily make this informed choice and find a way to make it work.

"We act as though comfort and luxury were the chief requirements of life, when all that we need to make us really happy is something to be enthusiastic about."
Charles Kingsley

"Only passions, great passions, can elevate the soul to great things."
Denis Diderot

© Iculig/Shutterstock.com

Mark Twain said, "The secret of success is making your vocation your vacation." Find what you like to do. Better yet, find your passion. If you can find your passion, it is easy to invest the time and effort necessary to be successful.

How do you know when you have found your passion? You have found your passion when you are doing an activity and you do not notice that the time is passing. The great painter Picasso often talked about how quickly time passed while he was painting. He said, "When I work, I relax; doing nothing or entertaining visitors makes me tired." Whether you are an artist, an athlete, a scientist, or a business entrepreneur, passion provides the energy needed to be successful. It helps you to grow and create. When you are using your talents to grow and create, you can find meaning and happiness in your life.

Psychologist Martin Seligman has written a book entitled *Authentic Happiness,* in which he writes about three types of work orientation: a job, a career, and a calling.[17] A job is what you do for the paycheck at the end of the week. Many college students have jobs to earn money for college. A career has deeper personal meaning. It involves achievement, prestige, and power. A calling is defined as "a passionate commitment to work for its own sake."[18] When you have found your calling, the job itself is the reward. He notes that people who have found their calling are consistently happier than those who have a job or even a career. One of the ways that you know you have found your calling is when you are in the state of "flow." The state of "flow" is defined as "complete absorption in an activity whose challenges mesh perfectly with your abilities."[19] People who experience "flow" are happier and more productive. They do not spend their days looking forward to

Friday. Understanding your personal strengths is the beginning step to finding your calling.

Seligman adds that any job can become a calling if you use your personal strengths to do the best possible job. He cited a study of hospital cleaners. Although some viewed their job as drudgery, others viewed the job as a calling. They believed that they helped patients get better by working efficiently and anticipating the needs of doctors and nurses. They rearranged furniture and decorated walls to help patients feel better. They found their calling by applying their personal talents to their jobs. As a result, their jobs became a calling.

Sometimes we wait around for passion to find us. That probably won't happen. The first step in finding your passion is to know yourself. Then find an occupation in which you can use your talents. You may be able to find your passion by looking at your present job and finding a creative way to do it based on your special talents. It has been said that there are no dead-end jobs, just people who cannot see the possibilities. Begin your search for passion by looking at your personal strengths and how you can apply them in the job market. If the job that you have now is not your passion, see what you can learn from it and then use your skills to find a career where you are more likely to find your passion.

> "Success is not the key to happiness; happiness is the key to success. If you love what you are doing, you will be successful."
> Anonymous

Stories from the Elders

Choosing a major may be more complicated than you thought when you first entered college. Taking the time to self-assess and learn more about your personality and interests will help you to discover a field of study that will enrich your life and provide a pathway to a career. As discussed in this chapter, you have had an opportunity look at your own personality type and how that relates to selecting a major. You have also had some exposure to new career opportunities you may not have known existed. Depending on your lifestyle and the community in which you have been raised, your career role models may have been limited. For some, you may be one of the first in your family to attend college, so you have a special opportunity to learn more about your own personal characteristics and explore career options that will offer you a great opportunity for success and happiness.

The story you are about to read comes to us from the Aztec/Mexica culture. This story's main characters may surprise you since their actions may not appear to be consistent with their public image.

The Creation of the Fifth Sun and Moon

Contributed by Dr. Mario E. Aguilar

In the great city of Teotihuacan, located in central Mexico, the gods found themselves in the dark. The Fourth Sun had ended, and the universe was cold and dark. The gods knew that without light, there could be no life.

The gods asked amongst themselves, "who shall sacrifice himself so that the universe has light and warmth?" No one spoke because they were afraid. Finally, Tecuciztecatl stood out amongst the gathered gods and said "I am the only one worthy to be the new sun."

Tecuciztecatl was very rich, handsome, and virile, and even though his ego could get the best of him, he was thought to be courageous. Surely he would be the new sun! Tecuciztecatl was told to prepare for his great sacrifice. Tecuciztecatl prepared his offerings with gold and silver adornments, precious jade and turquoise stones, and feathers from the great macaw and quetzal birds. He danced and sang great prayers.

Once all the preparations had been completed, the gods created a huge fire. They said to Tecuciztecatl, "Great proud warrior, with your fine preparations of precious materials, you will be a powerful sun. Jump into the fire and light the world!" He took a few steps back, and then charged toward the fire. To their horror, he stopped as soon as he felt the searing heat. Three times he ran toward the fire, but each time he failed. Tecuciztecatl stood shivering with fright. His great ornaments hid a heart of fear!

Suddenly, from the dark shadows, Nanahuatzin, a small, humble god with a pockmarked face, and simple clothes of paper, cloth, and feathers jumped out into the grand plaza. Then, taking a running leap, he jumped right into the heart of the fire. Suddenly, all around the sky, a new sun arose from the east, created by the humble but valiant Nanahuatzin. Then out of the fire flew a great golden eagle, forever to be the messenger of the sun.

Having seen this, and feeling humiliated, Tecuciztecatl, the proud and haughty god, jumped into the fire. Soon a bright white disk rose out of the fire. Then out rose a fierce animal that having stayed in the fire for too long, came out with burn spots all over its fur. It was the jaguar, the messenger of the moon.

Soon the gods had a new sun, but the moon was just as bright as the sun. One of the elderly gods could not sleep with all the light. One day a rabbit happened to hop by and the angry god grabbed the poor rabbit and threw him at the face of the moon. There the poor animal covered the face of the moon and darkened it. That is why today the sun is much brighter than the moon, and on every full moon you see the rabbit covering the moon's face.

> When you know who you are;
> when your mission is clear and you
> burn with the inner fire of unbreakable will;
> no cold can touch your heart;
> no deluge can dampen your purpose.
> You know that you are alive."
>
> Chief Seattle, Suquamis

Notes

Aztec/Mexica People

There are over 6 million people in Mexico who speak a native indigenous language and some who do not even speak Spanish. This is surprising to some people, but many Mexicans can trace at least 70% of their genetic heritage to an indigenous culture. Some of the indigenous people who inhabit Central Mexico are known as the Aztec/Nahua. Currently, there are over 2 million persons who are monolingual or bilingual in Nahuatl, the language of the Aztecs. Many of their descendants now live in the United States, predominately located in the Southwestern states of California, Arizona, New Mexico, and Colorado. For more information about the Nahuatl/Mexica culture, visit www.mexicayotl.com

Talking Circle

Use these questions for discussion in a talking circle or consider at least one of these questions as you respond in a journal entry:

1. Tecuciztecatl was seen by others as a strong, confident, and courageous god, but in the end he proved to be something other than the most valiant. How would you say your family and friends would describe your personal characteristics and traits? Would this be consistent with how your fellow students would describe you? Is it consistent with how you describe yourself?

2. Nanahuatzin surprised everyone with his courageous and valiant effort because he appeared shy, quiet, and simple. What personal ideal characteristics do you wish to possess? How consistent are these with the person you believe yourself to be? What will you need to do to be able to develop these characteristics?

3. Nanahuatzin, the humble and quiet god, became the strong and bright sun. Tecuciztecatl, the strong and confident god, became the subtle lighted moon. At first glance, you might not think their personality types fit the roles they eventually became. Can you relate this to yourself and to the career or major options you are considering?

4. What is the moral of this story? Can you relate this story to an experience you have had? Perhaps you have been misjudged or mislabeled by others and you surprised them with your behavior or actions? What did you learn about yourself through that experience?

5. The eagle is revered by many native cultures and in this story is considered a great messenger to the sun. The jaguar is described as a fierce animal with a spotted pelt and is the messenger to the moon. The rabbit is sacrificed for the good of the earth to cover the moon's bright light. Which of these animals do you think you are most like? What are some of the characteristics you share with the eagle, jaguar, or rabbit?

© Lyudmyla Kharlamova/
Shutterstock.com

College Success 1

The College Success 1 website is continually updated with supplementary material for each chapter including Word documents of the journal entries, classroom activities, handouts, videos, links to related materials, and much more. See http://www.collegesuccess1.com/.

Notes

1. Quoted in Rob Gilbert, ed., *Bits and Pieces*, November 4, 1999.

2. "Emotional Intelligence in Career Planning," available at https://www1.cfnc.org, accessed July 2017.

3. Angela Duckworth, Grit: The Power of Passion and Perseverance (New York: Simon & Schuster, 2016) p. 98.

4. U.S. Department of Labor, "O*Net Interest Profiler User's Guide, available at http://onetcenter.org

5. John L. Holland, *Making Vocational Choices: A Theory of Vocational Personalities and Work Environments* (2nd Ed.), (Englewood Cliffs, NJ: Prentice-Hall, 1985)..

6. U.S. Department of Labor, "O*Net Interest Profiler User's Guide."

7. Christopher Peterson, *A Primer in Positive Psychology* (New York: Oxford University Press, 2006) pp. 181–182.

8. Mark McCrindle and Ashley Fell, "Understanding the Impact of Covid-19 on the Emerging Generations," May 2020, https://mccrindle.com.au/wp-content/uploads/COVID19-Emerging-Generations-Report.pdf.

9. Shubhangi Srinivasan, "15 Employment Trends Shaping the Future of Jobs," December 7, 2019, https://www.feedough.com/employment-trends-2019/.

10. Ibid.

11. US Bureau of Labor Statistics, "Employment in Stem Occupations," last modified September 1, 2020, https://www.bls.gov/emp/tables/stem-employment.htm.

12. US Bureau of Labor Statistics, "Employment Projections: 2019 -2029 Summary," September 1, 2020, https://www.bls.gov/news.release/ecopro.nr0.htm.

13. Ibid.

14. Payscale, "College Salary Report 2020," https://www.payscale.com/college-salary-report/majors-that-pay-you-back/bachelors, accessed January, 2021.

15. Ibid.

16. Ibid

17. Martin Seligman, *Authentic Happiness* (Free Press, 2002).

18. Ibid.

19. Ibid.

Personality Preferences

Name _____ Date _____

Use the textbook and personality assessment to think about your personality type. Place an X on the scale to show your degree of preference for each dimension of personality.

Introvert _____|_____ Extravert

Sensing _____|_____ INtuitive

Thinking _____|_____ Feeling

Judging _____|_____ Perceptive

Write a key word or phrase to describe each preference.

Introvert

Extravert

Sensing

INtuitive

Thinking

Feeling

Judging

Perceptive

What careers are suggested by your personality assessment?

Was the personality assessment accurate and useful to you?

Multiple Intelligences Matching Quiz

Name _____   Date _____

Directions: Match the person with the intelligence at the right:

_____Michael Jordan   A. Musical: hearing and remembering musical patterns

_____Aristotle   B. Interpersonal: understanding other people

_____Martin Luther King, Jr. C. Mathematical: working with numbers

_____Sigmund Freud   D. Spatial: manipulating objects in space

_____William Shakespeare   E. Bodily-Kinesthetic: using your body

_____Albert Einstein   F. Linguistic: using language

_____William James "will.i.am" G. Intrapersonal: understanding yourself

_____Charles Darwin   H. Naturalist: understanding the environment

_____George Lucas   I. Existential: pondering the meaning of life and our place in the universe

Work with other students in a group to give examples of other famous person's in these categories.

Musical

Interpersonal

Mathematical

Spatial

Bodily Kinesthetic

Linguistic

Intrapersonal

Naturalist

Existential

Summing Up Values

Name _____ Date _____

Look at the "Values Checklist" you completed in this chapter. Choose the 10 values most important to you and list them here.

_____   _____

_____   _____

_____   _____

_____   _____

_____   _____

Next, pick out the value that is most important and label it 1. Label your second most important value 2, and so on, until you have picked out your top five values.

1. My most important value is _____.
   Why?

2. My second most important value is _____.
   Why?

3. My third most important value is _____.
   Why?

4. My fourth most important value is _____.
   Why?

5. My fifth most important value is _____.
   Why?

The Moon Will Smile at Your Courage: Managing Time and Money

Learning Objectives

Read to answer these key questions:

- ⌊What are the differences between Native and Western time perspectives?⌋
- What are my lifetime goals?
- How can I manage my time to accomplish my goals?
- How much time do I need for study and work?
- How can I make an effective schedule?
- What are some time management tricks?
- How can I deal with procrastination?
- How can I manage my money to accomplish my financial goals?
- What are some ways to save money?
- How can I pay for my education?
- How can I use priorities to manage my time?

Native peoples know that it is important to live in harmony with the earth and the universe. Building an awareness of new skills and the changes you are encountering will help you to remember that you are part of the universe, and your community will grow with you.

The Native Concept of Time

The concept of time is viewed differently by diverse people around the world, and it shapes their world view. The traditional Western concept of time, as described by astrophysicist Stephen Hawking, is the "arrow of time."[1] In this view, time is linear and sequential, like an arrow approaching a target; it is orderly, sequential, and chronological. This concept of time describes progress toward a clearly defined goal, and includes being on time and meeting deadlines.

Spiral circle of life petroglyph. Ancient Pueblo etching located at Petroglyph National Monument, Albuquerque, New Mexico.

The Native concept of time is described as circular and often represented by a circle or spiral. Circular time describes the natural world, including the seasons, biological events, and the cyclical passing of the sun and moon. Loren Spears, executive director of the Tomaquag Indian Museum, states that "We flow with the ebb and flow of nature, daylight and moonlight, with flow of seasons, not with modern Time Frames."[2]

The concept of circular time is sacred and reflected in songs, ceremonies, and creation stories. Rather than beginnings and endings, there is only what is, what always has been, and what will always be. Death is not an absolute; it is a passage into the next world, the next step in life. When storytellers describe time, they refer to seasons and observations of nature, rather than a specific time and date.

"More and more, I am convinced Indian time is just 'human time,'" said Native poet Sondra Ball of New Jersey. "Humans were not meant to keep exact times. We were meant to live within the confines of seasons, light and dark, and our own body's rhythms, which are not the same from day to day or from year to year."[3]

Native time describes the cycles of the past, including cycles of growth, renewal, and decline, and how these patterns will be repeated in the future. Because the events of the past have an influence on the present and future, the idea of circular time includes the recurrent obligations to care for the land and the natural environment. All life forms and human beings are connected. There is a responsibility for "right action" because present behavior will affect the future. If the land and its inhabitants are not respected, there will be dire consequences. For example, in Western society, animals are viewed as resources to be exploited, whereas Natives consider animals to have spirits that should be respected. If the animal is respected, it will return to feed and clothe the community.

The Native difference in time perspectives is sometimes referred to as "Indian Time." For example, tribal councils, cultural ceremonies, and pow wows have an announced time, but they begin when the participants are ready, depending on diverse priorities and travel distance.

When someone is running late, they sometimes say they are on Indian Time. However, if you have promised that you will pick up an elder for a doctor appointment at a certain time and you show up late, it shows disrespect to the elder.

One of the things I learned when I was in college was not to procrastinate. We get teased about being on Indian Time, but that's not a good way to be successful. I started out as a procrastinator, but I learned to create timelines for myself to stay on track.

–Elder Juanita Edaakie, Zuni, New Mexico

While learning to balance Native and Western time can be challenging, learning to work with Western time is important for success in schools, colleges, and workplaces. When you go home again you will notice the difference in time orientation and with awareness; you can learn to walk in both worlds, incorporating different approaches to time as defined by home, work, or college. This chapter presents some useful ideas on time management that will help in achieving your important lifetime goals.

You will need money to pay for your college education and to allow yourself time to focus on your college education. Students from traditional cultures have been taught to share and to be generous with the community, taking only what is needed at the time. But in college you will find that you must plan for the future, so that you will have the financial resources to pay for your books and tuition for the next session. Time and money management are concepts that may be different from your home culture. Learning time and money management techniques will be helpful in adapting to the college environment and will lead to greater academic and career success.

What Are My Lifetime Goals?

Setting goals helps you to establish what is important and provides direction for your life. Goals help you to focus your energy on what you want to accomplish. Goals are a promise to yourself to improve your life. Setting goals can help you turn your dreams into reality. Steven Scott, in his book *A Millionaire's Notebook,* lays out five steps in this process:

1. Dream or visualize.
2. Convert the dream into goals.
3. Convert your goals into tasks.
4. Convert your task into steps.
5. Take your first step, and then the next.[4]

As you begin to think about your personal goals in life, make your goals specific and concrete. Rather than saying, "I want to be rich," make your goal something that you can break into specific steps. You might want to start learning about money management or begin a savings plan. Rather than setting a goal for happiness, think about what brings you happiness. If you want to live a long and healthy life, think about the health habits that will help you to accomplish your goal. You will need to break your goals down into specific tasks to be able to accomplish them.

© winui/Shutterstock.com

Here are some criteria for successful goal setting:

1. **Is it specific and measurable?** Can it be counted or observed? The most common goal mentioned by students is happiness in life. What is happiness, and how will you know when you have achieved it? Is happiness a career you enjoy, owning your own home, or a travel destination?

2. **Is it achievable?** Do you have the skills, abilities, and resources to accomplish this goal? If not, are you willing to spend the time to develop the skills, abilities, and resources needed to achieve this goal?

3. **Is it realistic?** Do you believe that you can achieve it? Are you positive and optimistic about this goal?

4. **Is it timely?** When will you finish this goal? Set a date to accomplish your goal.

5. **What steps do you need to take to begin?** Are you willing to take action to start working on it?

6. **Do you want to do it?** Is this a goal you are choosing because it provides personal satisfaction, rather than meeting a requirement or expectation of someone else?

7. **Are you motivated to achieve it?** What are your rewards for achieving it?

8. **Does the goal match your values?** Is it important to you?

> "A goal is a dream with a deadline."
>
> Napoleon Hill

Journal Entry #1

Write a paragraph about your lifetime goals. Use any of these questions to guide your thinking:

- What is your career goal? If you do not know what your career goal is, describe your preferred work environment. Would your ideal career require a college degree?

- What are your family goals? Are you interested in marriage and family? What would be your important family values?

- What are your social goals (friends, community, and recreation)?

- When you are older and look back on your life, what are the three most important life goals that you want to have accomplished?

A Goal or a Fantasy?

One of the best questions ever asked in my class was, "What is the difference between a goal and a fantasy?" As you look at your list of lifetime goals, are some of these items goals or fantasies? Think about this question as you read the following scenario:

When Linda was a college student, she was walking through the parking lot, noticed a beautiful red sports car, and decided that it would become a lifetime goal for her to own a similar car one day. However, with college expenses and her part-time job, it was not possible to buy the car. She would have to be content with the used car that her dad had given her so that she could drive to college. Years passed by, and Linda now has a good job, a home, and a family. She is reading a magazine and sees a picture of a similar red sports car. She cuts out this picture and tapes it to the refrigerator. After it has been on the refrigerator for several months, her children ask her why the picture is on the refrigerator. Linda replies, "I just like to dream about owning this car." One day, as Linda is driving past a car dealership, she sees the red sports car on display and stops in for a test drive. To her surprise, she decides that she does not like driving the car. It doesn't fit her lifestyle, either. She enjoys outdoor activities that would require a larger car. Buying a second car would be costly and reduce the amount of money that the family could spend on vacations. She decides that vacations are more important than owning the sports car. Linda goes home and removes the picture of the red sports car from the refrigerator.

© Natursports/Shutterstock.com

There are many differences between a goal and a fantasy. A fantasy is a dream that may or may not become a reality. A goal is something that we actually plan to achieve. Sometimes we begin with a fantasy and later it becomes a goal. A fantasy can become a goal if steps are taken to achieve it. In the preceding example, the sports car is a fantasy until Linda actually takes the car for a test drive. After driving the car, she decides that she really does not want it. The fantasy is sometimes better than the reality. Goals and fantasies change over a lifetime. We set goals, try them out, and change them as we grow and mature and find out what is most important in life. Knowing what we think is important, and what we value most, helps us make good decisions about lifetime goals.

What is the difference between a goal and a fantasy? **A goal is something that requires action.** Ask yourself if you are willing to take action on the goals you have set for yourself. Begin to take action by thinking about the steps needed to accomplish the goal. Then take the first step and continue. Change your goals if they are no longer important to you.

"Vision without action is a daydream. Action without vision is a nightmare."
Japanese Proverb

"In life, as in football, you won't go far unless you know where the goalposts are."
Arnold Glasgow

Journal Entry #2

Write a paragraph about how you will accomplish one of your important lifetime goals. Start your paragraph by stating an important goal from the previous journal entry. What is the first step in accomplishing this goal? Next, list some additional steps needed to accomplish it. How can you motivate yourself to begin taking these steps?

For example:

One of my important lifetime goals is _____. The first step in accomplishing this goal is . . . Some additional steps are . . . I can motivate myself to accomplish this goal by . . .

The ABCs of Time Management

Using the **ABCs of time management** is a way of thinking about priorities. Priorities are what you think is important. An **A priority** is a task that relates to your lifetime goal. For example, if my goal is to earn a college degree, studying becomes an A priority. This activity would become one of the most important tasks that I could accomplish today. If my goal is to be healthy, an A priority would be to exercise and plan a healthy diet. If my goal is to have a good family life, an A priority would be to spend time with family members. Knowing about your lifetime goals and spending time on those items that are most important to you will help you to accomplish the goals that you have set for yourself. If you do not spend time on your goals, you may want to look at them again and decide which ones are fantasies that you do not really value or want to accomplish.

A **B priority** is an activity that you have to do, but that is not directly related to your lifetime goal. Examples of B priorities might be getting out of bed, taking a shower, buying groceries, paying bills, or getting gas for the car. These activities are less important, but still are necessary for survival. If I do not put gas in the car, I cannot even get to school or work. If I do not pay the bills, I will soon have financial difficulties. While we often cannot postpone these activities in order to accomplish lifetime goals, we can learn efficient time management techniques to accomplish these tasks quickly.

A **C priority** is something that I can postpone until later with no harmful effect. For example, I could wait until tomorrow or another day to wash my car, do the laundry, buy groceries, or organize my desk. As these items are postponed, however, they can move up the list to a B priority. If I cannot see out of my car window or have no clean clothes to wear, it is time to move these tasks up on my list of priorities. I can wait until I have finished studying to use my cell phone, social media, or video games.

Have you ever been a victim of "**C fever**"? This is an illness in which we do the C activities first and do not get around to doing the A activities that are connected to lifetime goals. Tasks required to accomplish lifetime goals are often ones that are more difficult, challenge our abilities, and take some time to accomplish. These tasks are often more difficult than the B or C activities. The C activities can fill our time and exhaust the energy we need to accomplish the A activities. An example of C fever is the student who cleans the desk, checks the cell phone, starts a video game, or checks Facebook or other social media before studying. C fever is doing the endless tasks that keep us from accomplishing goals that are really important to us. Why do we fall victim to C fever? C activities are often fun or easy and give us a sense of accomplishment. We can see immediate progress without too much effort. I can wash my car and get a sense of accomplishment and satisfaction in my shiny clean car. The task is easy and does not challenge my intellectual capabilities.

© iQoncept/Shutterstock.com

Setting Priorities

To see how the ABCs of time management work, read the profile of Justin, a typical college student, below.

Justin is a 19-year-old college student who plans to major in physical therapy. He is athletic and values his good health. He cares about people and likes helping others. He has a part-time job working as an assistant in the gym, where he monitors proper use of the weightlifting machines. Justin is also a member of the soccer team and practices with the team every afternoon.

Here is a list of activities that Justin would like to do today. Label each task as follows:

A if it relates to Justin's lifetime goals

B if it is something necessary to do

C if it is something that could be done tomorrow or later

_____ Get up, shower, get dressed	_____ Study for biology test that is tomorrow
_____ Eat breakfast	_____ Meet friends for pizza at lunch
_____ Go to work	_____ Call girlfriend
_____ Go to class	_____ Eat dinner
_____ Visit with friends between classes	_____ Unpack gear from weekend camping trip
_____ Do the laundry	_____ Watch football game on TV
_____ Go shopping for new gym shoes	_____ Play video games
_____ Attend soccer practice	_____ Do math homework
_____ Do weightlifting exercises	

While Justin is the only one who can decide how to spend his time, he can take some steps toward accomplishing his lifetime goal of being healthy by eating properly, exercising, and going to soccer practice. He can become a physical therapist by studying for the biology test and doing his math homework. He can gain valuable experience related to physical therapy by working in the gym. He cares about people and likes to maintain good relationships with others. Any tasks related to these goals are high-priority A activities.

What other activities are necessary B activities? He certainly needs to get up, shower, and get dressed. What are the C activities that could be postponed until tomorrow or later? Again, Justin needs to decide. Maybe he could postpone shopping for gym shoes until the weekend. He would have to decide how much time to spend visiting with friends, watching TV, or playing video games. Since he likes these activities, he could use them as rewards for studying for the biology test and doing his math homework.

Technology and Time Management

One of the great advantages of younger generations is their ease and proficiency with the use of technology in both their personal and professional lives. However, excessive time spent on technology can interfere with a healthy lifestyle and accomplishing lifetime goals. Research has shown that students with a technology addiction have lower academic success and higher levels of fatigue. Psychologists have identified some warning signs of addiction to technology.[5,6]

ACTIVITY

Are You Addicted to Technology?

Think about your use of television, cell phones, tablets, computers, video games, and other devices connected to the Internet. Rate the following items as true or false:

True	False	I have felt guilty about using my devices too much.
True	False	Using my devices has caused me to miss out on sleep.
True	False	I have tried to reduce the amount of time I spend on my devices but have not been successful.
True	False	I often experience an urge to use my devices and feel happier using them.
True	False	Use of my devices has left less time for physical fitness.
True	False	Being online has caused me to gain or lose weight.
True	False	I often experience eye strain, neck pain, or backaches after using my devices for a long time.
True	False	I am often distracted by my devices while driving.
True	False	I prefer communicating with my friends online.
True	False	I feel uncomfortable when I am not able to use my devices.
True	False	I lose track of time while using my devices.
True	False	People who care about me are concerned about how much time I spend online.
True	False	I miss school assignments and study time because of time spent online.

_____ Number of true responses. These responses indicate a possible addiction to technology.

_____ Number of false responses. These responses indicate that your technology use is under control.

Suggestions for Dealing with Technology Addiction

The first step in dealing with any addiction is increasing awareness of the problem. Keep a simple log of how many hours you spend watching television or using devices connected to the Internet. There are also apps you can use to track your time online.

If technology is causing you to fall behind on your schoolwork, remember to use priorities and rewards to accomplish your goals. Think about what is most important to you and the lifetime goals you have set for yourself. Give priority to tasks related to lifetime goals. It is also helpful to think of using technology as a reward. Finish your schoolwork first, and then reward yourself with watching television, using social media, or playing video games.

Living a balanced and healthy lifestyle is also important for your success. Studying is easier and more effective if you are well rested, have the proper nutrition, and have exercised during the day.

How to Estimate Study and Work Time

Students are often surprised at the amount of time necessary for study to be successful in college. A general rule is that you need to study two hours for every hour spent in a college class. A typical weekly schedule of a full-time student would look like this:

Typical College Schedule

15 hours of attending class
+30 hours of reading, studying, and preparation
45 hours total

A full-time job involves working 40 hours a week. A full-time college student spends 45 hours or more attending classes and studying. Some students will need more than 45 hours a week if they are taking lab classes, need help with study and learning skills, or are taking a heavy course load.

Some students try to work full-time and go to school full-time. While some are successful, this schedule is extremely difficult.

The Nearly Impossible Schedule

15 hours attending class
30 hours studying
+40 hours working
85 hours total

This schedule is the equivalent of having two full-time jobs! Working full-time makes it very difficult to find the time necessary to study for classes. Lack of study causes students to do poorly on exams and to doubt their abilities. Such a schedule causes stress and fatigue that make studying difficult. Increased stress can also lead to problems with personal relationships and emotional problems. These are all things that lead to dropping out of college.

Many students today work and go to college. Working during college can provide some valuable experience that will help you to find a job when you finish college. Working can teach you to manage your time efficiently and give you a feeling of independence and control over your own future. Many people need to work to pay for their education. A general guideline is to work no more than 20 hours a week if you plan to attend college full-time. Here is a workable schedule.

Part-Time Work Schedule

12 hours attending class
24 hours studying
+20 hours working
56 hours total

A commitment of 56 hours a week is like having a full-time job and a part-time job. While this schedule takes extra energy and commitment, many students are successful with it. Notice that the course load is reduced to 12 hours. This schedule involves taking one less class per semester. The class missed can be made up in summer school, or the time needed to graduate can be extended. Many students take five years to earn the bachelor's degree because they work part-time. It is better to take longer to graduate than to give up because of frustration and drop out of college. If you must work full-time, consider reducing your course load to one or two courses. You will gradually reach your goal of a college degree.

> "The key is not to prioritize what's on the schedule, but to schedule your priorities."
>
> Stephen Covey

> "When you do the things you have to do when you have to do them, the day will come when you can do the things you want to do when you want to do them."
>
> Zig Ziglar

Part-Time Student Schedule

     6 hours attending class
   12 hours studying
 +40 hours working
   58 hours total

Add up the number of hours you are attending classes, double this figure for study time, and add to it your work time, as in the above examples. How many hours of commitment do you have? Can you be successful with your current level of commitment to school, work, and study?

To begin managing your schedule, use the weekly calendar located at the end of this chapter to write in your scheduled activities such as work, class times, and athletics.

Schedule Your Success

What Is Your Chronotype?

It is interesting that scientists describe different time preferences or chronotypes as larks, owls, or hummingbirds.[7] Understanding your chronotype is important in scheduling your learning at a time when you can learn most efficiently and use the rest of the time for less important tasks.

- Larks like to get up and go to bed early. They are most alert during the day with productivity peaking about two hours before noon. If you are a lark or morning person, schedule your classes and study time for the morning.
- Owls prefer to get up and go to bed late. They are most productive around 6 pm. If you are an owl or evening person, schedule your classes and study time for later in the day or evening.
- Humming birds are combination types that tend to be more like larks or owls, or somewhere in between.

Another way to describe time of day preference is your prime time. Use your prime time for studying and you will accomplish more in less time.

Researchers have found that night owls often have lower GPAs because they are frequently sleep deprived. Did you know that sleep deprivation can reduce your intelligence, cause weight gain, and accelerate the aging process? Healthy 30-year-olds who slept for only four hours a night for six days had the body chemistry of a 60-year-old.[8] Loss of sleep interferes with attention, memory, mathematical skills, logical reasoning, and manual dexterity. If you are a night owl, consider changing your sleeping pattern to make sure you get enough sleep. This change will be helpful in your career after college. Here are some suggestions for getting more sleep:

Avoid

- Staying up all night or late in the night to study.
- Alcohol, nicotine, exercise, or food late in the evening. Note that alcohol initially makes you sleepy, but it interferes with sleep later in the night.

Do this

- Relax before bedtime by reading a good book or listening to soft music.
- Have a regular pattern of sleep. Go to bed at the same time each evening and get up at the same time each morning.
- Get some exercise every day so that you feel tired at night.

Using a Schedule

If you have not used a schedule in the past, consider trying a schedule for a couple of weeks to see if it is helpful in completing tasks and working toward your lifetime goals. There are several advantages to using a schedule:

- It gets you started on your work.
- It helps you avoid procrastination.
- It relieves pressure because you have things under control.
- It frees the mind of details.
- It helps you find time to study.
- It eliminates the panic caused by doing things at the last minute.
- It helps you find time for recreation and exercise.

Once you have made a master schedule that includes classes, work, and other activities, you will see that you have some blanks that provide opportunities for using your time productively. Here are some ideas for making the most of your schedule:

1. Fill in your study times. Use the time immediately before class for previewing and the time immediately after class for reviewing. Remember that you need to study two hours or more for each hour spent in a college class.

© Caroline Eibl/Shutterstock.com

2. Break large projects such as a term paper or studying for a test into small tasks and begin early. Double your time estimates for completion of the project. Larger projects often take longer than you think. If you finish early, use the extra time for something fun.

3. Set priorities. Make sure you include activities related to your lifetime goals.

4. Allow time for sleep and meals. It is easier to study if you are well rested and have good eating habits.

5. Schedule your time in manageable blocks of an hour or two. Having every moment scheduled leads to frustration when plans change.

6. Leave some time unscheduled to use as a shock absorber. You will need unscheduled time to relax and to deal with unexpected events.

7. Leave time for recreation, exercise, and fun.

See the weekly study schedule form at the end of this chapter.

© iQoncept/Shutterstock.com

If You Dislike Schedules

Some personality types like more freedom and do not like the structure that a schedule provides. There are alternatives for those who do not like to use a schedule. Here are some additional ideas.

1. A simple and fast way to organize your time is to use a to-do list. Take an index card or small piece of paper and simply write a list of what you need to do during the day. You can prioritize the list by putting an A or star by the most important items. Cross items off the list as you accomplish them. A list helps you focus on what is important and serves as a reminder not to forget certain tasks.

2. Another idea is to use monthly or yearly calendars to write down important events, tasks, and deadlines. Use these calendars to note the first day of school, when important assignments are due, vacations, and final exams. Place the calendars in a place where they are easily seen.

3. Use this simple question to keep you on track, "What is the best use of my time right now?"[9] This question works well if you keep in mind your goals and priorities.

4. Use reminders and sticky notes to keep on track and to remind yourself of what needs to be done each day. Place the notes in a place where you will see them, such as your computer, the bathroom mirror, or the dashboard of your car.

5. Some families use their refrigerators as time management devices. Use the refrigerator to post your calendars, reminders, goals, tasks, and to-do lists. You will see these reminders every time you open the refrigerator.

6. Invent your own unique ideas for managing time. Anything will work if it helps to accomplish your goals.

Manage Your Time with a Web Application

There are thousands of new web applications available to organize your life. You can use a web application on your phone, watch, laptop, computer, or other mobile device.

- Create a to-do list or schedule.
- Send reminders when assignments are due.
- Organize your calendar and plan your tasks.
- Organize your study time and plan assignments.
- Avoid procrastination.
- Create a virtual assistant to keep you organized.

Time Management Tricks

Life is full of demands for work, study, family, friends, and recreation. Time management tricks can help you get started on the important tasks and make the most of your time. Try the following techniques when you are feeling frustrated and overwhelmed.

Divide and Conquer

When large tasks seem overwhelming, think of the small tasks needed to complete the project and start on the first step. For example, suppose you have to write a term paper. You have to take out a paper and pencil, log onto your computer, brainstorm some ideas, go to the library to find information, think about your main ideas, and write the first sentence. Each of these steps is manageable. It's looking at the entire project that can be intimidating.

I once set out hiking on a mountain trail. When I got to the top of the mountain and looked down, I enjoyed a spectacular view and was amazed at how high I had climbed. If I had thought about how high the mountain was, I might not have attempted the hike. I climbed the mountain by taking it one step at a time. That's the secret to completing any large project: break it into small, manageable parts, then take the first step and keep going.

Learning a small part at a time is also easy and helps with motivation for learning. While in college, carry around some material that you need to study. Take advantage of five or ten minutes of time to study a small part of your material. In this way you make good use of your time and enhance memory by using distributed practice. Don't wait until you have large blocks of uninterrupted study time to begin your studies. You may not have the luxury of large blocks of time, or you may want to spend that time in other ways.

© iQoncept/Shutterstock.com

Time Management Tricks

- Divide and conquer
- Do the first small step
- 80/20 rule
- Aim for excellence, not perfection
- Make learning fun
- Take a break
- Study in the library
- Learn to say no

Do the First Small Step

The most difficult step in completing any project is the first step. If you have a challenging project to do, think of a small first step and complete that small step. Make the first step something that you can accomplish easily and in a short amount of time. Give yourself permission to stop after the first step. However, you may find that you are motivated to continue with the project. If you have a term paper to write, think about some small step you can take to get started. Log onto your computer and look at the blank screen. Start writing some ideas. Type the topic into a computer search engine and see what information is available. Go to the library and see what is available on your topic. If you can find some interesting ideas, you can motivate yourself to begin the project. Once you have started the project, it is easier to continue.

The 80/20 Rule

Alan Lakein is noted for many useful time management techniques. One that I have used over the years is the 80/20 rule. Lakein says, "If all items are arranged in order of value, 80 percent of the value would come from only 20 percent of the items, while the remaining 20 percent of the value would come from 80 percent of the items."[10] For example, if you have a list of ten items to do, two of the items on the list are more important than the others. If you were to do only the two most important items, you would have accomplished 80 percent of the value. If you are short on time, see if you can choose the 20 percent of the tasks that are the most valuable. Lakein noted that the 80/20 rule applies to many situations in life:

- 80 percent of file usage is in 20 percent of the files.
- 80 percent of dinners repeat 20 percent of the recipes.
- 80 percent of the washing is done on the 20 percent of the clothes worn most frequently.
- 80 percent of the dirt is on the 20 percent of the floor used most often.

Think about how the 80/20 rule applies in your life. It is another way of thinking about priorities and figuring out which of the tasks are C priorities. This prioritizing is especially important if you are short on time. The 80/20 rule helps you to focus on what is most important.

Aim for Excellence, Not Perfection

Are you satisfied with your work only if it is done perfectly? Do you put off a project because you cannot do it perfectly? Aiming for perfection in all tasks causes anxiety and procrastination. There are times when perfection is not necessary. Dave Ellis calls this time management technique "It Ain't No Piano."[11] If a construction worker bends a nail in the framing of a house, it does not matter. The construction worker simply puts in another nail. After all, "it ain't no piano." It is another matter if you are building a fine cabinet or finishing a piano. Perfection is more important in these circumstances. We need to ask: Is the task important enough to invest the time needed for perfection? A final term paper needs to be as perfect as we can make it. A rough draft is like the frame of a house that does not need to be perfect.

In aiming for excellence rather than perfection, challenge yourself to use perspective to see the big picture. How important is the project and how perfect does it need to be? Could your time be better invested accomplishing other tasks? This technique requires flexibility and the ability to change with different situations. Do not give up if you cannot complete a project perfectly. Do the best that you can in the time available. In some situations, if life is too hectic, you may need to settle for completing the project and getting it in on time rather than doing it perfectly. With this idea in mind, you may be able to relax and still achieve excellence.

Make Learning Fun by Finding a Reward

© carmen2011/Shutterstock.com

Time management is not about restriction, self-control, and deprivation. If it is done correctly, time can be managed to get more out of life and to have fun while doing it. Remember that behavior is likely to increase if followed by a reward. Think about activities that you find rewarding. In our time management example with Justin who wants to be a physical therapist, he could use many tasks as rewards for completing his studies. He could meet friends for pizza, call his girlfriend, play video games, or watch TV. The key idea is to do the studying first and then reward the behavior. Maybe Justin will not be able to do all of the activities we have mentioned as possible rewards, but he could choose what he enjoys most.

Studying first and then rewarding yourself leads to peace of mind and the ability to focus on tasks at hand. While Justin is out having pizza with his friends, he does not have to worry about work that he has not done. While Justin is studying, he does not have to feel that he is being deprived of having pizza with friends. In this way, he can focus on studying while he is studying and focus on having a good time while relaxing with his friends. It is not a good idea to think about having pizza with friends while studying or to think about studying while having pizza with friends. When you work, focus on your work and get it done. When you play, enjoy playing without having to think about work.

Take a Break

If you are overwhelmed with the task at hand, sometimes it is best to just take a break. If you're stuck on a computer program or a math problem, take a break and do

"Don't say you don't have enough time. You have exactly the same number of hours per day that were given to Helen Keller, Pasteur, Michelangelo, Mother Teresa, Leonardo da Vinci, Thomas Jefferson, and Albert Einstein."

H. Jackson Browne

© NorGal/Shutterstock.com

something else. As a general rule, take a break of 10 minutes for each hour of study. During the break, do something totally different. It is a good idea to get up and move around. Get up and pet your cat or dog, observe your goldfish, or shoot a few baskets. If time is really at a premium, use your break time to accomplish other important tasks. Put your clothes in the dryer, empty the dishwasher, or pay a bill.

Learn to Say No Sometimes

Learn to say no to tasks that you do not have time to do. Follow your statement with the reasons for saying no: you are going to college and need time to study. Most people will understand this answer and respect it. You may need to say no to yourself as well. Maybe you cannot go out on Wednesday night if you have a class early on Thursday morning. Maybe the best use of your time right now is to turn off the TV or get off the Internet and study for tomorrow's test. You are investing your time in your future.

Dealing with Time Bandits

Time bandits are the many things that keep us from spending time on the things we think are important. Another word for a time bandit is a time waster. In college, it is tempting to do many things other than studying. We are all victims of different kinds of bandits.

ACTIVITY

Put a checkmark next to the items that waste your time. Add your own personal time wasters at the end of the list.

_____ TV

_____ Other electronic devices

_____ Daydreaming

_____ Social media

_____ Saying yes when you mean no

_____ Friends

_____ Internet

_____ Social time

_____ Family

_____ Procrastination

_____ Household chores

_____ Roommates

_____ Video games

_____ Partying

_____ Children

_____ Cell phone

_____ Waiting time

_____ Girlfriend, boyfriend, spouse

_____ Sleeping in

_____ Shopping

_____ Being easily distracted

_____ Studying at a bad time

_____ Reading magazines

_____ Studying in a distracting place

_____ Movies

_____ Commuting time (travel)

List some of your personal time bandits here.

_____

_____

Here are some ideas for keeping time bandits under control:

- **Schedule time for other people.** Friends and family are important, so we do not want to get rid of them! Discuss your goal of a college education with your friends and family. People who care about you will respect your goals. You may need to use a Do Not Disturb sign at times. If you are a parent, remember that you are a role model for your children. If they see you studying, they are more likely to value their own education. Plan to spend quality time with your children and the people who are important to you. Make sure they understand that you care about them.

- **Remember the rewards.** Many of the time bandits listed above make good rewards for completing your work. Put the time bandits to work for you by studying first and then enjoying a reward. Enjoy the TV, Internet, cell phone, video games, or socializing with friends after you have finished your studies. Aim for a balance of work, study, and leisure time.

- **Remind yourself about your priorities.** When time bandits attack, remind yourself of why you are in college. Think about your personal goals for the future. Remember that college is not forever. By doing well in college, you will finish in the shortest time possible.

- **Use a schedule.** Using a schedule or a to-do list is helpful in keeping you on track. Make sure you have some slack time in your schedule to handle unexpected phone calls and deal with the unplanned events that happen in life. If you cannot stick to your schedule, just get back on track as soon as you can.

Journal Entry #3

Write a paragraph about how you will manage your time to accomplish your goal of a college education. Use any of these questions to guide your thinking:

- What are your priorities?
- How will you balance use of technology, school, work, and family/friends?
- What are some time management tools you plan to use?
- How can you deal with time bandits?

Dealing with Procrastination

Procrastination means putting off things until later. We all use delaying tactics at times. Procrastination that is habitual, however, can be self-destructive. Understanding some possible reasons for procrastination can help you use time more effectively and be more successful in accomplishing goals.

Why Do We Procrastinate?

There are many psychological reasons for procrastinating. Just becoming aware of these may help you deal with procrastination. If you have serious difficulty managing your time for psychological reasons, visit the counseling center at your college or university. Do you recognize any of these reasons for procrastination in yourself or others?

© bloomua/
Shutterstock.com

- **Fear of failure.** Sometimes we procrastinate because we are afraid of failing. We see our performance as related to how much ability we have and how worthwhile we are as human beings. We may procrastinate in our college studies because of doubts about our ability to do the work. Success, however, comes from trying and learning from mistakes. There is a popular saying: falling down is not failure, but failing to get up or not even trying is failure.

- **Fear of success.** Most students are surprised to find out that one of the reasons for procrastination is fear of success. Success in college means moving on with your life, getting a job, leaving a familiar situation, accepting increased responsibility, and sometimes leaving friends behind. None of these tasks is easy. An example of fear of success is not taking the last step required to be successful. Students sometimes do not take the last class needed to graduate. Some good students do not show up for the final exam or do not turn in a major project. If you ever find yourself procrastinating on an important last step, ask yourself if you are afraid of success and what lies ahead in your future.

- **Perfectionism.** Some people who procrastinate do not realize that they are perfectionists. Perfectionists expect more from themselves than is realistic and more than others expect of themselves. There is often no other choice than to procrastinate because perfectionism is usually unattainable. Perfectionism generates anxiety that further hinders performance. Perfectionists need to understand that perfection is seldom possible. They need to set time limits on projects and do their best within those time limits.

- **Need for excitement.** Some students can only be motivated by waiting until the last minute to begin a project. These students are excited and motivated by playing a game of "Beat the Clock." They like living on the edge and the adrenaline rush of responding to a crisis. Playing this game provides motivation, but it does not leave enough time to achieve the best results. Inevitably, things happen at the last minute to make the game even more exciting and dangerous: the printer breaks, the computer crashes, the student gets ill, the car breaks down, or the dog eats the homework. These students need to start projects earlier to improve their chances of success. It is best to seek excitement elsewhere, in sports or other competitive activities.

- **Excellence without effort.** In this scenario, students believe that they are truly outstanding and can achieve success without effort. These students think that they can go to college without attending classes or reading the text. They believe that they can pass the test without studying. They often do not succeed in college the first semester, which puts them at risk of dropping out of school. They often return to college later and improve their performance by putting in the effort required.

- **Loss of control.** Some students fear loss of control over their lives and procrastinate to gain control. An example is students who attend college because others (such as parents) want them to attend. Procrastination becomes a way of gaining control over the situation by saying, "You can't make me do this." They attend college but accomplish nothing. Parents can support and encourage education, but students need to choose their own goals in life and attend college because it is an important personal goal.

Tips for Dealing with Procrastination

When you find yourself procrastinating on a certain task, think about the consequences. Will the procrastination lead to failing an exam or getting a low grade? Think about the rewards of doing the task. If you do well, you can take pride in yourself and celebrate your success. How will you feel when the task is completed? Will you be able to enjoy your leisure time without guilt about not doing your work? How does the task help you to achieve your lifetime goals?

Maybe the procrastination is a warning sign that you need to reconsider lifetime goals and change them to better suit your needs.

Procrastination Scenario

George is a college student who is on academic probation for having low grades. He is required to make a plan for improving his grades in order to remain in college. George tells the counselor that he is making poor grades because of his procrastination. He is an accounting major and puts off doing homework because he dislikes it and does not find it interesting. The counselor asks George why he had chosen accounting as a major. He replies that accounting is a major that is in demand and has a good salary. The counselor suggests that George consider a major that he would enjoy more. After some consideration, George changes his major to psychology. He becomes more interested in college studies and is able to raise his grades to stay in college.

Most of the time, you will reap benefits by avoiding procrastination and completing the task at hand. Jane Burka and Lenora Yuen suggest the following steps to deal with procrastination:

1. Select a goal.

2. Visualize your progress.

3. Be careful not to sabotage yourself.

4. Stick to a time limit.

5. Don't wait until you feel like it.

6. Follow through. Watch out for excuses and focus on one step at a time.

7. Reward yourself after you have made some progress.

8. Be flexible about your goal.

9. Remember that it does not have to be perfect.[12]

© iQoncept/Shutterstock.com

Time Management, Part II

Test what you have learned by selecting the correct answers to the following questions.

1. To get started on a challenging project,

   a. think of a small first step and complete it.
   b. wait until you have plenty of time to begin.
   c. wait until you are well rested and relaxed.

2. If you are completing a to-do list of 10 items, the 80/20 rule states that

   a. 80% of the value comes from completing most of the items on the list.
   b. 80% of the value comes from completing two of the most important items.
   c. 80% of the value comes from completing half of the items on the list.

3. It is suggested that students aim for

   a. perfection.
   b. excellence.
   c. passing.

4. Sometimes students procrastinate because of

   a. fear of failure.
   b. fear of success.
   c. all of the above.

5. Playing the game "Beat the Clock" when doing a term paper results in

   a. increased motivation and success.
   b. greater excitement and quality work.
   c. increased motivation and risk.

How did you do on the quiz? Check your answers: 1. a, 2. b, 3. b, 4. c, 5. c

Journal Entry #4

Write a paragraph about how you will avoid procrastination. Consider these ideas when thinking about procrastination: fear of failure, fear of success, perfectionism, need for excitement, excellence without effort, and loss of control. How will you complete your assignments on time?

Managing Your Money

To be successful in college and in life, you will need to manage not only time, but money. One of the top reasons that students drop out of college is that they cannot pay for their education or that they have to work so much that they do not have time for school. Take a look at your lifetime goals. Most students have a goal related to money, such as becoming financially secure or becoming wealthy. If financial security or wealth is one of your goals, you will need to begin to take some action to accomplish that goal. If you don't take action on a goal, it is merely a fantasy.

© ARENA Creative/Shutterstock.com

Budgeting: The Key to Money Management

Money management begins with looking at your attitude toward money. Pay attention to how you spend your money so that you can accomplish your financial goals such as getting a college education, buying a house or car, or saving for the future. One of the most important things that you can do to manage your money and begin saving is to use a budget. A budget helps you become aware of how you spend your money and will help your make a plan for the future. It is important to control your money, rather than letting your money control you.

Monitor how you spend your money. The first step in establishing a workable budget is to monitor how you are actually spending your money at the present time. For one month, keep a list of purchases with the date and amount of money spent for each. You can do this on a sheet of paper, on your calendar, on index cards, or on a money management application for your phone. If you write checks for items, include the checks written as part of your money monitor. At the end of the month, group your purchases in categories such as food, gas, entertainment, and credit card payments, and add them up. Doing this will yield some surprising results. For example, you may not be aware of just how much it costs to eat at a fast-food restaurant or to buy lunch or coffee every day.

Managing Your Money

- Monitor your spending
- Prepare a budget
- Beware of credit and interest
- Watch spending leaks

© koya979/ Shutterstock.com

Prepare a budget. One of the best tools for managing your money is a budget. At the end of this chapter, you will find a simple budget sheet that you can use as a college student. After you finish college, update your budget and continue to use it. Follow these three steps to make a budget:

1. Write down your income for the month.

2. List your expenses. Include tuition, books, supplies, rent, phone, utilities (gas, electric, water, cable TV, Internet), car payments, car insurance, car maintenance (oil, repairs), parking fees, food, personal grooming, clothes, entertainment, savings, credit card payments, loan payments, and other bills. Use your money monitor to discover how you are spending your money and include categories that are unique to you.

3. Subtract your total expenses from your total income. You cannot spend more than you have. Make adjustments as needed.

Beware of credit and interest. College students are often tempted to use credit cards to pay for college expenses. This type of borrowing is costly and difficult to repay. It is easy to pull out a plastic credit card and buy items that you need and want. Credit card companies earn a great deal of money from credit cards. Jane Bryant Quinn gives an example of the cost of credit cards.[13] She says that if you owe $3,000 at 18 percent interest and pay the minimum payment of $60 per month, it will take you 30 years and 10 months to get out of debt! Borrowing the $3,000 would cost about $22,320 over this time! If you use a credit card, make sure you can pay it off in one to three months. It is good to have a credit card in order to establish credit and to use in an emergency.

Watch those spending leaks. We all have spending problem areas. Often we spend small amounts of money each day that add up to large spending leaks over time. For example, if you spend $3 on coffee each weekday for a year, this adds up to $780 a year! If you eat lunch out each weekday and spend $8 for lunch, this adds up to $2,080 a year. Here are some common areas for spending leaks:

- Fast food and restaurants
- Entertainment and vacations
- Clothing
- Miscellaneous cash
- Gifts

© Andrey Armyagov/Shutterstock.com

Need More Money?

You may be tempted to work more hours to balance your budget. Remember that to be a full-time college student, it is recommended that you work no more than 20 hours per week. If you work more than 20 hours per week, you will probably need to decrease your course load. Before increasing your work hours, see if there is a way you can decrease your monthly expenses. Can you make your lunch instead of eating out? Can you get by without a car? Is the item you are purchasing a necessity, or do you just want to have it? These choices are yours.

1. **Check out financial aid.** All students can qualify for some type of financial aid. Visit the Financial Aid Office at your college for assistance. Depending on your income level, you may qualify for one or more of the following forms of aid.

   - **Loans.** A loan must be paid back. The interest rate and terms vary according to your financial need. With some loans, the federal government pays the interest while you are in school.

   - **Grants.** A grant does not need to be repaid. There are both state and federal grants based on need.

   - **Work/study.** You may qualify for a federally subsidized job depending on your financial need. These jobs are often on campus and provide valuable work experience for the future.

   The first step in applying for financial aid is to fill out the Free Application for Federal Student Aid (FAFSA). This form determines your eligibility for financial aid. You can obtain this form from your college's financial aid office or over the Internet at https://fafsa.ed.gov/

   Here are some other financial aid resources that you can obtain from your financial aid office or over the Internet.

   - **Federal Student Aid Resources.** This site provides resources on preparing for college, applying for aid, online tools, and other resources: https://studentaid.ed.gov/sa/resources.

   - **How to apply for financial aid.** Learn how to apply for federal financial aid and scholarships at www.finaid.org.

> "Money is, in some respects, like fire; it is a very excellent servant, but a terrible master."
>
> P. T. Barnum

> "Empty pockets never held anyone back. Only empty heads and empty hearts can do that."
>
> Norman Vincent Peale

2. **Apply for a scholarship.** Applying for a scholarship is like having a part-time job, only the pay is often better, the hours are flexible, and you can be your own boss. For this part-time job, you will need to research scholarship opportunities and fill out applications. There are multitudes of scholarships available, and sometimes no one even applies for them. Some students do not apply for scholarships because they think that high grades and financial need are required. While many scholarships are based on grades and financial need, many are not. Any person or organization can offer a scholarship for any reason they want. For example, scholarships can be based on hobbies, parent's occupation, religious background, military service, and personal interests, to name a few.

There are several ways to research a scholarship. As a first step, visit the financial aid office on your college campus. This office is staffed with persons knowledgeable about researching and applying for scholarships. Organizations or persons wishing to fund scholarships often contact this office to advertise opportunities.

You can also research scholarships through your public or college library. Ask the reference librarian for assistance. You can use the Internet to research scholarships as well. Use any search engine such as Google.com and simply type in the keyword scholarships. The following websites index thousands of scholarships:

- The Federal Student Aid Scholarship site is located at https://studentaid.ed.gov/sa/types/grants-scholarships/finding-scholarships
- fastweb.com
- http://www.scholarships.com/
- studentscholarshipsearch.com
- collegeboard.com/paying

To apply for scholarships, start a file of useful material usually included in scholarship applications. You can use this same information to apply for many scholarships.

- Three current letters of recommendation
- A statement of your personal goals
- A statement of your financial need
- Copies of your transcripts
- Copies of any scholarship applications you have filled out

Be aware of scholarship scams. You do not need to pay money to apply for a scholarship. No one can guarantee that you will receive a scholarship. Use your college scholarship office and your own resources to research and apply for scholarships.

The Best Ideas for Becoming Financially Secure

Financial planners provide the following ideas as the best ways to build wealth and independence.[14] If you have financial security as your goal, plan to do the following:

1. **Use a simple budget to track income and expenses.** Do not spend more than you earn.

2. **Have a financial plan.** Include goals such as saving for retirement, purchasing a home, paying for college, or taking vacations.

3. **Save 10 percent of your income.** As a college student, you may not be able to save this much, but plan to do it as soon as you get your first good-paying job. If you cannot save 10 percent, save something to get in the habit of saving. Save to pay for your tuition and books.

4. **Don't take on too much debt.** Be especially careful about credit cards and consumer debt. Credit card companies often visit college campuses and offer high-interest credit cards to students. It is important to have a credit card, but pay off the balance each month. Consider student loans instead of paying college fees by credit card.

5. **Don't procrastinate.** The earlier you take these steps toward financial security, the better.

Scholarship

© mangostock/Shutterstock.com

Tips for Managing Your Money

Keeping these guidelines in mind can help you to manage your money.

- Don't let friends pressure you into spending too much money. If you can't afford something, learn to say no.
- Keep your checking account balanced or use online banking so you will know how much money you have.
- Don't lend money to friends. If your friends cannot manage their money, your loan will not help them.
- Use comparison shopping to find the best prices on the products that you buy.
- Get a part-time job while in college. You will earn money and gain valuable job experience.
- Don't use shopping as a recreational activity. When you visit the mall, you will find things you never knew you needed and will wind up spending more money than intended.
- Make a budget and follow it. This is the best way to achieve your financial goals.

Do What Is Important First

The most important thing you can do to manage time and money is to spend it on what is most important. Manage time and money to help you live the life you want. How can you do this? Author Stephen Covey wrote a book titled *The Seven Habits of Highly Effective People.* One of the habits is "Put first things first." Covey suggests that in time management, the "challenge is not to manage our time but to manage ourselves."[15]

How can you manage yourself? Our first thoughts in answering this question often involve suggestions about willpower, restriction, and self-control. Schedules and budgets are seen as instruments for self-control. It seems that the human spirit resists attempts at control, even when we aim to control ourselves. Often the response to control is rebellion. With time and money management, we may not follow a schedule or budget. A better approach to begin managing yourself is to know your values. What is important in your life? Do you have a clear mental picture of what is important? Can you describe your values and make a list of what is important to you? With your values and goals in mind, you can begin to manage both your time and your money.

When you have given some thought to your values, you can begin to set goals. When you have established goals for your life, you can begin to think in terms of what is most important and establish your priorities. Knowing your values is essential in making decisions about how to invest your time and money. Schedules and budgets are merely tools for helping you accomplish what you have decided is important. Time and money management is not about restriction and control, but about making decisions regarding what is important in your life. If you know what is important, you can find the strength to say no to activities and expenditures that are less important.

As a counselor, I have the pleasure of working with many students who have recently explored and discovered their values and are highly motivated to succeed. They are willing to do what is important first. I recently worked with a young couple who came to enroll in college. They brought their young baby with them. The new father was interested in environmental engineering. He told me that in high school, he never saw a reason for school and did just the minimum needed to get by. He was working as a construction laborer and making a living, but did not see a future in the occupation. He had observed an environmental engineer who worked for the company and decided that was what he wanted for his future. As he looked at his new son, he told me that he needed to have a better future for himself and his family.

He and his wife decided to do what was important first. They were willing to make the sacrifice to attend school and invest the time needed to be successful. The father planned to work during the day and go to school at night. Later, he would go to school full-time and get a part-time job in the evening. His wife was willing to get a part-time job also, and they would share in taking care of the baby. They were willing to manage their money carefully to accomplish their goals. As they left, they added that their son would be going to college as well.

How do you get the energy to work all day, go to school at night, and raise a family? You can't do it by practicing self-control. You find the energy by having a clear idea of what you want in your life and focusing your time and resources on the goal. Finding what you want to do with your life is not easy either. Many times people find what they want to do when some significant event happens in their lives.

Begin to think about what you want out of life. Make a list of your important values and write down your lifetime goals. Don't forget about the people who are important to you, and include them in your priorities. Then you will be able to do what is important first.

> "Fathers send their sons to college either because they went to college or because they didn't."
>
> L. L. Henderson

Journal Entry #5

What is your plan for managing your money? Consider these ideas when thinking about your plan: monitoring how you spend your money, using a budget, applying for financial aid and scholarships, saving money, and spending money wisely.

Stories from the Elders

This chapter has asked you to consider lifetime goals and developing a plan to reach those goals. This will take commitment, investment, and courage on your part. You have been asked to consider how you manage your time and how you define your priorities. Determining this will help you to understand the type of commitment of time that is needed for college success. Along with managing time is the need to manage your money wisely to allow yourself to accomplish your goals. As a student you will need to become knowledgeable about money resources like scholarships and financial aid. And, just as importantly, you may also need to learn to delay gratification, and put off large purchases until you have completed your education. Don't weigh yourself down with debt and worries now; focus on your goals and college success. Time, energy, and money are all part of the commitment and investment you are making to your future life success.

The story you are about to read comes to us from the Navajo, Dine, people of the Southwestern United States. The Navajo people live predominately in Arizona and New Mexico. They are well known as artisans of silver and turquoise jewelry, sand painting, and weaving. The weaving has become a tradition of the women of the tribe and they often utilize wool they harvest from their herds of sheep. Originally the weavers produced textiles used for blankets, cloaks, dresses, and saddle blankets. Today, it has become a highly regarded art form and produces much of the commercial enterprise for the Navajo economy.

How the Navajo Learned to Weave

In the Canyon de Chelley National Park stands a massive monolith made of sandstone known as Spider Rock. The Navajo or Dine people believe that this is the home of Spider Woman. The Dine believe that Spider Woman has strong spiritual powers and that she saved them as they entered this world.

One day a young girl feeling a bit lonely wanders into the dessert to look for cactus flowers. Soon she sees a trail of smoke coming out of the ground. "Hmm, how strange is this, how can fire be coming out of the ground?" she thinks to herself.

Being of a curious nature she runs over to take a look into the hole. She bends down and peers into the hole with one eye. Expecting to see fire or darkness underground, she is surprised to see Spider Woman spinning a blanket. The underground is lit up with a magical glow because Spider Woman is spinning on a loom made of sun rays and lightning bolts and the room glows with warm light.

Spider Woman senses the girl is near and without turning her head or looking away from her weaving, she says, "Who is it I feel close to me?" The girl is surprised that Spider Woman knows she is there and she quietly and shyly responds, "It is I, just a lonely girl walking about passing the day. The blanket you weave is more beautiful than any I have ever seen."

Spider Woman then says to the girl, "Would you like to come down and touch my blanket? You

"I seek strength, not to be greater than my brother, but to fight my greatest enemy—myself." Chief Yellow Lark, Lakota

"Those who have one foot in the canoe, and one foot on the boat, are going to fall into the water."

Tuscarora

will feel the power of the universe and the warm glow of the sun."

The girl joins Spider Woman and sits quietly as she listens to Spider Woman chant as she weaves. After some time, Spider Woman asks the girl, "Well, if you are feeling so lonely these days, maybe you would like to learn to weave?"

The girl is a quick learner and soon perfects her weaving skill. Later the girl returns home and begins to weave beautiful blankets for her friends and family. The Dine people are amazed at her skill and they ask her to tell them all about Spider Woman and to teach them to weave also. The girl shares her knowledge and skill with all who want to learn and becomes a friend to many. She is never lonely again.

Dine children are taught that if they do not behave well and listen to their parents and elders, Spider Woman would cover them with a web, entrap them, and eat them as a meal.

The Dine believe in the power of Spider Woman so much that they often rub the hands of their infant daughters with spider webs to ensure her weaver's spirit is passed on.

The Dine people believe to this day that Spider Woman lives in the Canyon de Chelley where her spirit still guides the weavers' hands.

Reference

Woodhead, Henry, and Jane Edwin. 1993. *The American Indians: The People of the Desert.* Richmond, Virginia: Time Life Books series.

Talking Circle

Use these questions for discussion in a talking circle or consider at least one of these questions as you respond in a journal entry:

1. In the story, lonely girl doesn't have a plan for her day or for her future. Yet, she luckily comes upon Spider Woman, and her life's plan unfolds. How will you go about planning your life? Will you hope to stumble upon the good fortune of lonely girl, or will you take a more strategic approach? How will you do that?

2. Lonely girl shares her knowledge freely and openly and as a result, is never lonely again. In some ways, lonely girl is a mentor to others and becomes a generous resource to her people. Have you had mentors in your life? Can you talk about someone you know who has been a successful college student and is now a working professional? What sacrifices did that person have to make to be able to complete their college educational goals?

3. Spider Woman is depicted as a strong and magical character. The Dine believe that she has created much of what lies upon the earth. Can you define your own character strengths? What are some deep beliefs you have in your own ability to weave a successful life?⌋

College Success 1

The College Success 1 website is continually updated with supplementary material for each chapter including Word documents of the journal entries, classroom activities, handouts, videos, links to related materials, and much more. See http://www.collegesuccess1.com/.

© Lyudmyla Kharlamova/
Shutterstock.com

Notes

1. Peter Knudtson and David Suzuki, *Wisdom of the Elders*, Toronto, Canada: Stoddart Publishing Company, 1993.

2. Britny Benson, "Native American Beliefs about Time and Death," Seven Ponds Blog, May 28, 2015, https://blog.sevenponds.com/cultural-perspectives/native-american-beliefs-about-time-and-death

3. John Hopkins, "A Look at Indian Time," Indian Country Today, updated September, 2018, https://indiancountrytoday.com/uncategorized/a-look-at-indian-time

4. Steven K. Scott, *A millionaire's Notebook,* quoted in Rob Gilbert, Editor, Bits & Pieces, November 4, 1999, 15.

5. Shainna Ali, "Could You Be Addicted to Technology?" Psychology Today, February 12, 2018, https://www.psychologytoday.com/us/blog/modern-mentality/201802/could-you-be-addicted-technology.

6. Havva Sert, Feride Taskin Yilmaz, Azime Karakoc Kumsar, and Dilek Aygin, "Effect of Technology Addiction on Academic Success and Fatigue among Turkish University Students," Fatigue: Biomedicine, Health & Behavior 7, no. 1 (2019), 41–51. https://www.researchgate.net/publication/331368453_Effect_of_technology_addiction_on_academic_success_and_fatigue_among_Turkish_university_students.

7. John Medina, *Brain Rules,* (Seattle: Pear Press, 2008), 157.

8. Ibid, pp. 162–163.

9. Alan Lakein, *How to Get Control of Your Time and Your life* (New York: Peter H. Wyden, 1973).

10. Ibid., 70–71.

11. Dave Ellis, *Becoming a Master Student* (Boston: Houghton Mifflin, 1998).

12. Jane Burka and Lenora Yuen, *Procrastination* (Reading, MA: Addison-Wesley, 1983).

13. Jane Bryant Quinn, "Money Watch," *Good Housekeeping*, November 1996, 80.

14. Robert Hanley, "Breaking Bad Habits," *San Diego Union Tribune*, September 7, 1992.

15. Stephen R. Covey, *The Seven Habits of Highly Effective People* (New York: Simon and Schuster, 1990), 150.

My Lifetime Goals: Brainstorming Activity

Name _____   Date _____

1. Think about the goals that you would like to accomplish in your life. At the end of your life, you do not want to say, "I wish I would have _____." Set a timer for five minutes and write whatever comes to mind about what you would like to do and accomplish over your lifetime. Include goals in these areas: career, personal relationships, travel, and financial security or any area that is important to you. Write down all your ideas. The goal is to generate as many ideas as possible in five minutes. You can reflect on which ones are most important later. You may want to do this as part of a group activity in your class.

Look over the ideas you wrote above and highlight or underline the goals that are most important to you.

2. Ask yourself what you would like to accomplish in the next five years. Think about where you want to be in college, what you want to do in your career, and what you want to do in your personal life. Set a timer and write whatever comes to mind in five minutes. The goal is to write down as many ideas as possible.

Again, look over the ideas you wrote and highlight or underline the ideas that are most important to you.

3. What goals would you like to accomplish in the next year? What are some steps that you can begin now to accomplish your lifetime goals? Consider work, study, leisure, and social goals. Set your timer for five minutes and write down your goals for the next year.

Review what you wrote and highlight or underline the ideas that are most important to you. When writing your goals, include fun activities as well as taking care of others.

Looking at the items that you have highlighted or underlined, make a list of your lifetime goals using the form that follows. Make sure your goals are specific enough so that you can break them into steps you can achieve.

My Lifetime Goals

Name _____   Date _____

Using the ideas that you brainstormed in the previous exercise, make a list of your lifetime goals. Make sure your goals are specific and concrete. Begin with goals that you would like to accomplish over a lifetime. In the second section, think about the goals you can accomplish over the next one to three years.

Long-Term Goals (lifetime goals)

Short-Term Goals (one to three years)

What are some steps you can take now to accomplish intermediate and long-term goals?

Successful Goal Setting

Name _____ Date _____

Look at your list of lifetime goals. Which one is most important? Write the goal here:

Answer these questions about the goal you have listed above.

1. What skills, abilities, and resources do you have to achieve this goal? What skills, abilities, and resources will you need to develop to achieve this goal?

2. Do you believe you can achieve it? Write a brief positive statement about achieving this goal.

3. State your goal in specific terms that can be observed or counted. Rewrite your goal if necessary.

4. Write a brief statement about how this goal will give you personal satisfaction.

5. How will you motivate yourself to achieve this goal?

6. What are your personal values that match this goal?

7. List some steps that you will take to accomplish this goal.

8. When will you finish this goal?

9. What roadblocks will make this goal difficult to achieve?

10. How will you deal with these roadblocks?

Weekly College Schedule

Name _____ Date _____

Copy the following schedule to use in future weeks or design your own schedule. Fill in this schedule and try to follow it for at least one week. First, fill in scheduled commitments (classes, work, activities). Next, fill in the time you need for studying. Put in some tasks related to your lifetime goals. Leave some blank time as a shock absorber to handle unexpected activities.

Time	Monday	Tuesday	Wednesday	Thursday	Friday	Saturday	Sunday
7 A.M.							
8							
9							
10							
11							
Noon							
1 P.M.							
2							
3							
4							
5							
6							
7							
8							
9							
10							
11							

Weekly To-Do Chart

Name _____   Date _____

Using a to-do list is an easy way to remind yourself of important priorities each day. This chart is divided into three areas representing types of tasks that college students need to balance: academic, personal, and social.

Weekly To-Do List

	Monday	Tuesday	Wednesday	Thursday	Friday
Academic					
Personal					
Social					

Study Schedule Analysis

Name _____ Date _____

Before completing this analysis, use the schedule form to create a master schedule. A master schedule blocks out class and work times as well as any regularly scheduled activities. Looking at the remaining time, write in your planned study times. It is recommended that you have two hours of study time for each hour in class. For example, a three-unit class would require six hours of study time. A student with 12 units would require 24 hours of study time. You may need more or fewer hours, depending on your study skills, reading skills, and difficulty of courses.

1. How many units are you enrolled in?

2. How many hours of planned study time do you have?

3. How many hours do you work each week?

4. How many hours do you spend in relaxation/social activities?

5. Do you have time planned for exercise?

6. Do you get enough sleep?

7. What are some of your time bandits (things that take up your time and make it difficult to accomplish your goals)?

Write a few discovery statements about how you use your time.

8. Are you spending enough time to earn the grades you want to achieve? Do you need to spend more time studying to become successful?

9. Does your work schedule allow you enough time to study?

10. How can you deal with your time bandits?

11. How can you use your time more effectively to achieve your goals?

Budgeting for College

Name _____ Date _____

Before you complete this budget, monitor your expenses for one month. Write down all expenditures and then divide them into categories that have meaning for you. Then complete the following budget and try to follow it for at least two months. Do this exercise on your own, since it is likely to contain private information.

College Student Monthly Budget

Monthly income for _____ (month)	
Income from job _____	
Money from home _____	**Total Income** [ ]
Financial aid _____	
Other _____	
Budgeted Monthly Expenses:	**Actual Monthly Expenses:**
Total Budgeted [ ]	**Total Actual**

Total Income [ ] **Minus Total Budgeted** [ ] **Equals** [ ]

CHAPTER 5

The Earth Sings the Same Song It Sang to My Ancestors: Improving Your Memory

Learning Objectives

Read to answer these key questions:

- ⌊What are some Native ways of knowing?⌋

- How does the memory work?

- How can I improve my memory?

- Why do I forget?

- What are some practical memory techniques based on brain science?

- What are some memory tricks?

- How can I optimize my brain power?

- Why is positive thinking important for improving memory and studying?

Acquiring Lwisdom is one of the Seven Grandfather teachings that also include love, respect, courage, honesty, humility, and truth. These teachings represent what is needed for survival and living the good life. Under these teachings, you are encouraged to use your inherent gifts and allow yourself to learn and live by your wisdom while observing and respecting all life around you. In the past, having a good memory was important for accurately sharing the stories and history.

Improving your memory is a great way to improve your academic success. When you listen and feel the songs of the earth—the wind blowing, the water flowing—you can remember that your ancestors heard these same songs. Acknowledging that your life is different from and yet the same as the past, can give you reassurance to develop new skills.

This chapter includes Native ways of knowing along with the latest findings in brain science translated into practical techniques for improving memory.

Petroglyphs on newspaper rock in Canyonlands national park, Utah, USA

Native Ways of Knowing

Students deserve a quality education that includes the contributions of Native peoples and an appreciation of their different world view. Indigenous knowledge is based on culture and includes community practices, rituals, and relationships. It is a way to make sense of the world. In this construct, human beings are connected to all other living beings. All life is revered and lives in balance and harmony. Learning is a foundation for sustainable ways of being, responsibility, and independence.

Traditional Indigenous knowledge is oral and symbolic. It is passed down to future generations through language, modeling, practice, animation, and stories.[1]

5 Characteristics of Indigenous Knowledge[2]

1. Personal

   No one person has the ultimate truth. Different voices and perceptions produce knowledge.

2. Orally transmitted

   Knowledge is passed down through story telling. These stories connect the speaker and listener and connect past and present memories.

3. Experiential

   Learning through the senses and experience are important ways of learning. Using all the senses brings together the physical and spiritual worlds. This way of learning includes the idea that the land is alive, and the only way to know is to be on the land.

   An elder is asked, "What do you mean by 'the land is alive'?" The elder says, "Come with me and I'll show you."

   After four or five days of walking through the forest and digging roots and doing work, the student says, "Are you ever going to tell me what is meant by 'the land is alive'?"

   The elder replies, "I see you need a few more days out here."

There is an emphasis on the practical application of skills and knowledge.

4. Holistic

Holistic means looking at all parts as interrelated. Ceremonies are used to share holistic knowledge. Ceremonies include fire, water, air, and land. Power comes from bringing these energies together.

The pipe is sacred, and, in the past, it was used to negotiate between different nations and set the stage for good talk to take place. As everyone touches the pipe, the circle is brought together. The sacred and physical realms are not separate.

5. Narrative

Stories are used to convey knowledge. These stories contain what is needed to live life in a good way. These stories use myth and metaphors to guide moral choice. They are connected to life, values, and proper behavior.

Knowledge comes in several forms:

- **Traditional knowledge** is carried forward from generation to generation. It describes the origins and achievements of Native people and is their record of allegiance to ancestral lands.
- **Empirical knowledge** is related to ecology and based on careful observation of living beings and their environment. Indigenous knowledge is closely related to the land, which provides food, shelter, clothing. The land is also related to social organization, ceremonies, and governance.
- **Revealed knowledge** comes through dreams, visions, and intuitions.

Native knowledge includes values, ethics and principles. The physical and metaphysical world are linked to a moral code. The nations of the Haudenosaunee believe that we borrow the earth from our children's children, and it is our duty to protect it and the culture for future generations. All decisions made now are made with the future generations who will inherit the earth in mind.

Here are some ideas for building on Native ways of knowing.

- Because no one person has the ultimate truth, seek different points of view before constructing your own reasonable view.
- The preservation of traditional stories and songs depended on practice. Review and practice the information you are learning in college.
- One way of practicing material is to say it out loud.
- Memory is connected to personal experience. Find a connection between your own experience and new knowledge.
- Seek to find practical applications of new knowledge.
- Because knowledge is holistic, try to understand how new knowledge fits with what you already know, as well as how it is connected to other new ideas you are learning.
- Learn new materials through the lens of your own cultural values. How will this new knowledge affect your future and the future of the earth?

Improving Your Memory

Memory: Short Term Versus Long Term

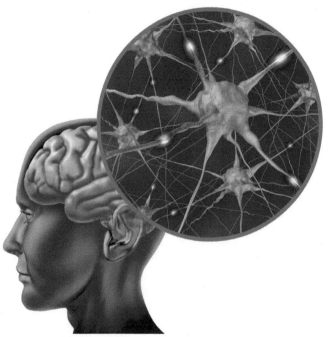

© Lightspring/Shutterstock.com

Effective studying in college involves transferring learning from short-term to long-term memory. Short-term memory is often called the working memory, which is a temporary space or desktop used to process information. The short-term memory has limited capacity and duration. If information is not transferred to long-term memory, it quickly disappears.

Through repetition or rehearsal, information is transferred to long-term memory, which has a higher capacity and duration. For example, if you just read your textbook, the information is stored in short-term memory and quickly disappears. Storing material in long-term memory is like making a trail through the jungle. The more the trail is used, the easier it is to follow and the more distinct it becomes. Learning requires effort; the more you practice or rehearse the more you learn.[3]

It is necessary to use some study strategies that involve repeating or reviewing the material to transfer the information to long-term memory available for passing tests and for later success in your career. To be most effective, this rehearsal or repetition must be done immediately and then at spaced intervals over time. Waiting to study just before a test by using intense marathon study sessions is not effective in transferring the material to long-term memory and is not very enjoyable either.

Forgetting

It was previously thought that once information was stored in long-term memory, it was there forever. However, scientists have found that our memories are often inaccurate and become distorted over time. Forgetting allows us to prioritize events. We forget items that are not important for our survival.

Examining the following lists of items frequently forgotten or remembered can give us insight into why forgetting occurs and how to minimize it.

We frequently forget these things:

- Names of people, places, or things

- Numbers and dates

- What we have barely learned

- Material we do not fully understand

- What we try to remember when embarrassed, frustrated, tired, or ill

- Material we have learned by cramming

- Ideas or theories that conflict with our beliefs

We tend to remember these things:

- Pleasant experiences

- Material that is important to us

- What we have put an effort into learning

- What we have reviewed or thought through often

- Material that is interesting to us

- Muscular skills such as riding a bike

- What we had an important reason to remember

- Items we discuss with others

- Material that we understand

- Frequently used information

Photo courtesy of First Nations University

To improve memory, you must first fully understand the material. Then convince yourself that the material you are learning is important and find something interesting about it. If you approach your studies with a positive attitude, it is easier to recall what you are studying. It is helpful if you can think about the material and discuss it with others. The critical step is putting in the effort to review the material you have learned so that it is transferred to long-term memory.

Minimizing Forgetting

Herman Ebbinghaus (1850–1909), a German psychologist and pioneer in research on forgetting, described a curve of forgetting.[4] He invented nonsense syllables such as WUX, CAZ, BIJ, and ZOL. He chose these nonsense syllables so that there would be no meaning, associations, or organizations that could affect the memory of the words. He would learn these lists of words and measure forgetting over time. The following is a chart of time and forgetting of nonsense syllables.

"Just as iron rusts from disuse, even so does inaction spoil the intellect."

Leonardo da Vinci

Time	Percent Forgotten
After 20 minutes	47
After 1 day	62
After 2 days	69
After 15 days	75
After 31 days	78

We can draw three interesting conclusions from examining these figures. First, **most of the forgetting occurs within the first 20 minutes**. Immediate review, or at least review during the first 20 minutes, would prevent most of the forgetting. Second, forgetting slows down over time. The third conclusion is that forgetting is significant after 31 days. Fortunately, we do not need to memorize nonsense syllables. We can use meaning, associations, organization, and proper review to minimize forgetting.

Review is important in transferring information from short-term to long-term memory. You can also minimize forgetting over time through the proper use of review.[5] Let's assume that you spend 45 minutes studying and learning something new. The optimum schedule for review would look like this:

After 10 minutes	Review for 5 minutes
After 1 day	Review for 5 minutes
After 1 week	Review for 3 minutes
After 1 month	Review for 3 minutes
After 6 months	Review for 3 minutes

Practical Memory Techniques Based on Brain Science

Remember that recitation or rehearsal of information is crucial in transferring information to long-term memory. Based on current research on brain science and psychology, here are some additional practical suggestions for improving memory.[6]

Memorization Tips

- Meaningful organization
- Visualization
- Recitation
- Develop an interest
- See the big picture first
- Intend to remember
- Learn small amounts frequently
- Basic background
- Relax

Think Positively about Learning

Positive emotions such as interest, joy, amusement, contentment, and relaxation optimize learning and memory. These positive emotions increase openness to new information as well as improve attention, memory, and verbal fluency. For greater success and achievement, it is important to think positively about learning. Rather than viewing learning as stressful or an unpleasant obligation, view it as a new and interesting adventure, and it can be easier and more rewarding.

Develop an Interest

We tend to remember what interests us. People often have phenomenal memories when it comes to sports, automobiles, music, stamp collecting, or anything they consider fun or pursue as a hobby. Find something interesting in your college studies. If you are not interested in what you are studying, look for something interesting or even pretend that you are interested and then reward yourself by doing something enjoyable.

Motivation and attitude have a significant impact on memory. Being highly motivated and approaching your studies with a positive attitude will help you to find something interesting and make it easier to remember. In addition, the more you learn about a topic, the more interesting it becomes. Often we judge a subject as boring because we know nothing about it.

Photo courtesy of First Nations University, Canada

Another way to make something interesting is to look for personal meaning. How can I use this information in my future career? Does the information relate to my personal experience in some way? How can I use this information? What is the importance of this information? And finally, is this information likely to be on the test?

See the Big Picture First

Imagine looking at a painting one inch at a time. It would be difficult to understand or appreciate a painting in this way. College students often approach reading a textbook in the same way. They focus on the small details without first understanding the main points. By focusing on the details without looking at the main points, it is easy to get lost. The first step in reading is to skim the chapter headings to form a mental outline of what you will be learning. Then read for detail.

Meaningful Organization

Another powerful memory technique is imposing your own form of personal organization on the material you are trying to remember. Psychologists have even suggested that your intelligence quotient (IQ) may be related to how well you have organized material you learned in the past. When learning new material, cluster facts and ideas into categories that are meaningful to you. Think of the mind as a file cabinet or a computer. Major topics are like folders in which we file detailed information. When we need to find the information, we think of the major topic and look in the folder to find the details. If we put all our papers into the file drawer without organization, it is difficult to find the information we need. Highlight or underline key ideas to focus on the main points and organize what you are learning.

The Magical Number 7 Theory

Grouping together or chunking bits of information together can make remembering easier. George Miller of the Harvard University found that the optimum number of chunks or bits of information that we can hold in short-term memory is five to nine.[7] It is much easier to remember material that is grouped in chunks of seven or less. You can find many examples of groups of seven used to enhance memory. There are seven digits in a phone number, seven days of the week, and seven numbers in your driver's license and license plate. There are also seven dwarfs, seven deadly sins, and Seven Wonders of the World!

Does this mean that we should try to remember only seven or less ideas in studying a textbook chapter? No, it is most efficient to identify seven or fewer key ideas and then cluster less important ideas under major headings. In this way, you can remember the key ideas in the chapter you are studying along with the details. The critical thinking required by this process also helps in remembering ideas and information.

Magical Number Seven

Remember George Miller's Magical Number Seven Theory? It is more efficient to limit the number of categories to seven or less, although you can have subcategories. Examine the following list of words.

goat	horse	cow
carrot	cat	lettuce
banana	tomato	pig
celery	orange	peas
cherry	apple	strawberry

Look at the list for one minute. Then look away from the list and write down all the words you can recall. Record the number of words you remembered: _____

Note that the following lists are divided into categories: animals, crops, and tropical fruits.

animals	crops	tropical fruits
lion	wheat	banana
giraffe	beans	kiwi
kangaroo	corn	mango
coyote	hay	guava
bear	oats	orange

Look at the above list for one minute. Then look away from the list and write down the words you recall. Record the number of words you remembered: _____

You probably remembered more from the second list because the list is organized into categories. Notice that there are only five words in each category. Remember that it is easier to remember lists with seven items or less. If these words have some meaning for you, it is easier to remember them. A farmer from the Midwest would probably have an easier time remembering the crops. A person from Hawai'i would probably remember the list of tropical fruits. We also tend to remember unusual items and the first and last items on the list. If you need to memorize a list, pay more attention to the mundane items and the items in the middle of the list.

Visualization

One of the most powerful memory techniques is visualization. If you can read the words and accompany them with pictures, you are using your brain in the most efficient way. Advertisers use pictures as powerful influences to motivate you to purchase their products. You can use the same power of visualization to enhance your studying. While you are studying history, picture what life would be like in that time period. In engineering, make pictures in your mind or on paper to illustrate scientific principles. Challenge yourself to see the pictures along with the words. Add movement to your pictures, as in a video. During a test, relax and recall the pictures.

© scyther5/Shutterstock.com

Intend to Remember

Tell yourself that you are going to remember. If you think you won't remember, you won't remember. This step also relates to positive thinking and self-confidence and will take some practice to apply. Once you have told yourself to remember, apply some of the above techniques such as organizing, visualizing, and reciting. If you intend to remember, you will pay attention, make an effort to understand, and use memory techniques to strengthen your memory.

One practical technique that involves intent to remember is the memory jogger. This involves doing something unusual to jog or trigger your memory. If you want to be sure to remember your books, place your car keys on the books. Since you cannot go anywhere without your keys, you will find them and remember the books too. Another application is putting your watch on your right hand to remember to do something. When you look at your left hand and notice that the watch is not there, the surprise will jog your memory for the item you wish to recall. You can be creative with this technique and come up with your own memory joggers.

Elaboration

Just as decorations or stories can be made more elaborate, learning can be made more elaborate too. The more you add details, connect the information, or make it personally meaningful, the easier it is to learn. Here are some ways to elaborate:[8]

- Write it in your own words. Look for personal meaning.

- Make a silly song or rhyme with the material.

- Rewrite your notes.

- Use flash cards to quiz yourself.

- Make a mind map.

- Underline the important points in the text and make notes in the margin about important points.

- Discuss the information with others.

- Study with a scented candle.

- Use multisensory learning including audio, visual, tactile, kinesthetic, and olfactory strategies.

- Associate the material learned to something you already know. How does the information match your experiences?

Distribute the Practice

Learning small amounts of material and reviewing frequently are more effective than a marathon study session. One research study showed that a task that took 30 minutes to learn in one day could be learned in 22 minutes if spread over two days. This is almost a 30 percent increase in efficiency.[9]

If you have a list of vocabulary words or formulas to learn, break the material into small parts and frequently review each part for a short period of time. Consider putting these facts or figures on index cards to carry with you in your purse or pocket. Use small amounts of time to quickly review the cards. This technique works well because it prevents fatigue and helps to keep motivation high. One exception to the distributed practice rule is creative work such as writing a paper or doing an art project, where a longer time period is needed for creative inspiration and immediate follow-through.

A learning technique for distributed practice is summed up in the acronym **SAFMEDS**, which stands for Say All Fast for one Minute Each Day and Shuffle.[10] With this technique, you can easily and quickly learn 100 or more facts. To use this technique, prepare flash cards that contain the material to be learned (vocabulary, foreign language words, numbers, dates, places, names, formulas). For example, if you are learning Spanish, place the Spanish word on one side of the card and the English word on the other side. Just writing out the flash cards is an aid to learning and is often sufficient for learning the material. Once the cards are prepared, *say* the Spanish word and see if you can remember what it means in English. Look at the back of the card to see if your answer is correct. Do this with *all* of the cards as *fast* as you can for *one minute each day*. Then *shuffle* the cards and repeat the process the next day.

It is important that you do this activity quickly. Don't worry if you do not know the answer. Just flip each card over, quickly look at the answer, and put the cards that you missed into a separate pile. At the end of the minute, count the number of cards you answered correctly. You can learn even faster if you take the stack of cards you missed and practice them quickly one more time. Shuffling the cards helps you to remember the actual meanings of the words, instead of just the order in which they appear. In the case of the Spanish cards, turn the cards over and say each English word to see if you can remember the equivalent word in Spanish. Each day, the number of correct answers will increase, and you will have a concrete measure of your learning. Consider this activity as a fun and fast-moving game to challenge yourself.

Create a Basic Background

You remember information by connecting it to things you already know. The more you know, the easier it is to make connections that make remembering easier. You will even find that it is easier to remember material toward the end of a college class because you have established a basic background at the beginning of the semester. With this in mind, freshman-level courses will be the most difficult in college because they form the basic background for your college education. College does become easier as you establish this basic background and practice effective study techniques.

You can enhance your basic background by reading a variety of books. Making reading a habit also enhances vocabulary, writing, and spelling. College provides many opportunities for expanding your reading horizons and areas of basic knowledge.

Stress and Emotions

Memory and learning are affected by stress and emotions. Moderate stress can be turned into motivation. For example, if you are moderately stressed over an exam, you may be more motivated to study for it. However, severe or chronic stress, along with the feeling that you have no control over it, results in a reduced ability to learn. If you are overly stressed, both short- and long-term memories are decreased as well as your ability to process language and do math.

Fear and stress are closely related. Fear causes us to run away from threatening or dangerous situations or to avoid them. Fear is one of the most powerful causes of academic failure. If you are fearful or doubt your ability to succeed in college, seek help from your counselor or advisor and use services such as tutoring to increase your self-confidence and minimize fear.

© Lightspring/Shutterstock.com

Using Mnemonics and Other Memory Tricks

Memory tricks can be used to enhance your memory. These memory tricks include acrostics, acronyms, peg systems, and loci systems. These systems are called *mnemonics*, from the Greek word *mneme* which means "to remember."

Mnemonic devices are very effective. A research study by Gerald R. Miller found that students who used mnemonic devices improved their test scores by up to 77 percent.[11] Mnemonics are effective because they help to organize material. They have been used throughout history, in part as a way to entertain people with amazing memory feats.

Mnemonics are best used for memorizing facts. They are not helpful for understanding or thinking critically about the information. Be sure to memorize your mnemonics carefully and review them right before exam time. Forgetting the mnemonic or a part of it can cause major problems.

Acrostics

Acrostics are creative rhymes, songs, poems, or sentences that help us to remember. Maybe you previously learned some of these in school.

Memorization Tricks
• Acrostics
• Acronyms
• Peg systems
• Loci systems
• Visual clues
• Say it aloud
• Have a routine
• Write it down

- Continents: Eat an Aspirin after a Nighttime Snack (Europe, Antarctica, Asia, Africa, Australia, North America, South America)
- Directions of the compass: Never Eat Sour Watermelons (North, East, South, West)
- Geological ages: Practically Every Old Man Plays Poker Regularly (Paleocene, Eocene, Oligocene, Miocene, Pliocene, Pleistocene, Recent)
- Guitar Strings: Eat All Dead Gophers Before Easter (E, A, D, G, B, E)
- Oceans: I Am a Person (Indian, Arctic, Atlantic, Pacific)
- Metric system in order: King Henry Drinks Much Dark Chocolate Milk (Kilometer, hectometer, decameter, meter, decimeter, centimeter, millimeter
- Notes on the treble clef in music: Every Good Boy Does Fine (E, G, B, D, F)
- Classification in biology: Kings Play Cards on Fairly Good Soft Velvet (Kingdom, Phylum, Class, Order, Family, Genus, Species, Variety)
- Order of operations in algebra: Please Excuse My Dear Aunt Sally (Parenthesis, Exponents, Multiplication, Division, Addition, and Subtraction)

An effective way to invent your own acrostics is to first identify key ideas you need to remember, underline these key words or write them down as a list, and think of a word that starts with the first letter of each idea you want to remember. Rearrange the words if necessary to form a sentence. The more unusual the sentence, the easier it is to remember.

In addition to acrostics, there are many other creative memory aids:

- Days in each month: Thirty days hath September, April, June, and November. All the rest have 31, except February which has 28 until leap year gives it 29.
- Spelling rules: *i* before *e* except after *c*, or when sounding like *a* as in neighbor and weigh.
- Numbers: Can I remember the reciprocal? To remember the reciprocal of pi, count the letters in each word of the question above. The reciprocal of pi = .3 1 8 3 10

Mnemonics become more powerful when used with visualization. For example, if you are trying to remember the planets, use a mnemonic and then visualize Saturn as a hula-hoop dancer to remember that it has rings. Jupiter could be a king with a number of maids to represent its moons.

Acronyms

Acronyms are commonly used as shortcuts in our language. The military is especially fond of using acronyms. For example, NASA is the acronym for the National Aeronautics and Space Administration. You can invent your own acronyms as a memory trick. Here are some common ones that students have used:

- The colors of the spectrum: Roy G. Biv (red, orange, yellow, green, blue, indigo, violet)
- The Great Lakes: HOMES (Huron, Ontario, Michigan, Erie, Superior)
- The stages of cell division in biology: IPMAT (interphase, prophase, metaphase, and telophase)

To make your own acronym, list the items you wish to remember. Use the first letter of each word to make a new word. The word you make can be an actual word or an invented word.

Peg Systems

Peg systems start with numbers, typically 1 to 100. Each number is associated with an object. The object chosen to represent each number can be based on rhyme or on a logical association. The objects are memorized and used with a mental picture to recall a list. There are entertainers who can have the audience call out a list of 100 objects and then repeat all of the objects through use of a peg system. Here is an example of a commonly used peg system based on rhyme:

One	Bun	Six	Sticks
Two	Shoe	Seven	Heaven
Three	Tree	Eight	Gate
Four	Door	Nine	Wine
Five	Hive	Ten	Hen

For example, if I want to remember a grocery list consisting of milk, eggs, carrots, and butter, I would make associations between the peg and the item I want to remember. The more unusual the association is, the better. I would start by making a visual connection between *bun*, my peg word, and *milk*, the first item on the list. I could picture dipping a bun into a glass of milk for a snack. Next I would make a connection between *shoe* and *eggs*. I could picture eggs being broken into my shoe as a joke. Next I would picture a *tree* with orange *carrots* hanging from it and then a *door* with *butter* dripping from the doorknob. The technique works because of the organization provided by the pegs and the power of visualization and association.

There are many variations of the peg system. One variation is using the letters of the alphabet instead of numbers. Another variation is to visualize objects and put them in a stack, one on top of the other, until you have a great tottering tower, like a totem pole telling a story. Still another variation is to use your body or your car as a peg system. Using our example of the grocery list above, visualize balancing the milk on your head, carrying eggs in your hands, having carrots tied around your waist and smearing butter on your feet. Remember that the more unusual the pictures, the easier they are to remember.

Loci Systems

Loci or location systems use a series of familiar places to aid the memory. The Roman orators often used this system to remember the outline of a speech. For example, the speaker might connect the entry of a house with the introduction, the living room with the first main point, and each part of the speech with a different room. Again, this technique works through organization and visualization.

Another example of using a loci system to remember a speech or dramatic production is to imagine a long hallway. Mentally draw a picture of each topic or section you need to remember, and then hang each picture on the wall. As you are giving your speech or acting out your part in the play, visualize walking down the hallway and looking at the pictures on the wall to remind yourself of the next topic. For multiple topics, you can place signs over several hallway entrances labeling the contents of each hallway.

Visual Clues

Visual clues are helpful memory devices. To remember your books, place them in front of the door so you will see them on your way to school. To remember to take your finished homework to school, put it in your car when you are done. To remember to fill a prescription, put the empty bottle on the front seat of your car. Tie a bright ribbon on your backpack to remind you to attend a meeting with your study group. When parking your car in the mall, look around and notice landmarks such as nearby stores or row numbers. When you enter a large department store, notice the items that are near the door you entered. Are you worried that you left the iron on? Tie a ribbon around the handle of the iron each time you turn it off or unplug it. To find out if you have all the items you need to go skiing, visualize yourself on the ski slope wearing all those items.

Say It Aloud

You can enhance memory by repeating aloud the items you are trying to remember. For example, if you want to remember where you hid your diamond ring, say it aloud a few times. Then reinforce the memory by making a visual picture of where you have hidden it. You can also make a rhyme or song to remember something. Commercials use this technique all the time to try to get you to remember a product and purchase it.

Have a Routine

Do you have a difficult time trying to remember where you left your keys, wallet, or purse? Having a routine can greatly simplify your life and help you to remember. As you enter your house, hang your keys on a hook each time. Decide where you will place your wallet or purse and put it in the same place each time. When I leave for work, I have a mental checklist with four items: keys, purse, glasses, and cell phone.

Write It Down

One of the easiest and most effective memory techniques is to simply write something down. Make a grocery list or to-do list, send yourself an email, or tape a note to your bathroom mirror or the dashboard of your car.

Remembering Names

Many people have difficulty remembering names of other people in social or business situations. The reason we have difficulty in remembering names is that we do not take the time to store the name properly in our memories. When we first meet someone, we are often distracted or thinking about ourselves. We are trying to remember our own names or wondering what impression we are making on the other person.

To remember a name, first make sure you have heard the name correctly. If you have not heard the name, there is no way you can remember it. Ask the person to repeat his or her name or check to see if you have heard it correctly. Immediately use the name. For example, say "It is nice to meet you, *Nancy*." If you can mentally repeat the name about five times, you have a good chance of remembering it. You can improve the chances of remembering the name if you can make an association. For example, you might think, "She looks like my daughter's friend Nancy." Some people remember names by making a rhyme such as "fancy Nancy."

Journal Entry #3

Review the material on using mnemonics and other memory tricks. List and explain at least three techniques that you find useful.

QUIZ

Memory Techniques

Test what you have learned by circling the letters of the correct answers to the following questions.

1. An effective memory technique is
   a. focusing on the details first.
   b. focusing on the main ideas first.
   c. realizing that learning in college is an unpleasant obligation.

2. Chunking information together can make learning easier. The optimum number of chunks which can be easily recalled is
   a. 10
   b. 20
   c. 7

3. To learn something new, it is helpful if you
   a. are interested in it.
   b. learn it right before the test.
   c. read it at least one time.

4. A mnemonic is
   a. a memory chip implanted in the brain to help you remember.
   b. a Greek word that means "repetition."
   c. an acrostic or acronym.

5. To remember names
   a. make sure you have heard the name correctly and repeat it.
   b. focus on the introduction and making a good impression.
   c. avoid saying the name aloud.

How did you do on the quiz? Check your answers: 1.b, 2.c, 3.a, 4.c, 5.a

Optimize Your Brain Power

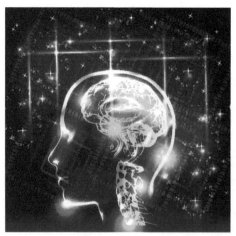

© Hubis/Shutterstock.com

The health of the body is connected to the health of your brain and your ability to learn. Specifically, brain health and optimal learning are affected by exercise, sleep, nutrition, hydration, stress, caffeine, alcohol, and drugs.[12]

Do aerobic exercise. Aerobic exercise is simply exercise that raises your heart rate, exercises your heart, and increases blood flow to the brain. It includes activities such as walking, running, swimming, dancing, and playing sports. The brain needs oxygen to function and exercise improves the flow of oxygen to the brain. Researchers have found that the human brain can grow new nerve cells by putting subjects on a three-month aerobic workout regimen. It is interesting to note that these new nerve cells can be generated at any age and are important in reversing the aging process. Exercise lowers your chance of getting Alzheimer's disease by 60%.[13] Exercise produces chemicals in the brain that help you to be alert, motivated, and pay attention. It has a positive effect on long-term memory, reasoning, and problem solving. For optimum health and learning, it is important to exercise the body as well as the mind. How much is needed? It is recommended that you do 30 minutes of aerobic exercise four to five times a week.

Sleep to remember and stay healthy. During sleep, we organize and consolidate learning from the previous day. It is important for transferring the information from short-term to long- term memory. During sleep, memories are sorted and stored according to their importance to you. One powerful learning strategy is to review the material you want to remember just before going to sleep. If sleep does not occur or is interrupted, it is more difficult to remember what has been studied the previous day. Lack of sleep negatively affects attention, memory, logical reasoning, mathematical skills, and manual dexterity. Scientists have found that lack of sleep decreases mental abilities:[14]

- There is a 30% decline in mental abilities after missing one night of sleep.
- There is a 60% decline in mental abilities after missing two nights of sleep.
- When sleep is restricted to six hours or less for five nights, mental abilities also decline 60%.

College students often miss out on sleep while cramming for exams, enjoying an active social life, and trying to balance work and school. Besides interfering with learning, lack of sleep has other detrimental effects on health:[15]

- The ability to utilize food declines by 30 percent, resulting in weight gain and an increase in fat instead of muscle.
- The level of stress hormones increases.
- The aging process is accelerated.
- Lack of sleep can make you less energetic, increase irritability, cause depression, and can make you accident-prone.
- The immune system is weakened, making you more susceptible to illness.

How much sleep do you need for optimum memory? It is recommended that adults have between 7.5 and 9 hours of sleep each night. The last two hours between 5.5 hours and 7.5 hours are the most important since it is during this time that rapid eye movement (REM) sleep occurs that the memories from the day are reviewed and stored in long-term memory. During sleep, the short-term memory is cleared out leaving space for new learning to occur. After the proper amount of sleep, you are able to remember more accurately and with less stress and anxiety.

Good nutrition and water are important. The brain learns easier if it is well hydrated and has the energy from good nutrition including whole grains, fruits, and vegetables. Low-fat diets have been shown to improve mental performance.

Drink caffeine in moderation. Caffeine can make you feel stressed, making it difficult to think.

Avoid smoking. Smoking blocks the carotid artery that supplies oxygen to the brain. Smoking also contributes to cognitive decline as you get older. Smokers also have a 30 percent increased risk of dementia, a condition that affects memory, thinking, and language skills.[16] Tobacco use is the leading cause of preventable illness and death in the United States, and one out of every five deaths in the United States is related to smoking.

Limit alcohol. Researchers have found that heavy drinking over a long period of time shrinks brain volume and can speed up memory loss with aging. One study showed that people who had more than fourteen drinks per week over twenty years had 1.6 percent smaller brains.[17]

Excessive drinking is a factor in poor college performance and high dropout rates.[18] College students who are considered binge drinkers are at risk for many alcohol-related problems. Binge drinking is simply drinking too much alcohol at one time. In men, binge drinking is defined by researchers as drinking five or more drinks in a row. For women, it is drinking four or more drinks in a row. Students who are binge drinkers are more likely to

- fall behind in schoolwork.
- miss class.
- be hurt or injured.
- experience sexual assault or date rape.
- drive a car after drinking.
- get in trouble with campus or local police.
- engage in unprotected sex.
- damage property.
- die from alcohol poisoning.

Don't abuse drugs. Drug abuse causes changes in the brain's chemical systems and circuits and can harm judgment, decision making, memory, and the ability to learn. It causes problems with concentration, reasoning, and problem solving. Abusing drugs increases the risk for heart attacks, strokes, brain damage, seizures, and death from accidental overdose.[19]

Use safety gear. Wear a seat belt when driving and a helmet when biking, boarding, or skating to reduce head injuries.

Keep active. Do puzzles, play a musical instrument, take something apart and fix it, draw or paint, dance, make friends with interesting people, read challenging books, or take a college course.

Stress, Relaxation, and Learning

One of the major challenges in life is dealing with stress and being able to relax. For college students, it is important to realize that too much stress interferes with memory, concentration, and learning. Chronic stress, which we do not feel we can control, interferes with both short- and long-term memory. Studies have shown that adults with high stress performed 50 percent worse on cognitive tests as compared with adults with low stress.[20] Learning to deal with stress is important for college, career, and lifelong success.

What Is Stress?

Imagine a world where there is absolutely no stress. While the thought is intriguing, it would probably be very boring. Some stress is positive and essential for well-being. For example, when we run a race, play a game of football, or act in a play, we experience stress, but it provides excitement and motivation. When a teacher announces a test, a little stress can cause the student to study for the test. Hans Selye, a famous researcher on stress, called this positive type of stress "eustress." He even went so far as to suggest, "Without stress, there could be no life."[21]

Hans Selye described negative stress as "distress." Distress has several physical symptoms that are uncomfortable and detract from good health. These symptoms can range from headaches, stomachaches, and sleeplessness to serious health problems such as high blood pressure, heart disease, and stroke. It is helpful to know some relaxation techniques to deal with the distress.

Relax While Studying

As you become more confident in your study techniques, you can become more relaxed. Here are some suggestions to help you relax during study time.

- Use distributed practice to take away some of the pressure of learning; take breaks between periods of learning. Give yourself time to absorb the material.
- Plan ahead so that you do not have to cram. Waiting until the last minute to study produces anxiety that is counterproductive.
- If you are feeling frustrated, it is often a good idea to stop and come back to your studies later. You may gain insight into your studies while you are more relaxed and doing something else. You can often benefit from a fresh perspective.

Practice Stress-Reducing Thoughts

When you are trying to deal with a stressful situation, listen to your self-statements. What are you saying to yourself? If these statements are negative, you will have negative emotions and will be stressed out. Think of some positive, stress-reducing thoughts that you can use in stressful situations. Here are some examples, but you will be better off to think up some of your own:

- That's the way it goes. No use getting upset.
- It's not the end of the world.
- Keep cool.
- It's no big deal.
- Relax.
- Life's too short to let this bother me.
- It's their problem.
- Life's like that.

- Be happy.
- I'll just do the best I can.
- No need to worry.

Take Action to Resolve Your Problems

If you have problems that are causing stress, take action to resolve them. Here are some steps you can take to solve problems and reduce stress:

- Concentrate your efforts on doing something about the problem.
- Seek information on how to solve the problem. This step may involve doing research or speaking to others.
- Make a plan of action.
- Make it a priority to solve the problem.
- Do what needs to be done to solve the problem, one step at a time.

Using Mindfulness to Relax

Mindfulness is a relaxation technique that involves **being aware of what is going on in a particular moment** and can be used as a quick break when you are feeling stressed and overwhelmed. It is effective because it temporarily takes your mind away from the everyday stresses of life. Living in the moment can be invigorating and help you to stay on task, as well as increasing focus and engagement. It can be as simple as stopping for a few moments to pay attention to your breathing. Here are a few ideas for taking a quick break by using mindfulness:[22]

© Gustavo Frazao/Shutterstock.com

- Focus on your breathing. When your attention wanders to your worries, bring it back to your breathing. Focus on your breathing for at least two minutes.
- Notice your surroundings. Look around and focus on the details in your surroundings.
- Practice savoring the moment. Take a piece of chocolate and unwrap it carefully. Feel the texture and notice the smell. Take a small bite and savor it as it melts on your tongue. Practice enjoying the present moment.
- Make it new. Whether working on a term paper, doing a presentation, or working on a project, think about how you can do it differently and make it new. This will increase the enjoyment and quality of the project.
- Mind the gap. Instead of being impatient at a red light or any other times when you have to wait, use the time as a break from stress. Breathe in and out. Savor the moment.
- Focus on the soles of your feet. Move your toes, feel your socks and shoes, and breathe naturally until you feel calm.
- Focus on your senses. Carefully observe your surroundings in detail including sounds and smell. Make a mental photograph. Close your eyes and see if you can remember all the details. Open your eyes and see what you missed. Mentally list the things you can appreciate in your surroundings.

- Imagine yourself in a pleasant place. When you are actually in a beautiful place, take the time to make a mental photograph. Memorize each detail so that you can return to this place in your mind when you feel stressed. Some people visualize the mountains, the beach, the ocean, a mountain stream, waterfalls, a tropical garden, or a desert scene. Choose a scene that works for you.
- Take a short walk. Pay attention to your breathing, the sensation of wind on your skin, and what you can see and hear.

Other Relaxation Techniques

Another way to deal with stress is to practice some physical and mental relaxation techniques. Here are a few suggestions:

- Listen to soothing music. Choose music that has a beat that is slower than your heart rate. Classical or New Age music can be very relaxing.
- Lie down in a comfortable place and tense and relax your muscles. Start with the muscles in your head and work your way down to your toes. Tense each muscle for five to 10 seconds and then release the tension completely.
- Use positive thinking. Look for the good things in life and take the time to appreciate them.
- Maintain a healthy diet and get enough exercise.
- Practice yoga or tai chi.
- Keep things in perspective. Ask yourself, "Will it be important in 10 years?" If so, do something about it. If not, just relax.
- Focus on the positives. What have you learned from dealing with this problem? Has the problem provided an opportunity for personal growth?
- Discuss your feelings with a friend who is a good listener or get professional counseling.
- Keep your sense of humor. Laughter actually reduces the stress hormones.
- Maintain a support network of friends and loved ones.
- Get a massage or give one to someone else.

Journal Entry #4

What is your plan for keeping your brain healthy throughout life? Include some of these ideas: keeping mentally active, exercise, getting enough sleep, nutrition, drinking water, relaxation, avoiding addictions, and using safety gear.

Positive Thinking

You can improve your memory as well as your life by using positive thinking. Positive thinking involves two aspects: thinking about yourself and thinking about the world around you. When you think positively about yourself, you develop confidence in your abilities and become more capable of whatever you are attempting to do. When you think positively about the world around you, you look for possibilities and find interest in what you are doing.

Golfer Arnold Palmer has won many trophies but places high value on a plaque on his wall with a poem by C.W. Longenecker:

If you think you are beaten, you are.
If you think you dare not, you don't.
If you like to win but think you can't,
It's almost certain that you won't.
Life's battles don't always go
To the stronger woman or man,
But sooner or later, those who win
Are those who think they can.[23]

Success in athletics, school, or any other endeavor begins with positive thinking. To remember anything, first, you have to believe that you can remember. Trust in your abilities. Then apply memory techniques to help you to remember.

If you think that you cannot remember, you will not even try.

The second part of positive thinking involves thinking about the world around you. If you can convince yourself that the world and your college studies are full of interesting possibilities, you can start on a journey of adventure to discover new ideas. For example, it is easier to remember what you read if you find the subject interesting. If the topic is interesting, you will learn more about it. The more you learn about a topic, the more interesting it becomes, and you are well on your way in your journey of discovery. If you tell yourself that the task is boring, you will struggle and find the task difficult. You will also find it difficult to continue.

To find something interesting, look for personal meaning. How can I use this information? Does it relate to something I know? Will this information be useful in my future career? Why is this information important? Write down your personal goals and remind yourself of your purpose for attending college. You are not just completing an assignment: you are on a path to discovery.

To be successful in college, start with the belief that you can be successful. Anticipate that the journey will be interesting, challenging, and full of possibilities. Enjoy the journey!

© Anson0618/Shutterstock.com

How can you use positive thinking to improve your memory and success in college? Use any of these questions to guide your thinking:

- How can I think positively about myself?
- How can I think positively about my college experience?
- What is the connection between belief and success?
- How can positive thinking make college more fun?

Stories from the Elders

Wesakechak e-pwekitot

This story is written by Larry Gauthier based on stories from the elders of the Canadian Woodland Cree.

Kiyas maga, a long time ago in the days of our ancestors, when humans could talk to animals, when humans learned from animals, in the days when Wesakechak walked on mother earth, this story was told.

As we all know Wesakechak does not like to work and is always travelling from tribe to tribe, living off the people of the tribe. Most tribes take him in without questions, but because he never helps out, he eventually overstays his welcome. The good thing about this is that Wesakechak always knows when to leave and when he has overstayed his welcome.

One time he had again overstayed his welcome. He could tell because no one placed food in front of him that day. He decided to pack what little belongings he had, and said good-bye to everyone. He began to walk in the direction of the south, not for any particular reason, just that it looked like an easier trail.

He walked and walked and walked, for two days and nights he walked. Finally he was so tired he just laid down; he didn't even build a shelter, he just laid down and went to sleep. He probably didn't even know how to build a shelter.

He slept and slept and slept. Sun woke him up early, but he was too lazy to get up. He just rolled over and kept on sleeping. Finally when Sun was at her highest, Wesakechak's eyes opened wide, his senses became alert, and he could smell the most beautiful smell he had ever smelled. He got up and began to follow his nose.

In a short time he came to camp, and immediately saw what was making that beautiful aroma. He saw a duck roasting on the fire. He called out, "Tansi, tansi, hello, hello," but no one answered. He looked at the duck and his mouth began to water. "Tansi tansi," he called out. Still no one answered. That gave Wesakechak time to think and he began to have selfish thoughts. If no one is around, he thought, I can just take that duck and run away and have it all to myself. So he took the duck from the fire and was about to run away with it, but thought he would just give it a little taste. It smelled so good, he wanted to taste it. So he had a little taste, next thing he knew he had eaten the whole duck. I had better leave before the people come home and see that I ate their dinner. Off he ran, but Wesakechak, being the character he was, didn't run too far before he got tired. He wanted to have a nap; he was so full from eating the whole duck. He spied a nice grassy area and walked over and promptly fell asleep.

> "People must pursue, acquire, and own knowledge to achieve freedom; otherwise we are mere slaves."
>
> Janine Pease-Pretty on Top, Crow

(continued)

Nokum, the old lady, whose duck Wesakechak ate, returned to her camp and found her duck had disappeared. She looked around and found the pile of duck bones surrounded by tracks. She recognized the tracks as Wesakechak as he was the only person who walked around with holy moccasins. She followed Wesakechak's tracks and soon heard him snoring. She saw him asleep with a look of complete satisfaction. "Hmmm," Nokum thought, "I am going to teach Wesakechak a lesson." She went back to her camp and got some medicine powder and threw it in the air and began to sing a song. The medicine drifted to Wesakechak and soon he breathed it in. The smell woke him up.

"Now what is that awful smell?" He asked out loud. He then remembered what he had done and thought he better put some distance between himself and the camp from which he stole the duck. He rose up and as he was took his first step, this loud noise escaped from his backside, phooot. . . He stopped, froze still. "What was that?" he asked himself. He took another step. . . phooot. Again he was startled. He was getting scared. He took another step and sure enough a loud noise escapes. . . PHHOOOOT. . . He bolts and with each step he lets out a loud fart. That is how humans come to pass gas.

Talking Circle

Use these questions for discussion in a talking circle or consider at least one of these questions as you respond in a journal entry.

1. Many of the stories from the elders use humor to teach morality. What is the moral of this story?

2. In this story, Wesakechak takes the easiest path. Developing good memory and good reading skills takes practice and self-discipline. Consider the path you will take on this journey, will you go the way of Wesakechak?

3. Wesakechak does not work for his food. In fact, Wesakechak is kind of lazy and wanders about without a purpose. What happens as a result? What would Wesakechak need to do to become a successful college student?

4. As you are attending college, you may find that you have to take the more difficult path and invest a lot of your time studying and improving basic skills in reading and mathematics. What is the payoff for you?⌋

College Success 1

The College Success 1 website is continually updated with supplementary material for each chapter including Word documents of the journal entries, classroom activities, handouts, videos, links to related materials, and much more. See http://www.collegesuccess1.com/.

© Lyudmyla Kharlamova/ Shutterstock.com

Notes

1. "Indigenous Ways of Knowing," University of Toronto, https://www.oise.utoronto.ca/abed101/indigenous-ways-of-knowing/, accessed March, 2021

2. Castellano, M.B (2000). Updating Aboriginal traditions of knowledge, In G.J.S. Dei, B.L. Hall, &D.G. Rosenburg (Eds.), *Indigenous knowledges in global contexts*. Toronto, Ontario, Canada: University of Toronto Press.

3. Terry Doyle and Todd Zakrajsek, *The New Science of Learning, How to Learn in Harmony with Your Brain*, (Sterling, VA: Stylus, 2013), 6–7.

4. Colin Rose, *Accelerated Learning*, (New York: Dell Publishing, 1985), 33–36.

5. Ibid., 50–51.

6. Doyle and Zakrajsek, *The New Science of Learning, How to Learn in Harmony with Your Brain*, 77.

7. G.A. Miller, "The Magical Number Seven, Plus or Minus Two: Some Limits on Our Capacity for Processing Invformation," *Psychological Review* 63 (March 1956): 81–97.

8. Doyle and Zakrajsek, *The New Science of Learning, How to Learn in Harmony with Your Brain*, 49–50.

9. Adapted from Paul Chance, *Learning and Behavior* (Pacific Grove, CA: Brooks/Cole, 1979), 301.

10 Walter Pauk, *How to Study in College* (Boston: Houghton Mifflin, 1989), 108.

11 Colin Rose, *Accelerated Learning* (New York: Dell Publishing, 1985), 33–36.

12. John Medina, *Brain Rules: 12 Principles for Surviving and Thriving at Work, Home, and School*, (Seattle, WA: Pear Press, 2008).

13. Ibid., p. 16.

14. Ibid., p. 162.

15. Ibid., p. 178.

16. John Medina, Ibid., p. 178.

17. Sara Lindberg, "What You Need to Know About Smoking and Your Brain," Healthline, August 23, 2019, https://www.healthline.com/health/smoking/smoking-effects-on-brain#cognitive-decline.

18. Amanda MacMillan, "Here's What Really Happens to Your Brain When You Drink Too Much Alcohol," April 24, 2018, https://www.health.com/condition/alcoholism/effects-of-alcohol-on-the-brain.

19. American Addiction Centers, "Binge Drinking on College Campuses," January 15, 2020, https://www.alcohol.org/teens/college-campuses/.

20. WebMD, "What Is Drug Addiction?" https://www.webmd.com/mental-health/addiction/drug-abuse-addiction#1.

21. John Medina, Ibid., p. 178.

22. "What is Stress", January 2021, http://www.stress.org

23. Rob Gilbert, ed., *Bits and Pieces* (Fairfield, NJ: The Economics Press, 1998), Vol. R, No. 40, p. 12.

Scenarios

Name _____ Date _____

Review the main ideas on improving memory and reading. Based on these ideas, how would you be successful in the following situations? You may want to do this as a group activity in your class.

1. You just read the assigned chapter in economics and cannot remember what you read. It went in one ear and out the other.

2. In your anatomy and physiology class, you are required to remember the scientific names for 100 different muscles in the body.

3. You signed up for a philosophy class because it meets general education requirements. You are not interested in the class at all.

4. You have a midterm in your literature class and have to read 400 pages in one month.

5. You must take American history to graduate from college. You think that history is boring.

6. You have been introduced to an important business contact and would like to remember his/her name.

7. You are enrolled in an algebra class. You continually remind yourself that you have never been good at math. You don't think that you will pass this class.

8. You have noticed that your grandmother is becoming very forgetful. You want to do whatever is possible to keep your mind healthy as you age.

Memory Test

Name _____ Date _____

Part 1. Your professor will read a list of 15 items. Do not write them down. After listening to this list, see how many you can remember and write them here.

1.   6.   11.

2.   7.   12.

3.   8.   13.

4.   9.   14.

5.   10.   15.

After your professor has given you the answers, write the number of words you remembered: _____

Part 2. Your professor will discuss memory techniques that you can use to improve your test scores and then will read another list. Again, do not write the words down, but try to apply the recommended techniques. Write as many words as you can remember.

1.   6.   11.

2.   7.   12.

3.   8.   13.

4.   9.   14.

5.   10.   15.

How many words did you remember this time? _____

Practice with Mnemonics

Name _____ Date _____

Join with a group of students in your class to invent some acrostics and acronyms.

Acrostics

Acrostics are creative rhymes, songs, poems, or sentences that help us to remember. To write an acrostic, think of a word that starts with the same letter as each idea you want to remember. Sometimes you can rearrange the words if necessary to form a sentence. At other times, it is necessary to keep the words in order. The more unusual the sentence, the easier it is to remember.

> **Example:** Classification in biology: Kings Play Cards on Fairly Good Soft Velvet (Kingdom, Phylum, Class, Order, Family, Genus, Species, Variety)

Create an acrostic for the planets in the solar system. Keep the words in the same order as the planets from closest to the sun to farthest from the sun.

Mercury, Venus, Earth, Mars, Jupiter, Saturn, Uranus, Neptune, Pluto (now a dwarf planet)

_____

_____

_____

Acronyms

To make your own acronym, list the items you wish to remember. Use the first letter of each word to make a new word. The new word you invented can be an actual word or an invented word.

> **Example:** The Great Lakes: HOMES (Huron, Ontario, Michigan, Erie, and Superior)

The following are the excretory organs of the body. Make an acronym to remember them. Rearrange the words if necessary.

intestines, liver, lungs, kidneys, skin

_____

_____

_____

Write down any acrostics or acronyms that you know. Share them with your group.

The Rainbow Will Rise Full Circle: Improving Study Skills

Learning Objectives

Read to answer these key questions:

- What are some learning strategies based on brain science?

- How can I apply memory techniques to reading?

- What is a reading system for college texts?

- What are some reading strategies for different subjects?

- What are some e-learning strategies?

- What are the best ways to study math?

- How can I create my success in college, careers, and life?

Learning how to learn is not only important in college but also in your future career. The world is in a constant state of change requiring continued learning on the job. Learning strategies based on current research in neuroscience, psychology, and education can make studying easier, more effective, and more productive. This chapter explores some key ideas that can make you an efficient lifelong learner. Apply these memory strategies to improve study skills, make reading more effective, and increase your success in math.

⌐Indigenous knowledge is experiential; it places an emphasis on learning through the senses and the power of observation. This chapter helps you to become aware of how you can use all your senses to improve study skills and make learning more effective.

Scientifically, we know that the rainbow is a full circle, but we can only see half of the rainbow with our eyes. The rainbow is a beautiful symbol of the richness of life and the power of the circle. All things of importance are done in a circle, and one step connects to the next. Let your new study skills guide your success and know that the power of the circle is with you in each phase of your growth.⌐

Neuroscience and Practical Learning Strategies

Recent discoveries in neuroscience can be translated into practical and efficient learning strategies for students. Neuroscientists have shown that learning can be increased by **using and integrating all the senses**, not just the preferred ones. This process is called **multi-sensory integration**. It is important to emphasize that multi-sensory integration is based on current research and is different from traditional learning style theory.

Learning is optimized when more senses are used when trying to remember what we are studying. Researchers note that "it is likely that the human brain has evolved to develop, learn, and operate optimally in multi-sensory environments."[1]

The senses work together as a team to optimize learning by encoding the information into the brain in the form of long-term memories. Sensory inputs include

- **Visual:** learning through reading, observing, or seeing things.
- **Auditory:** learning through listening and talking.
- **Tactile:** learning through touching the material or using a "hands-on approach."
- **Kinesthetic:** learning through movement as in learning to ride a bicycle.
- **Olfactory:** learning by smell.
- **Gustatory:** learning through taste.

The TruTalent Learning & Productivity assessment located in your career portfolio offers suggestions on how to make your learning easier and more productive.

Use all of your senses to help you to remember. For example, when studying Spanish, motivate yourself to learn by watching videos of Spanish speaking countries, listen to the words and say them out loud, use flash cards you can touch to practice the vocabulary, imagine the smell of Mexican food, eat some salsa and chips, and if possible, travel to a Spanish speaking country where you can practice the language.

Are there differences between the left brain and right brain that affect how we learn? Educators have often taught students that there is a difference between the right brain and left brain, with one side being more creative and the other more analytical. This idea is not supported by current brain research that shows that **both sides of the brain work together**. New findings show that the right side of the brain tends to remember the main ideas and the left side remembers the details, but every brain is unique.[2] It is suggested that to improve memory, it is important to begin with the main idea (right brain) and then remember the details (left brain).

Visual Learning Strategies

Some scientists have found that vision is the best tool for learning anything. The more visual the input, the more likely it is to be remembered. It was found that 72 hours after learning something, people recalled only 10% of material presented orally versus 65% recollection when a picture was added.[3] When we animate the pictures, learning is further improved. It is important to use visualization as an aid to studying and remembering. Make a visual picture of what you need to remember. If you can make a mental video, recall is further enhanced.

Here are some visual learning strategies. Highlight or place a checkmark in front of the learning strategies that you can use:

_____Make a visual image of what you are learning. For example, while reading history, picture in your mind's eye what it would be like to live in that historical period. Even better, make a video.

_____If you are having difficulties understanding a concept, find an online video that explains it.

_____Use color to highlight the important points in the text while reading. Review the important points by looking at the highlighted passages again.

_____Take notes and use underlining and highlighting in different colors to highlight the important points. Include flow charts, graphs, and pictures in your notes.

_____Make summary sheets or mind maps to summarize and review your notes.

_____Use pictures, diagrams, flow charts, maps, graphs, time lines, videos, and multimedia to aid in learning and preparing for exams.

_____Use flash cards to remember the details.

_____Sit in front of the class so you can carefully observe the professor. Copy what is written on the board or use your cell phone to photograph it.

_____Create visual reminders to keep on track. Make lists on note pads or use sticky notes as reminders.

_____Before answering an essay question, picture the answer in your mind and then make an outline or mind map.

_____Use mind maps and outlines to review for exams.

_____When learning new material, begin with visual learning strategies and then reinforce them with audio, kinesthetic, tactile, or olfactory strategies.

Audio Learning Strategies

Audio learning strategies involve using the sense of hearing to learn new information. Use these techniques to reinforce visual learning. Highlight or place a checkmark next to the strategies you can use.

_____As you are reading, ask questions or say out loud what you think will be important to remember.

_____Make it a priority to attend lectures and participate in classroom discussions.

_____To prepare for exams, rehearse or say the information verbally. For example, while studying math, say the equations out loud.

_____Discuss what you are learning with other students or friends. Form a study group.

____Use memory devices, rhymes, poems, rhythms, or music to remember what you are studying. For example, turn facts into a rap song or musical jingle to aid in recall.

____Memorize key concepts by repeating them aloud.

____If you are having problems reading your textbook or understanding the directions, read them out loud.

____Some students can study better with music. However, if your attention shifts to the music, you are multi-tasking and it will take longer to complete your work. On the other hand, some students use music for relaxation, which can be beneficial to studying. Experiment to see if you can be more efficient with the music on or off.

Tactile Learning Techniques

You can increase your learning by using your sense of touch to learn new information. Here are some tactile learning strategies: highlight or place a checkmark next to the ones you can use:

____Writing is one of the best tactile learning strategies. Take notes, write a journal, list key ideas, make an outline, or create a mind map.

____Use real objects to help you learn. For example, in a physics course, if you are studying levers, make a simple lever and observe how it works. If you are studying geography, use a globe or map to aid in studying.

____Use flash cards to review the key ideas as well as the details.

Kinesthetic Learning Strategies

These strategies involve moving around while studying. Highlight or place a checkmark in front of the strategies that you can use.

____Move while studying. For example, review material while on your exercise bike or stair stepper.

____Participate in kinesthetic learning experiences such as drama, building, designing, visiting, interviewing, and going on field trips.

____Take frequent breaks and study in different locations.

____Use a study group to teach the material to someone else.

Olfactory Learning Strategies

Olfactory refers to our sense of smell and is strongly associated with learning and memory. Marketing companies are using this sense to increase sales. For example, bakeries often distribute the smells from baking outside as a way of drawing in customers. Perfumes and body sprays are often advertised as a way to attract the opposite sex. Researchers had two groups watch a movie and tested them for recall. One group was tested without smell, and one was tested with the smell of popcorn in the room. The group with the popcorn smell had significantly increased recall.[4] Smells are powerful because they are often connected to emotions. In our previous example, movies and popcorn are positive experiences. Can you think of creative ways to use smell to increase memory? When creating that visual picture or video to enhance memory, include the sense of smell. Make it a four-dimensional movie (visual, audio, kinesthetic and olfactory!). You can use smells to create a positive learning environment.

Gustatory Learning Strategies

Gustatory refers to our sense of taste and can be used to enhance recall. You can eat your favorite piece of candy or chewing gum when trying to remember something that is difficult or seems uninteresting to you. Your sense of taste can be used to stimulate the reward center of the brain which regulates motivation, learning, memory, and goal-directed behavior. A caution on this technique is to avoid overeating and the resultant weight gain. One piece of candy or sugarless gum will do!

Journal Entry #1

Neuroscientists have discovered that learning is increased by using and integrating all the senses. How would you study a chapter in history, biology, or one of your current courses by using all your senses?

Applying Memory Strategies to Reading

You can apply memory strategies to store information from reading in your long-term memory.

A Study System for Reading a College Textbook: SQ4R

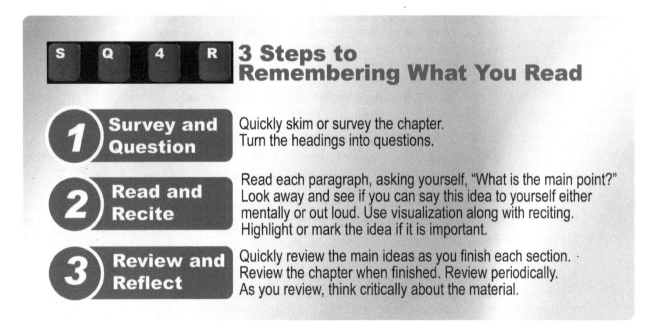

Figure 6.1 The SQ4R System for reading a college textbook.
Courtesy of Charlotte Moore. © Kendall Hunt Publishing Company.

Many students spend time reading their college textbooks with little benefit. Often students say that they cannot remember the material they have just read. The reason for this problem is not lack of intelligence, but rather a simple lack of rehearsal. If you are just reading the material, you are placing it in short-term memory, which quickly disappears. Effective study systems for reading a college textbook include techniques for storing information in long-term memory including recognizing major points, organizing the material to be learned, reviewing, intending to remember, and critical thinking about reading. It helps to think positively about the material and look for something interesting or meaningful in it. The essential point is that you must repeat or rehearse the material to transfer it to long-term memory. The **SQ4R system** (**Survey**, **Question**, **Read**, **Recite**, **Review**, and **Reflect**) is a simple and effective way to store information in long-term memory. This system can be broken down into three steps.

Step 1: Survey and Question. Finding the important points and understanding the organization of the reading is essential for learning and recall. The typical pattern of a college text is title, subtitle, paragraph, and topic sentence. **Learn to focus on the pattern and major points and then add the details.** This is accomplished by surveying and questioning the chapter before you begin reading it in detail. Read the title and first paragraph or introduction to the chapter and then look quickly through the chapter, letting your eyes glide across bold headings, diagrams, illustrations, and photos. Read the last paragraph or summary of the chapter. This process should take five minutes or less for a typical chapter in a college textbook. It is time well spent for transferring the information to your long-term memory.

While you are surveying the chapter, ask yourself questions. Take each major heading in the chapter and turn it into a question. For example, in this section of the book you might ask: What is a system for reading a college text? Why do I need a system? What is SQ4R? What is the first step of SQ4R? You can also ask some general questions as you survey the chapter: What is the main point? What will I learn? Do I know something about this? Can I find something that interests me? How can I use this? Does this relate to something said in class? What does this mean? Is this a possible test question? Asking questions will help you to become an active reader and to find some personal meaning in the content that will help you remember it. If you at least survey and question the relevant textbook material before you go to class, you will have the advantage of being familiar with some of the key ideas to be discussed.

There are several benefits to taking this first step:

- This is the first step in rehearsal for storage of information into long-term memory.
- The quick survey is a warmup for the brain, similar to an athlete's warmup before exercise.
- A survey step is also good practice for improving your reading speed.
- Reading to answer questions increases comprehension, sparks interest, and has the added bonus of keeping you awake while reading.

"The important thing is to not stop questioning."
Albert Einstein

If you want to be able to read faster, improve your reading comprehension, and increase retention of your reading material, practice the survey and question step before you begin your detailed reading.

Step 2: Read and recite. The second step in reading a text is to read and recite. Read each paragraph and look for the most important point or topic sentence. If the point is important, highlight or underline it. You might use different colors to organize the ideas. You can also make a notation or outline in the margin of the text if the point is especially significant, meaningful, useful, or likely to appear on an exam. A picture, diagram, or chart drawn in the margin is a great way to use visualization to improve retention of the material. If you are reading online, take notes on the important points or use cut and paste to collect the main ideas in a separate document.

Next, look away and see if you can say the main point to yourself either silently or out loud. Reciting is even more powerful if you combine it with visualization. Make a video in your head to illustrate what you are learning. Include color, movement, and sound if possible. Reciting is crucial to long-term memory storage. It will also keep you awake. Beginning college students will find this step a challenge, but practice makes it a habit that becomes easier and easier.

Photo courtesy of William Bright of Connors State College.

If you read a paragraph or section and do not understand the main point, try these techniques:

1. **Notice any vocabulary or technical terms that are unfamiliar.** Look up these words in a dictionary or in the glossary at the back of the book. Use index cards; write the words on one side and the definition on the other side. Use the SAFMEDS technique (Say All Fast in one Minute Each Day Shuffle) discussed earlier in this textbook. You are likely to see these vocabulary words on quizzes and exams.

2. **Read the paragraph again.** Until you get into the habit of searching for the main point, you may need to reread a paragraph until you understand. If this does not work, reread the paragraphs before and after the one you do not understand.

3. **Write a question in the margin and ask your instructor or tutor to explain.** College instructors have office hours set aside to assist students with questions, and faculty are generally favorably impressed with students who care enough to ask questions. Most colleges offer tutoring free of charge.

4. **If you are really frustrated, put your reading away and come back to it later.** You may be able to relax and gain some insight about the material.

5. **Make sure you have the proper background for the course.** Take the introductory course first.

6. **Assess your reading skills.** Colleges offer reading assessments, and counselors can help you understand your skill level and suggest appropriate courses. Most colleges offer reading courses that can help you to be successful in college.

7. **If you have always had a problem with reading, you may have a learning disability.** A person with a learning disability is of average or higher-than-average intelligence, but has a problem that interferes with learning. Most colleges offer assessment that can help you understand your learning disability and tutoring that is designed to help you to compensate for the disability.

Step 3: Review and reflect. The last step in reading is to review and reflect. After each section, quickly review what you have highlighted or underlined. Again, ask questions. How can I use this information? How does it relate to what I already know? What is most important? What is likely to be on the exam? Is it true? Learn to think critically about the material you have learned.

When you finish the chapter, quickly (in a couple of minutes) look over the highlights again. This last step, review and reflect, is another opportunity for rehearsal. At this point, you have stored the information in long-term memory and want to make sure that you can access the information again in the future. Think of this last step as a creative step in which you put the pieces together, gain an understanding, and begin to think of how you can apply your new knowledge to your personal life. This is the true reward of studying.

Review is faster, easier, and more effective if done immediately. As discussed previously, most forgetting occurs in the first 20 minutes after exposure to new information. If you wait 24 hours to review, you will probably have forgotten 80 percent of the material and will have to spend a longer time in review. Review periodically to make sure that you can access the material easily in the future, and review again right before the test.

As you read about the above steps, you may think that this process takes a lot of time. Remember that it is not how much you read, but how you read that is important. In reality, the SQ4R technique is a time-saver in that you do not have to reread all the material before the test. You just need to quickly review information that is stored in long-term memory. Rereading can be purely mechanical and consume your time with little payoff. Rather than rereading, spend your time reciting the important points. With proper review, you can remember 80 to 90 percent of the material.

Research has shown that you can retain 88% of the material you study using the following review schedule.[5] The rate of retention using this schedule is four times better.

1. Review immediately within 30 seconds.

2. Review after a few minutes.

3. Review after one hour.

4. Review a day later after an overnight rest.

5. Review after a week.

6. Review after one month.

Suggestions for review schedules vary, but the key point is that review is most effective when it is done in short sessions spaced out over time. The review can be done quickly; it is probably the most important investment you can make in remembering what you have read.

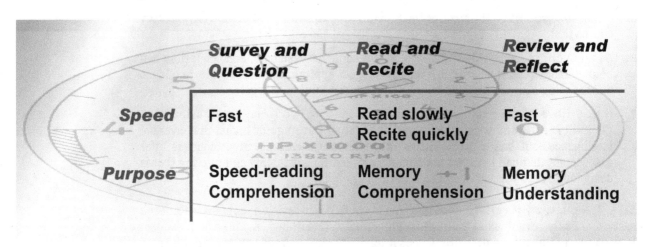

	Survey and Question	Read and Recite	Review and Reflect
Speed	Fast	Read slowly Recite quickly	Fast
Purpose	Speed-reading Comprehension	Memory Comprehension	Memory Understanding

Figure 6.2 This chart summarizes the speed and purpose of each SQ4R step.

What to Do If Your Reading Goes in One Ear and Out the Other

1. **Silence your inner critic.**
   If you have always told yourself that you are a poor reader or hate reading, these thoughts make it difficult to read. Think positively and tell yourself that with some effort, you can read and understand. Focus on what you can do, rather than what you can't do.

2. Look for the key ideas and underline them.

3. **Try visualization.**
   Make a mental picture or video with the material you are reading.

4. **Look for personal meaning.**
   Can you relate the material to your life in any way?

5. Do a quick scan of the material to find some major points and then reread the material closely.

6. Try talking to the text as you read it. Ask questions. Why is this important? Do you know anything about this? Do you agree or disagree? Do you think it is a good or bad idea? Can you use this information in the future? Can you find something interesting in the text? Challenge the material and think critically about it. Make humorous remarks. Imagine yourself in the situation. What would it be like and what would you do? You can write your comments in the text or do this silently in your head.

© wavebreakmedia/Shutterstock.com

Reading Strategies for Different Subjects

Math

1. Skimming the textbook can help you to decide if you are enrolled in the correct course. While skimming a math book, keep in mind that many of the topics will be unfamiliar to you. You should be able to understand the first few pages and build your knowledge from there. If you do not understand these first few pages, you may need to go back and take a review math course, especially if there has been a gap in studying math. If all the concepts are familiar to you, you may be taking a class that you do not need.

2. It is helpful to read your math textbook before you go to class so you can begin to understand key concepts and vocabulary. Make note of areas that need special attention to increase your understanding. Pre-reading or at least skimming the text will help you to understand the lecture better.

3. As you are reading, make flash cards to review important formulas, vocabulary, and definitions.

4. It is not enough to read and understand mathematical concepts. Make sure that you add practice to your study system. Practice builds self-confidence needed for success on math exams.

5. Focus on understanding math concepts rather than on memorizing problems.

Science

1. In science classes, the scientific method is used to describe the world. The scientific method relies on questioning, observing, hypothesizing, researching, and analyzing. You will learn about theories and scientific principles. Highlight or mark theories, names of scientists, definitions, concepts, and procedures.

2. Understand the scientific principles and use flash cards to remember details and formulas.

3. Study the charts, diagrams, tables, and graphs. Draw your own pictures and graphs to get a visual picture of the material.

4. Use lab time as an opportunity to practice the theories and principles that you have learned.

Social and Behavioral Sciences

1. Social and behavioral scientists focus on principles of behavior, theories, and research. Notice that there are different theories that explain the same phenomena. Highlight, underline, and summarize these theories in your own words.

2. When looking at the research, ask yourself what the point of the research was, who conducted the research, when the research was completed, what data was collected, and what conclusions were drawn.

3. Think of practical applications of theories.

4. Use flash cards to remember details.

Literature Courses

When taking a course in literature, you will be asked to understand, appreciate, interpret, evaluate, and write about the literature.

1. Underline the names of characters and write plot summaries.

2. Write notes about your evaluation of literary works.

3. Make flash cards to remember literary terms.

4. Write down important quotes or note page numbers on a separate piece of paper so that you don't have to go back and find them later when you are writing about a work.

Foreign Language Courses

Foreign language courses require memorization and practice.

1. Distribute the practice. Practice a small amount each day. It is not possible to learn everything at once.

2. Complete the exercises as a way to practice and remember.

3. Study out loud.

4. Practice speaking the language with others.

5. Use flash cards to remember vocabulary.

6. Make charts to practice verb conjugations.

7. Ask for help if you do not understand.

8. Learn to think in the foreign language. Translating from English causes confusion because the structures of languages are different.

> "Whatever the mind of man can conceive and believe, it can achieve."
> Napoleon Hill

Improving Reading Concentration

Hank Aaron said that what separates the superstar from the average ballplayer is that the superstar concentrates just a little longer. Athletes are very aware of the power of concentration in improving athletic performance. Coaches remind athletes to focus on the ball and to develop good powers of concentration and visualization. Skilled athletes, musicians, and artists don't have any trouble concentrating. Think about a time when you were totally focused on what you were doing. You were motivated to continue.

Being able to concentrate on your reading helps you to study more efficiently. You can set the stage for paying attention by focusing on your goals, getting some exercise, being well-rested, and avoiding multi-tasking. Here are some suggestions for managing the distractions and improving concentration.

Manage your external environment. Find an environment that minimizes distractions. One idea is to study in the library where there are many cues that remind you to study. There are books and learning resources and other people studying. Concentration and motivation can be increased by varying the places where you study. You may be able to set up a learning environment in your home where you can place a desk or table, your computer, and your materials for learning. Vary your routine by finding a quiet place outside to study, or any place where you can focus your attention. Avoid studying in the kitchen, in your bed, or in front of the TV where you can be distracted by food, sleep, or an interesting program on TV.

Manage Your Internal Distractions

1. **Become an active reader.** Read to answer questions. Search for the main idea. Recite or re-say the main idea in your mind. Reflect and think critically about the material you are reading. Mark or highlight the text. Visualize what you are reading.

2. **Remind yourself of your purpose for reading.** Think of your future college and career goals.

3. **Give yourself permission to daydream once in a while.** Use daydreaming as a break from your studies. Come back to your studies with a relaxed attitude.

4. **Break the task into small parts.** If the task seems overwhelming, break it into small parts and do the first part. If you have 400 pages to read in 10 days, read 40 pages each day. Make a schedule that allows time to read each day until you have accomplished your goal. Use distributed practice in your studies. Study for a short time each day rather than holding a marathon study session just before the test.

5. **Vary the content and subjects that you are studying.** Athletes maintain concentration and motivation by including strength, speed, and skill practice in each workout. Musicians practice scales, different musical pieces, and rhythm exercises in one practice session. In your studies, you can do the same. For example, when studying a foreign language, spend some time on reading, some time on learning vocabulary, and some practice in speaking the language. Then do some problems for your math class.

6. **Be here now.** Choose where you will place your attention. Your body can be attending a lecture or be at the desk reading, but your mind can be in many different and exciting places. You can tell yourself, "Be here now." You cannot force yourself to pay attention, but when your mind wanders, notice that you have drifted off and gently return your attention to your lecture or reading. This will take some practice, since attention tends to wander often.

© Diego Cervo/Shutterstock.com

7. **The spider technique.** If you hold a tuning fork to a spider web, the web vibrates and the spider senses that it has caught some tasty food and goes looking for it. After a while the spider discovers that there is no food and learns to ignore the vibrations caused by the tuning fork. When you are sitting in the library studying and someone walks in talking and laughing, you can choose to pay attention either to the distraction or to the studying. Decide to continue to pay attention to the studying.

8. **Set up a worry time.** Many times, worries interfere with concentration. Some people have been successful in setting up a worry time. Here's how it works:

   a. Set a specific time each day for worrying.

   b. When worries distract you from your studies, remind yourself that you have set aside time for worrying.

   c. Tell yourself, "Be here now."

   d. Keep your worry appointment.

   e. During your worry time, try to find some solutions or take some steps to resolve the things that cause you to worry.

9. **Take steps to solve personal problems.** If you are bothered by personal problems, take steps to solve them. See your college counselor for assistance. Another strategy is to plan to deal with the problem later so you can study now.

10. **Use the checkmark technique.** When you find yourself distracted from a lecture or from studying, place a checkmark on a piece of paper and refocus your attention on the task at hand. You will find that your checkmarks decrease over time and your attention improves.

Journal Entry #2

What are the six steps of SQ4R? Write four intention statements about improving your reading.

The six steps of SQ4R are . . .

I intend to . . .

© SnowWhiteimages/
Shutterstock.com

Guidelines for Marking Your Textbook

Marking your textbook can help you pick out what is important, save time, and review the material. It is a great way to reinforce your memory. In high school, you were given the command, "Thou shalt not mark in thy book!" College is different. You have paid for the book and need to use it as a tool. Even if you plan to sell your book, you can still mark it up. Here are some guidelines for marking your book:

- Underline or mark only the key ideas in your text. You don't have to underline complete sentences; just underline enough to make sense when you review your markings. If reading online, use the highlighter tool to mark the main points and then cut and paste the main points into a separate document.

- Aim for marking or highlighting about 20 percent of the most important material. If you mark too much of your reading, it will be difficult to review the main points.

- Read each paragraph first. Ask yourself, "What is the main point?" Highlight or mark the main point if it is important. Not every paragraph has a main point that needs to be marked.

- Use other marks to help you organize what you have read. Write in numbers or letters and use different colors to help you organize ideas.

- Most college texts have wide margins. Use these margins to write down questions, outlines, or key points to remember.

- Learn to be brief, fast, and neat in your marking or highlighting.

- If you are tempted to mark too much, use the double system of first underlining with a pencil as much as you want and then using a highlighter to pick out the most important 20 percent of the material in the chapter.

QUIZ

Learning Strategies and Reading

Test what you have learned by selecting the correct answers to the following questions.

1. For optimal learning, brain scientist believe that it is best to use

   a. your left brain.
   b. your right brain.
   c. multisensory input.

2. Brain scientists have recently found that you learn best by using

   a. your preferred learning style.
   b. all of your senses to remember.
   c. auditory techniques.

3. Most scientists believe that the most powerful strategy for learning anything is

   a. visual.
   b. auditory.
   c. kinesthetic.

4. If you have read the chapter and can't remember what you have read,

   a. read the chapter again.
   b. remember to select important points and review them.
   c. the material is stored in long-term memory.

5. When you start reading a new textbook,

   a. begin with chapter one.
   b. focus on the details you will need to remember.
   c. skim over the text to get a general idea of what you will be reading.

How did you do on the quiz? Check your answers: 1. c, 2. b, 3. a, 4. b, 5. c

Journal Entry #3

You have just read a chapter in your economics textbook and can't remember what you have just read. How can you apply the ideas in this chapter to improve your reading comprehension?

Photo courtesy of Navajo Technical University.

Tips for Online Learners

There are many advantages to online learning, but knowing good online study strategies is essential for success. Using these tips can help you to enjoy the advantages of online learning while becoming a successful online learner.

Advantages of Online Learning

Thinking about the advantages of online learning can help to increase motivation. With online learning, you don't have to travel to class or spend time in a classroom. You can learn at your own pace and in the privacy of your own home. Online courses are convenient and save time and money.

New advances in technology have provided powerful tools for online learning. Students from the New Millennial Generation and Generation Z already understand, use, and enjoy the social media and technology used for online education.

Challenges of Online Learning

Learning in a classroom provides opportunities for interaction with the instructor and other students. Some students may miss the opportunities for social interaction and asking questions. Remember to take advantage of online opportunities for interaction and ask questions if needed.

Discussion boards and chats are the most frequently used tools for interaction. These tools are often required, and points are awarded for participation.

Face-to-face courses have a definite schedule of meetings. Online courses are more flexible. Getting assignments done with a flexible schedule can be challenging for some students.

Balance Freedom with Responsibility

Online courses generally have weekly learning objectives and modules. This gives students the freedom to choose when they are going to complete coursework. There are generally no set days and times for learning. This freedom can lead to procrastination. Students who wait until just before an assignment is due have increased stress and lower performance. Procrastination is the leading reason for lack of success in an online course. One way to avoid procrastination is to think about how online learning is important to accomplishing your lifetime goals. Spend your time on what is most important, and then reward yourself for getting the work done.

Establish a Personal Schedule

Log in to your online course at the beginning of the week to see what is expected. Some professors may expect you to log in more frequently. Then create a plan or schedule for completing the work before it is due. List due dates on a calendar, and check them off as they are completed.

Minimize Distractions

We have more distractions in our personal spaces than in a classroom. The most common distractions are related to the technology we are using to learn. While learning online, we are distracted by phones, messages, notifications, and the myriad of connections through social media. Minimize these distractions by putting your phone in another room or turning it off. Avoid browsing the Internet, checking your email, or responding to social media while studying. Use these potential distractions as a reward for completing your work. Work first, and then reward yourself by checking your phone or browsing the Internet.

Read the Syllabus

Begin your online course by reading the syllabus. It contains important information and explains what is required in the course and how you can earn a good grade.

Online Learning and Memory

The brain learns best with distributed practice and frequent review. This means that it is important to break learning tasks into small parts and review them frequently. It is stressful and ineffective to study or complete projects for large amounts at a time right before an assignment is due.

Review Tools

Review is important to store information in long-term memory. Here are some review tools you can use online:

- Take notes on any videos or presentations. Write down the most important ideas. Review these ideas immediately and then periodically to store the information in long-term memory. The physical act of writing notes reinforces memory.
- Some students find it helpful to read the material out loud, especially if it is complex or difficult to understand.
- If you are reading online text, see if there is an option for highlighting. Some programs allow you to highlight important points and then print out the highlights. Review what you have highlighted immediately after reading, and then review it again periodically.
- If there is no option for highlighting, print the material and highlight it.
- Another option is to copy and paste important points into a separate document for review.
- When reading online, it is helpful to read a small amount at a time rather than having marathon reading sessions. Reading a small amount helps with motivation and retention of the material.
- If you are required to learn detailed information, make flash cards and review them frequently.

Online Assessment

Online assessments generally de-emphasize objective exams and rely on creative projects. For example, in the place of a final exam, a final creative project may be required. Spend the time needed to complete these creative projects and showcase your best work. Ask your professor if you can use creative media or videos to complete your project.

Expect More Writing

A classroom involves more speaking in contrast to an online course, which requires more writing. If you dislike writing or find it difficult, try these ideas:

- Understand what is required. Is there a grading rubric that details how points are earned and what is expected? Is there a requirement for a certain number of words or pages in your paper? Are you required to write a formal paper, or is it a more informal response to a discussion that requires your personal thoughts?
- Begin with freewriting. Freewriting is just writing down whatever comes to mind, without worrying about perfection. This technique can be helpful to get started and come up with ideas for writing. Freewriting is not the finished product. It is a way to begin.
- Organize your thoughts into paragraphs with a main idea and supporting details.
- If you are writing a paper, put your first draft away and look at it another day. This will help you to review and edit your work.
- Begin early.

How to Be Successful in Your Math Courses

To improve math study, it is helpful to begin by realizing the importance of math. The careers with the highest salaries require math and it is a requirement for graduation from college. However, students often have math phobia and postpone taking math courses until the end of their college studies. This can result in limited choice of a college major, dropping out of college, or a delay in graduation. It is important to take math early in your college studies and to enroll in math courses each semester until your math requirement is complete.

If you struggle with math and avoid the subject, examine your thoughts about math. It is often assumed that some people are born with a talent for math and others are not. Even worse, it is sometimes assumed that men are better at math than women. It is important to understand that both men and women develop the skill to succeed in math by having a positive attitude and practicing math problems. As your skills develop, your self-confidence increases along with your success in math. Another barrier to success in math is the fear of asking questions or asking for extra help. Students often fear that asking for help is a sign of lacking the intelligence to succeed in math. Faculty appreciate students who ask questions in class or ask for extra help because it shows they are interested in learning.

Researchers have studied the variables contributing to success in math.[6] About 50% of math success depends on your previous knowledge of math skills and how fast you can learn math. For this reason, it is important to take a math placement test and start at the level that is right for you. If you have had a gap in your math studies, you may need to go back and enroll in math review courses. About 25% of success in math depends on the quality of instruction in math. You may need to find the math instructor who matches how you learn best. The remaining 25% of success depends on math study skills and personal characteristics related to success in math. Successful students:

- Think positively about their ability to succeed in math. If you have had difficulties with math in the past and believe that you may not be successful in your college math courses, you will not take the steps needed to be successful in math. If you have self-statements such as "I hate math" or "I'm not good at math," change your statement to "I can learn to be successful in math."
- Use an internal locus of control, which means taking responsibility for your own success. Rather than blaming a teacher or past bad experiences, take the steps necessary to be successful.
- Use the motivation techniques from the second chapter to increase success, especially growth mindset and grit. Realize that you can learn to be good at math. Stay positive, be gritty and don't give up.

- Prepare adequately for math courses to minimize test anxiety. This topic is covered more in depth in the test-taking chapter.
- Make it a goal to earn an A or a B in their math courses. Lower grades will make it difficult to succeed in the next level.

Here are some tips for improving your math success:

It is estimated that you will need to spend at least 10 hours a week studying math to be successful in a college math course. College math courses go four times faster than high-school math courses and require more work outside of class.[7] Make a study schedule and plan the time needed for reading your math text, reviewing your notes, doing your homework, and practicing math problems. Invest the time and effort needed to be successful.

Make studying math a priority. Study math first and then study subjects that are easier for you. Make use of your prime time when you are most alert to study math.

Math involves practice. Unlike other courses that rely on critical thinking, memorization, and recall, math also requires the application of math concepts to solving problems. To be successful on math exams, practice solving problems until you feel comfortable with them. Make practice tests to prepare for exams. It is important to apply the concept of distributed practice to study math. Study frequently over a period of time and review what you have learned in the past. Massed study will not work in a math course. Math can be compared to success in sports or music in that they all require practice to be successful. Rehearsal and practice are needed to store math concepts in long-term memory.

Use effective review techniques. It is important to review what is learned in your math classes as soon as practical after class. Remember that most of the forgetting occurs immediately after learning something new. Review your notes right after class, review what you have read in your math text at the end of your reading session, and use small amounts of time to quickly review important concepts on flash cards. Immediate review is a powerful memory technique.

Realize that math is sequential. You must understand the first step before you can go on to the next. For this reason, start at your level, attend every class, and make it your goal to earn an A or a B on your first test. If you miss any step, see a tutor early in the semester or use online resources to fill in the gap.

Math is like a foreign language. Math uses specialized vocabulary that you must understand in order to do your math problems. Make sure to write down the definitions of math terms in your notes and review these terms. Use flash cards to review the vocabulary.

Use a study group. Choose two to six students who are serious about math success. Have each group member bring note cards with sample questions for the group to practice. Create practice tests and practice taking the tests. Sometimes it is easier learning from your peers and you may be more comfortable asking questions.

Use additional resources. Find out about tutoring in your college and use these services early in your math course. If you are stuck on a problem, use Google or You Tube to find out how to solve the problems.

Ask questions in class. As soon as you don't understand something in class, ask questions. Other students probably have the same question and may be thankful that you asked it. Faculty generally appreciate questions because it shows you are paying attention and interested in the course. Student questions help faculty to make sure students understand what they are teaching.

Use multisensory techniques to study math. Remember that learning is easier if you use all of your senses. Highlight or place a checkmark in front of the study techniques that you can use:

_____ Read important math concepts out loud.

_____Use flash cards make from note cards or virtual flashcards from Study Stacks: http://www.studystack.com/.

_____Watch YouTube videos on math concepts and solving problems.

_____Use different colors of ink to take notes on math.

_____Take pictures of the board with your cell phone.

_____Say important concepts, formulas, or definitions out loud.

_____Record important concepts and listen to them in your car.

_____Teach group members how to solve problems.

_____Use math manipulatives to understand problems. Math manipulatives are letters, numbers, magnetic boards, and other pieces that help to understand math concepts. They are available at learning stores. There are also virtual manipulative sites such as the Computing Technology for Math Excellence site at: http://www.ct4me.net/math_manipulatives_2.htm.

_____Use Facebook to post pictures of your math homework and discuss it with friends.

_____Move around while studying.

_____Rewrite or highlight your math notes.

_____Use a math app to learn how to solve problems.

Some Useful Math Apps

Search for math apps on any search engine such as Google. Here are some useful ones:

MyScript Calculator allows you to write problems on your tablet screen and the built in calculator solves the problem.

Algebra Tutor includes many different apps to solve algebra problems.

Algeo is an online graphing calculator.

Photomath allows you to take a photo of a problem and solve it with the app.

Wolfram Alpa is a collection of data and algorithms used to solve problems. It is used in Siri to calculate the answers to problems.

*A Student Perspective: How to Be Successful in Math

Personally, I had always experienced immense anxiety around the subject of mathematics since I was a young child. Just as the text suggested, I had an experience in the first grade trying to do addition with some blocks. I struggled a bit from what I can remember, and the experience altered my perceptions of mathematics for many, many years.

Courtesy of Aaron Dressin

When I started college, I was tested on my mathematic skills for placement, and fell into the remedial math course. It was difficult at first, but I knew that to succeed I needed to put in a lot of work to get through it, and just do the best I could.

Funny enough, I have successfully completed all my math courses to include statistics with "passing" and "A" grades. This wasn't the result of luck, but the result of effort, positivity, understanding, time, patience, and learning when to ask for help.

Because of my personal awareness of my mathematics struggles, I put in an immense amount of effort. I practiced A LOT. If I didn't understand something, I worked with tutors, sought help from co-workers, and stayed after class to work with the professors. I would also look up information on how to solve a problem on YouTube and the Khan Academy.

I would take a break when I was frustrated, remain positive during difficult times, and further, I thought of the work as little puzzles. Thinking of mathematics as puzzles to be solved versus hard work changed my perception of math. I would get excited when I solved long math equations!

Also, I attended every single class and completed all my homework for all my math classes. I knew that if failed to do just that, I would fail the class. You can't miss a class or skip your homework. It's that simple. Math will snowball on you as it is truly a class that builds off the previous ones. You can't miss a segment or you will be totally lost. It's also important to take your math courses as close to the other as possible. We tend to forget the things that we don't use often or that we don't like. So, if you wait a year or so to take a different math course, you could be lost because you forgot everything you learned in your previous math course.

All I know is that it takes a crazy amount of work, practice, and dedication to succeed in math. It's work, but in the end, you will realize that are you weren't so bad at math after all. It was just all in your head like it was mine. My math courses are my proudest accomplishments in college thus far.

*Courtesy of Sasha Zimmerman

Math Success

1. About 50% of your success in math depends on

   a. placement in the proper level of math.
   b. your attitude toward math.
   c. your math study skills.

2. The estimated time needed per week to study for a college math course is

   a. 3 hours.
   b. 10 hours.
   c. 6 hours.

3. Preparation for exams in math is different from other subjects. To be successful on math exams, the most important strategy is

   a. memorization.
   b. recall.
   c. practice.

4. The best time to review in your math class is

   a. a marathon study session just before the test.
   b. as soon as possible after learning new material.
   c. on weekends when you are relaxed.

5. Learning in math is sequential which means

   a. it is OK to miss your math class once in awhile.
   b. it is not too important to do the math homework if it is not collected.
   c. you must understand the first step before you can understand the next step.

How did you do on the quiz? Check your answers: 1. a, 2. b, 3. c, 4. b, 5. c

Journal Entry #4

List five ideas for improving your math success.

KEYS TO SUCCESS

Create Your Success

We are responsible for our success in college as well as what happens in our lives. We make decisions and choices that create the future. Our behavior leads to success or failure. Too often we believe that we are victims of circumstance. When looking at our lives, we often look for others to blame for how our lives are going.

- I failed math. I had a bad math teacher.

- My grandparents did it to me. I inherited these genes.

- My parents did it to me. My childhood experiences shaped who I am.

- It was my teacher's fault. He gave me a bad grade.

- My boss did it to me. She gave me a poor evaluation.

- The government did it to me. All my money goes to taxes.

- Society did it to me. I have no opportunity.

These factors are all powerful influences in our lives, but we are still left with choices. You can study independently and be successful in math in spite of your math teacher. You can ask yourself how you created your failing grade and how you can improve in the future. You can use your job evaluation as a way to improve your job performance. You can create your own opportunity.

Concentration camp survivor Viktor Frankl wrote a book, *Man's Search for Meaning*, in which he describes his experiences and how he survived his ordeal in a concentration camp. His parents, brother, and wife died in the camps. He suffered starvation and torture. Through all of his sufferings and imprisonment, he still maintained that he was a free man because he could make choices.

We who lived in concentration camps can remember the men who walked through the huts comforting others, giving away their last piece of bread. They may have been few in number, but they offer sufficient proof that everything can be taken from a man but one thing: the last of the human freedoms—to choose one's attitude in any given set of circumstances, to choose one's own way. . . . Fundamentally, therefore, any man can, even under such circumstances, decide what shall become of him—mentally and spiritually. He may retain his human dignity even in a concentration camp.[7]

Viktor Frankl could not choose his circumstance at that time, but he did choose his attitude. He decided how he would respond to the situation. He realized that he still had the freedom to make choices. He used his memory and imagination to exercise his freedom. When times were the most difficult, he would imagine that he was in the classroom lecturing to his students about psychology. He eventually did get out of the concentration camp and became a famous psychiatrist.

Hopefully, none of you will ever have to experience the circumstances faced by Viktor Frankl, but we all face challenging situations. It is empowering to think that our behavior is more a function of our decisions than of our circumstances. It is not productive to look around and find someone to blame for your problems. Psychologist Abraham Maslow says that instead of blaming, we should see how we can make the best of the situation.

One can spend a lifetime assigning blame, finding a cause, "out there" for all the troubles that exist. Contrast this with the responsible attitude of confronting the situation,

bad or good, and instead of asking, "What caused the trouble? Who was to blame?" asking, "How can I handle the present situation to make the best of it?"[9]

Author Stephen Covey suggests that we look at the word responsibility as "response-ability."[10] It is the ability to choose responses and make decisions about the future. When you are dealing with a problem, it is useful to ask yourself what decisions you made that led to the problem. How did you create the situation? If you created the problems, you can create a solution.

At times, you may ask, "How did I create this?" and find that the answer is that you did not create the situation. We certainly do not create earthquakes or hurricanes, for example. But we do create or at least contribute to many of the things that happen to us. Even if you did not create your circumstances, you can create your reaction to the situation. In the case of an earthquake, you can decide to panic or find the best course of action at the moment.

Author Steven Covey relates this concept to careers:

© Sylvie Bouchard/Shutterstock.com

But the people who end up with the good jobs are the proactive ones who are solutions to problems, not problems themselves, who seize the initiative to do whatever is necessary, consistent with correct principles, to get the job done.[11]

Use your resourcefulness and initiative to create the future that you want.

Journal Entry #5

Give your thoughts on the following:

Each of us is responsible for what happens in our life. We make decisions and choices that create the future. We create our own success.

Stories from the Elders

This chapter has presented many new learning strategies that can help you to be successful in challenging college courses. You have also been challenged to apply these strategies to improve your reading.

Some of the most difficult courses you may encounter are math and science. These courses can lead to high paying and satisfying careers. You need some positive thinking to develop your confidence in these areas as well as spending enough time to practice and learn these subjects to accomplish your educational and career goals.

The story you are about to read comes to us from the Cherokee Nation. The story tells about how the Spider Woman came up with a new method for stealing the Sun for the good of all the people. These stories are common among all tribes and help us to understand how people and creatures are all part of the living Universe.

How Spider Stole the Sun

When the world was new, it was so very dark. The animals could not see anything and they were always bumping into each other, tripping and falling down, and just making a mess of everything. One evening, they gathered together and decided that something had to change. Life would be no good if they had no light; besides, it was so very cold in the dark. As they sat in the faint light of the moon, they said, "What are we to do? How can we find more light?"

"I remember hearing that there is light on the other side of the world. Since I have the best eyes for the night and I can see so much better than you in the dark, I will go and see what I can find out. Maybe I can lure the light over our way. Those creatures over there are holding all the light for their very own and that's just not right!" said owl with a shiver.

Owl set out and flew as fast as he could. Soon he began to see light, and this light was far greater than any he had ever seen. As he approached closer, he saw a huge ball of gleaming, radiating light perched upon a tree. With all of his excitement, he flew right to the light and swooped a bit into his wing. To his surprise it was teeming with heat and he tossed it from one wing to the other, "Ouch!" he screeched. Upon hearing his screech, the people saw the owl and snatched back their sunlight, right from his winged tips.

Owl returned to his world empty handed and ever since that time, he hides from the light and only shows himself in the dark of night.

Once again the creatures gathered, "Now, we know there is light to be had and someone else has got to go and bring back that radiance." Opossum went and came back with a hole in his tail and to this day, his relatives have no tails. Raven, Buzzard, Fox, Frog, they all tried, but not one brought back the light.

Finally, Old Lady Spider said, "I have been watching you all, and I think with my eight legs, even though they are not as strong as they once were, perhaps I have a way to capture that sunlight. Will you let me try? My days on this earth are not long; let me do this for you while I still can."

So, Old Lady Spider set out to bring the sun back. She quickly spun a web as long and strong as she could. It reached to the other side of the earth! She pulled out a large iron pot and tied it around her back. Off she went. Quietly and swiftly

"What is life? It is the flash of a firefly in the night. It is the breath of a buffalo in the wintertime. It is the little shadow which runs across the grass and loses itself in the sunset."

Eagle Chief, Pawnee

she found the sun and swooped up a bit into the pot. So smooth were her movements that the people never even sensed she was near.

Old Lady Spider came back home and opened the lid of the pot and out peered the sun. She threw it into the air and out came the sun. And they say that since that time the sun never stays on one side of the earth, but travels back and forth to grace all the creatures of the earth with warmth.

Notes

The Cherokee Nation is the second-largest Indian tribe in the United States with more than 300,000 tribal citizens. Over 70,000 Cherokee reside within a 7,000 square mile geographical area, which is *not* a reservation but rather a federally-recognized, truly sovereign nation covering most of northeast Oklahoma. The tribe has taken the lead in self-governance through the enactment of a tax code and the re-establishment of the tribe's district court, law enforcement, and judicial systems. In addition, the nation operates several successful enterprises, including Cherokee Nation Enterprises (CNE), and Cherokee Nation Industries, Inc. CNE operates the Cherokee casino facilities, two convenience store/gas stations, and a Cherokee gift shop located at the tribal complex in Tahlequah. This information is provided by the Cherokee Nation Cultural Resource Center. For information regarding culture and language, please email cultural@cherokee.org or contact communications@cherokee.org.

References

Ferguson, Diana. 2001. *Native American Myths.* London: Collins and Brown.

Talking Circle

Use these questions for discussion in a talking circle or consider at least one of these questions as you respond in a journal entry:

1. The creatures in this story had a problem to solve. They needed light. Think about how they worked together to solve this problem. Have you had a problem in your personal or educational life that you have worked with others to solve? If you are having difficulties in any of your courses, what services does your college provide to help you to succeed?

2. The creatures in this story attempt many different ways to solve this problem. If something did not work, they kept trying something new. What different strategies can you use to learn the challenging material in college?

3. Old Lady Spider watched other creatures fail in their quest for the Sun. While watching these failures, she devised a new method to capture the Sun so that she could share it with all humanity. How is this story related to the role of science and math in finding discoveries that can improve the lives of all people? Have you considered a career in math or science? How can you use the material in this chapter to improve your chances of success in these fields?

4. Old Lady Spider devises a plan to solve the problem. How did she create her success as suggested in this chapter? She has a certain wisdom and has learned patience through her long life. How can you use the wisdom of Old Lady Spider to stay in college and accomplish your goals?

College Success 1

The College Success 1 website is continually updated with supplementary material for each chapter including Word documents of the journal entries, classroom activities, handouts, videos, links to related materials, and much more. See http://www.collegesuccess1.com/.

© Lyudmyla Kharlamova/
Shutterstock.com

Notes

1. Terry Doyle and Todd Zakrajsek, *The New Science of Learning, How to Learn in Harmony with Your Brain*, (Sterling, Virginia: Stylus), 45.

2. John Medina, *Brain Rules*, (Seattle: Pear Press, 2008), 250.

3. Ibid., 233–234.

4. Ibid., 212.

5. Colin Rose, *Accelerated Learning*, (New York: Dell Publishing, 1985), 51.

6. Paul Nolting, *Winning at Math*, (Bradenton, FL: Academic Success Press, 2014), 37.

7. Ibid., 19.

8. Viktor Frankl, *Man's Search for Meaning* (New York: Pocket Books, 1963), 104–105.

9. Quoted in Rob Gilbert, ed., *Bits and Pieces*, November 4, 1999.

10. Stephen Covey, *The Seven Habits of Highly Effective People* (New York: Simon and Schuster, 1989), 71.

11. Ibid., 75

Check Your Textbook Reading Skills

Name _____ Date _____

As you read each of the following statements, mark your response using this key:

1   I seldom or never do this.

2   I occasionally do this, depending on the class.

3   I almost always or always do this.

_____   **1.**   Before I read the chapter, I quickly skim through it to get main ideas.

_____   **2.**   As I skim through the chapter, I form questions based on the bold printed section headings.

_____   **3.**   I read with a positive attitude and look for something interesting.

_____   **4.**   I read the introductory and summary paragraphs in the chapter before I begin reading.

_____   **5.**   As I read each paragraph, I look for the main idea.

_____   **6.**   I recite the main idea so I can remember it.

_____   **7.**   I underline, highlight, or take notes on the main ideas.

_____   **8.**   I write notes or outlines in the margin of the text.

_____   **9.**   After reading each section, I do a quick review.

_____   **10.**   I quickly review the chapter immediately after reading it.

_____   **11.**   During or after reading, I reflect on how the material is useful or meaningful to me.

_____   **12.**   I read or at least skim the assigned chapter before I come to class.

_____   **13.**   I have planned reading time in my weekly schedule.

_____   **14.**   I generally think positively about my reading assignments.

_____   **Total points**

Check your score.
42–36   You have excellent college reading skills.
35–30   You have good skills, but can improve.
29–24   Some changes are needed.
23–14   Major changes are needed.

Becoming an Efficient College Reader

Name _____   Date _____

1. Based on your responses to the reading skills checklist on the previous page, list some of your good reading habits.

2. Based on this same checklist, what are some areas you need to improve?

3. Review the material on SQ4R and reading for speed and comprehension. Write five intention statements about how you plan to improve your reading. I intend to . . .

4. Review the material on how to concentrate while reading. List some ideas that you can use.

Surveying and Questioning a Chapter

Name _____ Date _____

Using the *next chapter* assigned in this class or any other class, answer these questions. Again, challenge yourself to do this activity quickly. Can you finish the exercise in five to seven minutes? Notice your beginning and end times.

1. What is the title of the chapter? For example, the title of this chapter is "Using Brain Science to Improve Study Skills." A good question would be, "How can I use brain science to improve my study skills?"

2. Briefly list one key idea mentioned in the introduction or first paragraph.

3. Write five questions you asked yourself while surveying this chapter. Read the bold section headings in the chapter and turn them into questions. For example, one heading in this chapter is "Neuroscience and Practical Learning Strategies." This heading might prompt you to ask, "What are some new findings in neuroscience? How can this help me to improve study skills?"

4. List three topics that interest you.

5. Briefly write one key idea from the last paragraph or chapter summary.

6. How long did it take you to do this exercise? Write your time here.

7. What did you think of this exercise on surveying and questioning a chapter?

CHAPTER 7

Listen to the Trees Talk: Taking Notes, Writing, and Speaking

Learning Objectives

Read to answer these key questions:

- Why is it important to take notes?

- What are some good listening techniques?

- What are some tips for taking good lecture notes?

- What are some note-taking systems?

- What is the best way to take notes in math?

- What is the best way to review my notes for the test?

- What is power writing?

- How can I make a good speech?

Knowing how to listen and take good notes can make your college life easier and may help you in your future career as well. Professionals in many occupations take notes as a way of recording key ideas for later use. Whether you become a journalist, attorney, architect, engineer, or other professional, listening and taking good notes can help you to get ahead in your career.

Good writing and speaking skills are important to your success in college and in your career. In college, you will be asked to write term papers and complete other writing assignments. The writing skills you learn in college will be used later in jobs involving high responsibility and good pay; on the job, you will write reports, memos, and proposals. In college, you will probably take a speech class and give oral reports in other classes; on the job, you will present your ideas orally to your colleagues and business associates.

⌊Reading, writing, and listening are important skills for college success. Learning to listen to the trees talk is a way to think about patience and understanding. Trees can take many years to grow to a point that they have large trunks and branches filled with leaves. When the wind comes through and rustles the leaves, you can hear their song, but you must sit quietly, observe the wind, and listen patiently to the music.⌋

Why Take Notes?

The most important reason for taking notes is to remember important material for tests or for future use in your career. If you just attend class without taking notes, you will forget most of the material by the next day.

How does taking notes enhance memory?

* In college, the lecture is a way of supplementing the written material in the textbook. Without good notes, an important part of the course is missing. Note taking provides material to rehearse or recite, so that it can be stored in long-term memory.
* When you take notes and impose your own organization on them, the notes become more personally meaningful. If they are meaningful, they are easier to remember.
* Taking notes helps you to make new connections. New material is remembered by connecting it to what you already know.
* The physical act of writing the material is helpful in learning and remembering it.
* Notes provide a visual map of the material to be learned.
* Taking notes is a way to listen carefully and record information to be stored in the memory.
* Note taking helps students to concentrate, maintain focus, and stay awake.
* Attending the lectures and taking notes helps you to understand what the professor thinks is important and to know what to study for the exam.

Photo courtesy of William Bright of Connors State College.

The College Lecture

You will experience many different types of lectures while in college. At larger universities, many of the beginning-level courses are taught in large lecture halls with 300 people or more. More advanced courses tend to have fewer students. In large lecture situations, it is not always possible or appropriate to ask questions. Under these circumstances, the large lecture is often supplemented by smaller discussion sessions where you can ask questions and review the lecture material. Although attendance may not be checked, it is important to attend both the lectures and the discussion sessions.

A formal college lecture is divided into four parts. Understanding these parts will help you to be a good listener and take good notes.

> "Education is not a problem. It is an opportunity."
> Lyndon B. Johnson

1. **Introduction.** The professor uses the introduction to set the stage and to introduce the topic of the lecture. Often an overview or outline of the lecture is presented. Use the introduction as a way to begin thinking about the organization of your notes and the key ideas you will need to write down.

2. **Thesis.** The thesis is the key idea in the lecture. In a one-hour lecture, there is usually one thesis statement. Listen carefully for the thesis statement and write it down in your notes. Review the thesis statement and related ideas for the exam.

3. **Body.** The body of the lecture usually consists of five or six main ideas with discussion and clarification of each idea. As a note taker, your job is to identify the main ideas, write them in your notes, and put in enough of the explanation or examples to understand the key ideas.

4. **Conclusion.** In the conclusion, the professor summarizes the key points of the lecture and sometimes asks for questions. Use the conclusion as an opportunity to check your understanding of the lecture and to ask questions to clarify the key points.

How to Be a Good Listener

Effective note taking begins with good listening. What is good listening? Sometimes students confuse listening with hearing. Hearing is done with the ears. Listening is a more active process done with the ears and the brain engaged. Good listening requires attention and concentration. Practice these ideas for good listening:

- **Be physically ready.** It is difficult to listen to a lecture if you are tired, hungry, or ill. Get enough sleep so that you can stay awake. Eat a balanced diet without too much caffeine or sugar. Take care of your health and participate in an exercise program so that you feel your best.

- **Prepare a mental framework.** Look at the course syllabus to become familiar with the topic of the lecture. Use your textbook to read, or at least survey, the material to be covered in the lecture. If you are familiar with the key concepts from the textbook, you will be able to understand the lecture and know what to write down in your notes. If the material is in your book, there is no need to write it down in your notes.

  The more complex the topic, the more important it is for you to read the text first. If you go to the lecture and have no idea what is being discussed, you may be overwhelmed and find it difficult to take notes on material that is totally new to you. Remember that it is easier to remember material if you can connect it to material you already know.

- **Find a good place to sit.** Arrive early to get a good seat. The best seats in the classroom are in the front and center of the room. If you were buying concert tickets, these would be the best and most expensive seats. Find a seat that will help you to hear and focus on the speaker. You may need to find a seat away from your friends to avoid distractions.

- **Have a positive mental attitude.** Convince yourself that the speaker has something important to say and be open to new ideas. This may require you to focus on your goals and to look past some distractions. Maybe the lecturer doesn't have the best speaking voice or you don't like his or her appearance. Focus on what you can learn from the professor rather than outward appearances.

- **Listen actively to identify the main points.** As you are listening to the lecture, ask yourself, "What is the main idea?" In your own words, write the main points down in your notes. Do not try to write down everything the professor says. This will be impossible and unnecessary. Imagine that your mind is a filter and you are actively sorting through the material to find the key ideas and write them down in your notes. Try to identify the key points that will be on the test and write them in your notes.

- **Stay awake and engaged in learning.** The best way to stay awake and focused is to listen actively and take notes. Have a mental debate with the professor. Listen for the main points and the logical connection between ideas. The physical act of writing the notes will help to keep you awake.

Handwritten Notes and Memory

Cognitive scientists have found that writing your notes by hand can improve your memory because it causes the brain to be more active.[1] Writing notes by hand requires listening, processing, prioritizing, and summarizing the information in your own words. Handwritten notes involve more thought and reorganization, which promote understanding and retention. While writing your notes, you are holding the ideas in your mind longer. This improves short- and long-term memory. Handwritten notes work best for in-depth conceptual learning and complex material.

Using a laptop, tablet, or other digital device can be distracting. Research shows that students who use digital devices in class are likely to use them for non-class-related activities 40 percent of the time. Digital note taking does not involve processing information. If you type your notes, it is likely that you record them verbatim, without actively summarizing and synthesizing key points.

Digital notes have a place, depending on the situation. For factual learning that does not require in-depth comprehension, digital note taking works well. Digital note taking is faster, and you can share your notes and store them online. If you type faster than you write, consider a handwritten summary of the notes with important points to remember.

Tips for Good Note Taking

Here are some suggestions for taking good notes:

1. Attend all of the lectures. Because many professors do not take attendance, students are often tempted to miss class. If you do not attend the lectures, however, you will not know what the professor thinks is important and what to study for the test. There will be important points covered in the lectures that are not in the book.

2. Have the proper materials. A three-ring notebook and notebook paper are recommended. Organize notes chronologically and include any handouts given in class. You can have a small notebook for each class or a single large notebook with dividers for each class. Just take the notebook paper to class and later file it in your notebook at home. Use your laptop as an alternative to a paper notebook.

3. Begin your notes by writing the date of the lecture, so you can keep your notes in order.

4. Write notes on the front side only of each piece of paper. This will allow you to spread the pages out and see the big picture or pattern in the lectures when you are reviewing.

Photo courtesy of William Bright of Connors State College.

5. Write notes neatly and legibly so you can read and review them easily.

6. Do not waste time recopying or typing your notes. Your time would be better spent reviewing your notes.

7. As a general rule, do not rely on an audio recorder for taking notes. With an audio recorder, you will have to listen to the lecture again on tape. For a semester course, this would be about 45 hours of recording! It is much faster to review carefully written notes.

8. Copy down everything written on the board and the main points from PowerPoint or other visual presentations. If it is important enough for the professor to write on the board, it is important enough to be on the test.

9. Use key words and phrases in your notes. Leave out unimportant words and don't worry about grammar.

10. Use abbreviations as long as you can read them. Entire sentences or paragraphs are not necessary and you may not have time to write them.

11. Don't loan your whole notebook to someone else because you may not get it back. If you want to share your notes, make copies.

12. If the professor talks too fast, listen carefully for the key ideas and write them down. Leave spaces in your notes to fill in later. You may be able to find the information in the text or get the information from another student.

13. Explore new uses of technology for note taking. Students are taking notes and sharing them on Facebook and GradeGuru, for example.

Journal Entry #1

Write one paragraph giving advice to a new student about taking notes in college. Use any of these questions to guide your thinking:

- Why is note taking necessary in college?
- How can you be a good listener?
- What are some tips for taking good notes?
- What are some ideas that don't work?

Note-Taking Systems

- Cornell format
- Outline method
- Mind map

Note-Taking Systems

We remember by finding patterns in new information including similarities, differences, hierarchy, and relationships among items. Recognizing patterns is useful in taking good notes. There are several systems for taking notes, depending on the patterns and organization that make sense to you. The most familiar pattern is using your own words to record the important points.

The Cornell Format

The Cornell format is an efficient method of taking notes and reviewing them. It appeals to students who are logical, orderly, and organized and have lectures that fit into this pattern. The Cornell format is especially helpful for thinking about key points as you review your notes.

Step 1: Prepare. To use the Cornell format, you will need a three-ring notebook with looseleaf paper. Draw or fold a vertical line 2½ inches from the left side of the paper. This is the recall column that can be used to write key ideas when reviewing. Use the remaining section of the paper for your notes. Write the date and title of the lecture at the top of the page.

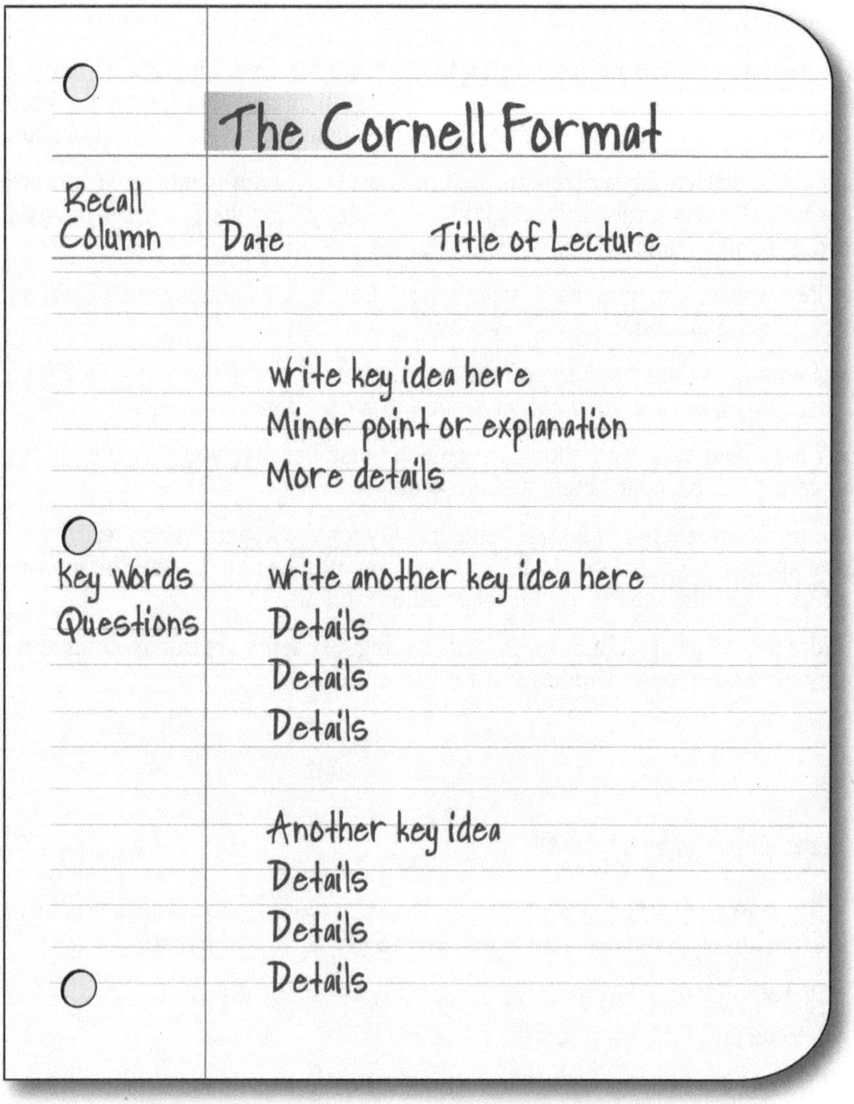

Figure 7.1 The Cornell format is an efficient way of organizing notes and reviewing them.

Courtesy of Charlotte Moore. © Kendall Hunt Publishing Company.

Step 2: Take notes. Use the large area to the right of the recall column to take notes. Listen for key ideas and write them just to the right of the recall column line, as in the diagram above. Indent your notes for minor points and illustrative details. Then skip a space and write the next key idea. Don't worry about using numbers or letters as in an outline format. Just use the indentations and spacing to highlight and separate key ideas. Use short phrases, key words, and abbreviations. Complete sentences are not necessary, but write legibly so you can read your notes later.

Step 3: Use the recall column for review. Read over your notes and write down key words or ideas from the lecture in the recall column. Ask yourself, "What is this about?" Cover up the notes on the right-hand side and recite the key ideas of the lecture. Another variation is to write questions in the margin. Find the key ideas and then write possible exam questions in the recall column. Cover your notes and see if you can answer the questions.

The Outline Method

If the lecture is well organized, some students just take notes in outline format. Sometimes lecturers will show their outline as they speak.

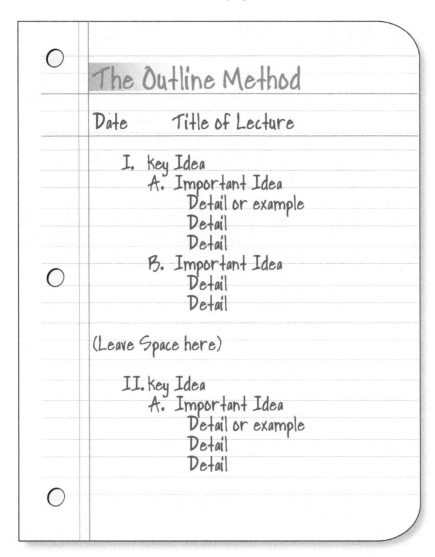

Figure 7.2 If a lecture is well organized, the outline format of taking notes works well.

Courtesy of Charlotte Moore. © Kendall Hunt Publishing Company.

- Use Roman numerals to label main topics. Then use capital letters for main ideas and Arabic numerals for related details or examples.
- You can make a free-form outline using just indentation to separate main ideas and supporting details.
- Leave spaces to fill in material later.
- Use a highlighter to review your notes as soon as possible after the lecture.

The Mind Map

A mind map shows the relationship between ideas in a visual way. It is much easier to remember items that are organized and linked together in a personally meaningful way. As a result, recall and review is quicker and more effective. Mind maps can be used show the contents of a lecture in a visual way and appeal to those who do not want to be limited to a set structure, as in the outline formats. They can also be used for lectures that are not highly structured. Here are some suggestions for using the mind-mapping technique:

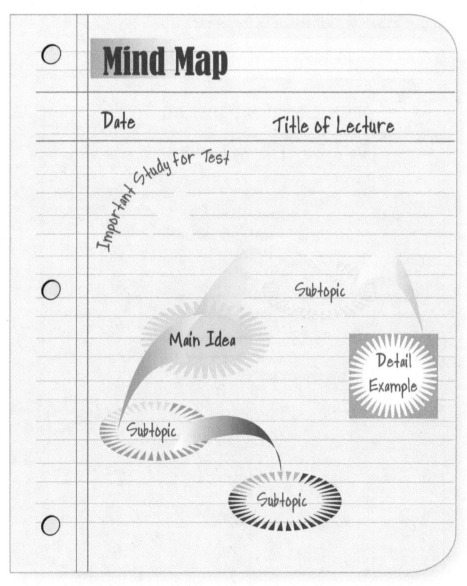

Figure 7.3 The mind map format of taking notes shows the relationship between ideas in a visual way.

Courtesy of Charlotte Moore. © Kendall Hunt Publishing Company.

- Turn your paper sideways to give you more space. Use standard-size notebook paper or consider larger sheets if possible.
- Write the main idea in the center of the page and circle it.
- Arrange ideas so that more important ideas are closer to the center and less important ideas are farther out.
- Show the relationship of the minor points to the main ideas using lines, circles, boxes, charts, and other visual devices. Here is where you can use your creativity and imagination to make a visual picture of the key ideas in the lecture.
- Use symbols and drawings.
- Use different colors to separate main ideas.
- When the lecturer moves to another main idea, start a new mind map.
- When you are done with the lecture, quickly review your mind maps. Add any written material that will be helpful in understanding the map later.
- A mind map can also be used as:
  - a review tool for remembering and relating the key ideas in the textbook;
  - a preparation tool for essay exams in which remembering main ideas and relationships is important; and
  - the first step in organizing ideas for a term paper.

Taking Notes in Math

Prepare for note-taking in math by prereading the chapter. This will help you to understand key ideas and areas where you need help. As you are reading, note some areas for asking questions in class. It is also a good idea to review the notes from the previous lecture so you can build on previous knowledge. Make sure to copy down anything written on the board or use your cell phone to photograph the board and write notes later. The Modified Three Column Note-Taking Method is recommended for taking notes in a math class.[2] Once you are used to using this system, you may no longer need to label the columns.

There are three steps to using this format. Begin with writing the example in the middle of the page. Next write the explanation, and lastly, write down the key words to the left. To review the notes, cover up the examples and explanations and say the meaning of the key word or term. Then place a checkmark next to the terms you don't know so you can review them again. Make note cards or use the StudyStack website (http://www.studystack.com/ to create flashcards for review.

Improving Note-Taking Efficiency

Improve note-taking efficiency by listening for key words that signal the main ideas and supporting details. Learn to write faster by using telegraphic sentences, abbreviations, and symbols.

Telegraphic Sentences

Telegraphic sentences are short, abbreviated sentences used in note taking. They are very similar to the text messages sent on a cell phone. There are four rules for telegraphic sentences:

1. Write key words only.
2. Omit unnecessary words (*a, an, the*).
3. Ignore rules of grammar.
4. Use abbreviations and symbols.

Modified Three Column Note-Taking Method

Key words/Rules	Examples	Explanations
Solve a linear equation	$5(x + 4) + 3(x - 4) = 2(x - 2)$	Have to get x on one side of the = and numbers on the other side of the =.
Distributive Property	$5x + 20 + 3x - 12 = 2x - 4$	Multiply numbers to the left of the () by each variable and number in the ().
Commutative Property	$5x + 3x + 20 - 12 = 2x - 4$	Regroup numbers and variables
Combine Like Terms	$8x + 8 = 2x - 4$	Add x's together and numbers together.

Adapted from *Winning at Math* by Paul Nolting. Courtesy of Charlotte Moore.
© Kendall Hunt Publishing Company.

© Lightspring/Shutterstock.com

Here is an example of a small part of a lecture followed by a student's telegraphic notes:

Heavy drinking of alcoholic beverages causes students to miss class and to fall behind in schoolwork. College students who are considered binge drinkers are at risk for many alcohol-related problems. Binge drinking is simply drinking too much alcohol at one time. Binge drinking is defined by researchers as drinking five or more drinks in a row for men or four or more drinks in a row for women. Researchers estimate that two out of five college students (40 percent) are binge drinkers.

Binge drinking—too much alcohol at one time
Men = 5 in row
Women = 4
2 out of 5 (40%) college students binge

Signal Words

Signal words are clues to the patterns, structure, and content of a lecture. Recognizing signal words can help you to identify key ideas and organize them in your notes. The table on the following page lists some common signal words and their meaning.

Signal Words

Type	Examples	Meaning
Main idea words	And most important A major development The basic concept is Remember that The main idea is We will focus on The key is	Introduce the key points that need to be written in your notes.
Example words	To illustrate For example For instance	Clarify and illustrate the main ideas in the lecture. Write these examples in your notes after the main idea. If multiple examples are given, write down the ones you have time for or the ones that you understand the best.
Addition words	In addition Also Furthermore	Add more important information. Write these points down in your notes.
Enumeration words	The five steps First, second, third Next	Signal a list. Write down the list in your notes and number the items.
Time words	Before, after Formerly Subsequently Prior Meanwhile	Signal the order of events. Write down the events in the correct order in your notes.
Cause and effect words	Therefore As a result If . . ., then	Signal important concepts that might be on the exam. When you hear these words, label them "cause" and "effect" in your notes and review these ideas for the exam.
Definition words	In other words It simply means That is In essence	Provide the meanings of words or simplify complex ideas. Write these definitions or clarifications in your notes.
Swivel words	However Nevertheless Yes, but Still	Provide exceptions, qualifications, or further clarification. Write down qualifying comments in your notes.
Compare and contrast words	Similarly Likewise In contrast	Present similarities or differences. Write these similarities and differences in your notes and label them.
Summary words	In conclusion To sum up In a nutshell	Restate the important ideas of the lecture. Write the summaries in your notes.
Test words	This is important. Remember this. You'll see this again. You might want to study this for the test.	Provide a clue that the material will be on the test. Write these down in your notes and mark them in a way that stands out. Put a star or asterisk next to these items or highlight them. Each professor has his or her own test clue words.

How to Review Your Notes

Immediate review. Review your notes as soon as possible after the lecture. The most effective review is done immediately or at least within 20 minutes. If you wait until the next day to review, you may already have forgotten much of the information. During the immediate review, fill in any missing or incomplete information. Say the important points to yourself. This begins the process of rehearsal for storing the information in long-term memory.

Intermediate review. Set up some time each week for short reviews of your notes and the key points in your textbook from previous weeks. Quickly look over the notes and recite the key points in your mind. These intermediate reviews will help you to master the material and avoid test anxiety.

Test review. Complete a major review as part of your test preparation strategy. As you look through your notes, turn the key ideas into possible test questions and answer them.

Final review. The final review occurs after you have received the results of your test. Ask yourself these questions:

- What percentage of the test questions came from the lecture notes?
- Were you prepared for the exam? If so, congratulate yourself on a job well done. If not, how can you improve next time?
- Were your notes adequate? If not, what needs to be added or changed?

> "You have to get your education. Then nobody can control your destiny."
> Charles Barkley

© Terence/Shutterstock.com

Listening and Note Taking

Test what you have learned by selecting the correct answer to the following questions.

1. When taking notes on a college lecture, it is most important to

   a. write down everything you hear.
   b. write down the main ideas and enough explanation to understand them.
   c. write down names, dates, places, and numbers.

2. To be a good listener,

   a. read or skim over the material before you attend the lecture.
   b. attend the lecture first and then read the text.
   c. remember that listening is more important than note taking.

3. To stay awake during the lecture,

   a. drink lots of coffee.
   b. sit near your friends so you can make some comments on the lecture.
   c. listen actively by taking notes.

4. Since attendance is not always checked in college classes,

   a. it is not necessary to attend class if you read the textbook.
   b. it is acceptable to miss lectures as long as you show up for the exams.
   c. it is up to you to attend every class.

5. The best time to review your notes is

   a. as soon as possible after the lecture.
   b. within 24 hours.
   c. within one week.

How did you do on the quiz? Check your answers: 1. b, 2. a, 3. c, 4. c, 5. a

---

Journal Entry #2

Write five intention statements about improving your note-taking skills. Consider your note-taking system, how to take notes more efficiently, and the best way to review your notes. I intend to . . .

> "The highest reward for a person's toil is not what they get for it, but what they become by it."
> John Ruskin

Power Writing

Effective writing will help you in school, on the job, and in your personal life. Good writing will help you to create quality term papers. The writing skills that you learn in college will be used later in jobs involving high responsibility and good pay. You can become an excellent writer by learning about the steps in POWER writing: prepare, organize, write, edit, and revise.

Power Writing
- Prepare
- Organize
- Write
- Edit
- Revise

Prepare

Plan your time. The first step in writing is to plan your time so that the project can be completed by the due date. Picture this scene: It is the day that the term paper is due. A few students proudly hand in their term papers and are ready to celebrate their accomplishments. Many of the students in the class are absent, and some will never return to the class. Some of the students look as though they haven't slept the night before. They look stressed and weary. At the front of the class is a line of students wanting to talk with the instructor. The instructor has heard it all before:

- I had my paper all completed and my printer jammed.
- My hard drive crashed and I lost my paper.
- I was driving to school and my paper flew off my motorcycle.
- I had the flu.
- My children were sick.
- I had to take my dog to the vet.
- My dog ate my paper.
- My car broke down and I could not get to the library.
- My grandmother died and I had to go to the funeral.
- My roommate accidentally took my backpack to school.
- I spilled salad dressing on my paper, so I put it in the microwave to dry it out and the writing disappeared!

© Benjamin Howell/Shutterstock.com

To avoid being in this uncomfortable and stressful situation, plan ahead. Plan to complete your project at least one week ahead of time so that you can deal with life's emergencies. Life does not always go as planned. You or your children may get sick, or your dog may do strange things to your homework. Your computer may malfunction, leading you to believe it senses stress and malfunctions just to frustrate you even more.

To avoid stress and do your best work, start with the date that the project is due and then think about the steps needed to finish. Write these dates on your calendar or on your list of things to do. Consider all these components:

Project due date:

To do	By when?
1. Brainstorm ideas.	_____
2. Choose a topic.	_____
3. Gather information.	_____
4. Write a thesis statement.	_____
5. Write an outline.	_____
6. Write the introduction.	_____
7. Write the first draft.	_____
8. Prepare the bibliography.	_____
9. Edit.	_____
10. Revise.	_____
11. Print and assemble.	_____

You can also try an assignment calculator app that helps you to develop a timeline such as the one created at the University of Minnesota at https://www.lib.umn.edu/apps/ac/

Find a space and time. Find a space where you can work. Gather the materials that you will need to write. Generally, writing is best done in longer blocks of time. Determine when you will work on your paper and write the time on your schedule. Start right away to avoid panic later.

Choose a general topic. This task will be easy if your topic is already clearly defined by your instructor or your boss at work. Make sure that you have a clear idea of what is required, such as length, format, purpose, and method of citing references and topic. Many times the choice of a topic is left to you. Begin by doing some brainstorming. Think about topics that interest you. Write them down. You may want to focus your attention on brainstorming ideas for five or 10 minutes, and then put the project aside and come back to it later. Once you have started the process of thinking about the ideas, your mind will continue to work and you may have some creative inspiration. If inspiration does not come, repeat the brainstorming process.

Gather information. Go to your college library and use the Internet to gather your information. As you begin, you can see what is available, what is interesting to you, and what the current thinking is on your topic. Note the major topics of interest that might be useful to you. Once you have found some interesting material, you will feel motivated to continue your project. As you find information relevant to your topic, make sure to write down the sources of your information to use in your bibliography. The bibliography contains information about where you found your material. Write down the author, the title of the publication, the publisher, and the place and date of publication. For Internet resources, list the address of the website and the date accessed.

Write the thesis statement. The thesis statement is the key idea in your paper. It provides a direction for you to follow. It is the first step in organizing your work. To write a thesis statement, review the material you have gathered and then ask these questions:

- What is the most important idea?
- What question would I like to ask about it?
- What is my answer?

Photo courtesy of William Bright of Connors State College

For example, if I decide to write a paper for my health class on the harmful effects of smoking, I would look at current references on the topic. I might become interested in how the tobacco companies misled the public on the dangers of smoking. I would think about my thesis statement and answer the questions stated above.

- **What is the most important idea?** Smoking is harmful to your health.
- **What question would I like to ask about it?** Did the tobacco companies mislead the public about the health hazards of smoking?
- **What is my answer?** The tobacco companies misled the public about the hazards of smoking in order to protect their business interests.
- **My thesis statement:** Tobacco companies knew that smoking was hazardous to health, but to protect their business interests, they deliberately misled the public.

The thesis statement helps to narrow the topic and provide direction for the paper. I can now focus on reference material related to my topic: research on health effects of smoking, congressional testimony relating to regulation of the tobacco industry, and how advertising influences people to smoke.

Organize

Organize

- List related topics
- Arrange in logical order
- Have an organizational structure

At this point you have many ideas about what to include in your paper, and you have a central focus, your thesis statement. Start to organize your paper by listing the topics that are related to your thesis statement. Here is a list of topics related to my thesis statement about smoking:

- Tobacco companies' awareness that nicotine is addictive
- Minimizing health hazards in tobacco advertisements
- How advertisements encourage people to smoke
- Money earned by the tobacco industry
- Health problems caused by smoking
- Statistics on numbers of people who have health problems or die from smoking
- Regulation of the tobacco industry
- Advertisements aimed at children

Think about the topics and arrange them in logical order. Use an outline, a mind map, a flowchart, or a drawing to think about how you will organize the important topics. Keep in mind that you will need an introduction, a body, and a conclusion.

Having an organizational structure will make it easier for you to write because you will not need to wonder what comes next.

Write

Write the First Sentence
Begin with the main idea.

Write the Introduction
This is the road map for the rest of the paper. The introduction includes your thesis statement and establishes the foundation of the paper. It introduces topics that will be discussed in the body of the paper. The introduction should include some interesting points that provide a "hook" to motivate the audience to read your paper. For example, for a paper on the hazards of smoking, you might begin with statistics on how many people suffer from smoking-related illnesses and premature death. Note the large profits earned by the tobacco industry. Then introduce other topics: deception, advertisements, and regulation. The introduction provides a guide or outline of what will follow in the paper.

Write
• First sentence
• Introduction
• Body
• Conclusion
• References

Write the Body of the Paper
The body of the paper is divided into paragraphs that discuss the topics that you have introduced. As you write each paragraph, include the main idea and then explain it and give examples. Here are some good tips for writing:

1. **Good writing reflects clear thinking.** Think about what you want to say and write about it so the reader can understand your point of view.

2. **Use clear and concise language.** Avoid using too many words or scholarly-sounding words that might get in the way of understanding.

3. **Don't assume that the audience knows what you are writing about.** Provide complete information.

4. **Provide examples, stories, and quotes to support your main points.** Include your own ideas and experiences.

5. **Beware of plagiarism.** Plagiarism is copying the work of others without giving them credit. It is illegal and can cause you to receive a failing grade on your project or even get you into legal trouble. Faculty regularly uses software programs that identify plagiarized material in student papers. You can avoid plagiarism by using quotation marks around an author's words and providing a reference indicating where you found the material. Another way to avoid plagiarism is by carefully reading your source material while using critical thinking to evaluate it. Then look away from the source and write about the ideas in your own words, including your critical thinking about the subject. Don't forget to include a reference for the source material in your bibliography.

Write the Conclusion
The conclusion summarizes the topics in the paper and presents your point of view. It makes reference to the introduction and answers the question posed in your thesis statement. It often makes the reader think about the significance of your point and the implications for the future. Make your conclusion interesting and powerful.

Include References
No college paper is complete without references. References may be given in footnotes, endnotes, a list of works cited, or a bibliography. You can use your computer to insert these references. There are various styles for citing references depending on your subject area.

There are computer programs that put your information into the correct style. Ask your instructor which style to use for your particular class or project. Three frequently used styles for citing references are APA, Chicago, and MLA.

1. The American Psychological Association (APA) style is used in psychology and other behavioral sciences. Consult the *Publication Manual of the American Psychological Association*, 7th ed. (Washington, DC: American Psychological Association, 2020). You can find this source online at www.apastyle.org.

2. Chicago style is used by many professional writers in a variety of fields. Consult the *Chicago Manual of Style*, 17th ed. (Chicago: University of Chicago Press, 2017). You can find this source online at www.chicagomanualofstyle.org/home.html.

3. The Modern Language Association (MLA) style is used in English, classical languages, and the humanities. Consult the *MLA Handbook for Writers of Research Papers*, 8th ed. (New York: Modern Language Association, 2016). This source is available online at www.mla.org/style.

Each of these styles uses a different format for listing sources, but all include the same information. Make sure you write down this information as you collect your reference material. If you forget this step, it is very time-consuming and difficult to find later.

- Author's name
- Title of the book or article
- Journal name
- Publisher
- City where book was published
- Publication date
- Page number (and volume and issue numbers, if available)

You can find free online information to assist with your citations.

- The Citation Machine at https://www.citationmachine.net/ can be used to automatically generate citations in any format. Just enter the requested details, and the proper citation is generated.
- The Purdue University Online Writing Lab at https://owl.purdue.edu/owl/research_and_citation/resources.html has helpful information on citations in any format.

Save Your Work

As soon as you have written the first paragraph, save it on your computer. If your computer is not backed up by a remote server such as iCloud, save another copy on a flash drive. When you are finished, print your work and save a paper copy. Then, if your hard drive crashes, you will still have your work at another location. If your file becomes corrupted, you will still have the paper copy. Following these procedures can save you a lot of headaches. Any writer can tell you stories of lost work because of computer problems, lightning storms, power outages, and other unpredictable events.

Put It Away for a While

The last step in writing the first draft is to take a break. Put it away for a while and come back to it later. In this way, you can relax and gain some perspective on your work. You will be able to take a more objective look at your work to begin the process of editing and revising.

"All things are difficult before they are easy."
John Norley

© Creativa/Shutterstock.com

Writer's Block

Many people who are anxious about writing experience "writer's block." You have writer's block if you find yourself staring at that blank piece of paper or computer screen not knowing how to begin or what to write. Here are some tips for avoiding writer's block.

- **Write freely.** Just write anything about your topic that comes to mind. Don't worry about organization or perfection at this point. Don't censure your ideas. You can always go back to organize and edit later. Free-writing helps you to overcome one of the main causes of writer's block: you think it has to be perfect from the beginning. This expectation of perfection causes anxiety. You freeze up and become unable to write. Perhaps you have past memories of writing where the teacher made many corrections on your paper. Maybe you lack confidence in your writing skills. The only way you will become a better writer is to keep writing and perfecting your writing skills. Don't worry how great it is. You can fix it later. Just begin.

- **Use brainstorming if you get stuck.** For five minutes, focus your attention on the topic and write whatever comes to mind. You don't even need to write full sentences; just jot down ideas. If you are really stuck, try working on a different topic or take a break and come back to it later.

- **Realize that it is only the first draft.** It is not the finished product and it does not have to be perfect. Just write some ideas on paper; you can revise them later.

- **Read through your reference materials.** The ideas you find can get your mind working. Also, reading can make you a better writer.

- **Break the assignment up into small parts.** If you find writing difficult, write for five minutes at a time. Do this consistently and you can get used to writing and can complete your paper.

- **Find a good place for writing.** If you are an introvert, look for a quiet place for concentration. If you are an extrovert, go to a restaurant or coffee shop and start your writing.

- **Beware of procrastination.** The more you put off writing, the more anxious you will become and the more difficult the task will be. Make a schedule and stick to it.

Tips to Overcome Writer's Block

1. Write freely
2. Use brainstorming
3. Realize it's a first draft
4. Read reference materials
5. Break up assignment
6. Find a good place to write
7. Beware of procrastination

Photo courtesy of William Bright of Connors State College.

Edit and Revise

The editing and revising stage allows you to take a critical look at what you have written. It takes some courage to do this step. Once people see their ideas in writing, they become attached to them. With careful editing and revising, you can turn in your best work and be proud of your accomplishments. Here are some tips for editing and revising:

1. **Read your paper as if you were the audience.** Pretend that you are the instructor or another person reading your paper. Does every sentence make sense? Did you say what you meant to say? Read what you have written, and the result will be a more effective paper.

2. **Read paragraph by paragraph.** Does each paragraph have a main idea and supporting details? Do the paragraphs fit logically together? Use the cut-and-paste feature on your computer to move sentences and paragraphs around if needed.

3. **Check your grammar and spelling.** Use the spell check and grammar check on your computer. These tools are helpful, but they are not thorough enough. The spell check will pick up only misspelled words. It will skip words that are spelled correctly but not the intended word—for example, if you use "of" instead of "on" or "their" instead of "there." To find such errors, you need to read your paper after doing a spell check.

4. **Check for language that is biased in terms of gender, disability, or ethnic group.** Use words that are gender neutral. If a book or paper uses only the pronoun "he" or "she," half of the population is left out. You can often avoid sexist language by using the plural forms of nouns:

(singular)   The successful student knows *his* values and sets goals for the future.

(plural)   Successful students know *their* values and set goals for the future.

After all, we are trying to make the world a better place, with opportunity for all. Here are some examples of biased language and better alternatives.

Biased Language	*Better Alternatives*
policeman	police officer
chairman	chair
fireman	firefighter
postman	mail carrier

mankind	humanity
manmade	handcrafted
housewife	homemaker

5. **Have someone else read your paper.** Ask your reader to check for clarity and meaning. After you have read your paper many times, you do not really see it anymore. If you need assistance in writing, colleges offer tutoring or writing labs where you can get help with editing and revising.

6. **Review your introduction and conclusion.** They should be clear, interesting, and concise. The introduction and conclusion are the most powerful parts of your paper.

7. **Prepare the final copy.** Check your instructor's instructions on the format required. If there are no instructions, use the following format:

   - Use double-spacing.

   - Use 10- or 12-point font.

   - Use one-inch margins on all sides.

   - Use a three-inch top margin on the first page.

   - Single-space footnotes and endnotes.

   - Number your pages.

8. **Prepare the title page.** Center the title of your paper and place it one third of the page from the top. On the bottom third of the page, center your name, the professor's name, the name of the class, and the date.

Final Steps

Make sure you follow instructions about using a folder or cover for your paper. Generally professors dislike bulky folders or notebooks because they are difficult to carry. Imagine your professor trying to carry 50 notebooks to his or her office! Unless asked to do so, do not use plastic page protectors. Professors like to write comments on papers, and it is extremely difficult to write on papers with page protectors.

If you are submitting your paper online, check to make sure you have submitted the correct document and that is was successfully uploaded.

Turning your paper in on time is very important. Some professors do not accept late papers. Others subtract points if your paper is late. Put your paper in the car or someplace where you will have to see it before you go to class. **Then reward yourself for a job well done!**

Journal Entry #3

Write five intention statements about improving your writing. While thinking about your statements, consider the steps of POWER writing: prepare, organize, write, edit, and revise. Do you need to work on problems such as writer's block or getting your writing done on time? I intend to . . .

Effective Public Speaking

You may need to take a speech class in order to graduate from college, and many of your classes will require oral presentations. Being a good speaker can contribute to your success on the job as well. A study done at Stanford University showed that one of the top predictors of success in professional positions was the ability to be a good public speaker.[3] You will need to present information to your boss, your colleagues, and your customers or clients.

Photo courtesy of William Bright of Connors State College.

Learn to Relax

Students often panic when they find out that they have to make a speech. Good preparation can help you to feel confident about your oral presentation. Professional speaker Lilly Walters believes that you can deal with 75 percent of your anxiety by being well prepared.[4] You can deal with the remaining 25 percent by using some relaxation techniques.

- If you are anxious, admit to yourself that you are anxious. If it is appropriate, as in a beginning speech class, you can even admit to the audience that you are anxious. Once you have admitted that you are anxious, visualize yourself confidently making the speech.
- You do not have to be perfect; it is okay to make mistakes. Making mistakes just shows you are human like the rest of us.
- If you are anxious before your speech, take three to five deep breaths. Breathe in slowly and hold your breath for five seconds, and then breathe out slowly. Focus your mind on your breathing rather than your speech.
- Use positive self-talk to help you to relax. Instead of saying to yourself, "I will look like a fool up there giving the speech," tell yourself, "I can do this" or "It will be okay."
- Once you start speaking, anxiety will generally decline.
- With experience, you will gain confidence in your speaking ability and will be able to relax more easily.

Preparing and Delivering Your Speech

Write the Beginning of the Speech

The beginning includes a statement of your objective and what your speech will be about. It should prepare the audience for what comes next. You can begin your speech with a personal experience, a quote, a news article, or a joke. Jokes can be effective, but they are risky. Try out your joke with your friends to make sure that it is funny. Do not tell jokes that put down other people or groups.

Write the Main Body of the Speech

The main body of the speech consists of four or five main points. Just as in your term paper, state your main points and then provide details, examples, or stories that illustrate them. As you present the main points of your speech, consider your audience. Your speech will be different depending on whether it is made to a group of high school students, your college classmates, or a group of professionals. You can add interest to your speech by using props, pictures, charts, PowerPoint, music, or video clips. College students today are increasingly using PowerPoint software to make classroom presentations. If you are planning to enter a professional career, learning how to make PowerPoint presentations will be an asset.

Write the Conclusion

In your conclusion, summarize and review the key points of your speech. The conclusion is like the icing on a cake. It should be strong, persuasive, and interesting. Invest some time in your ending statement. It can be a call to action, a recommendation for the future, a quote, or a story.

Practice Your Speech

Practice your speech until you feel comfortable with it. Prepare a memory system or notes to help you deliver your speech. You will want to make eye contact with your audience, which is difficult if you are trying to read your speech. A memory system useful for delivering speeches is the loci system. Visualize a house, for example: the entryway is the introduction, and each room represents a main point in the speech. Visualize walking into each room and what you will say in each room. Each room can have items that remind you of what you are going to say. At the conclusion, you say good-bye at the door. Another technique is to prepare brief notes or outlines on index cards or sheets of paper. When you are practicing your speech, time it to see how long it is. Keep your speech within the time allowed. Most people tend to speak longer than necessary.

Review the Setup

If you are using props, make sure that you have them ready. If you are using equipment, make sure it is available and in working condition. Make arrangements in advance for the equipment you need and, if possible, check to see that it is running properly right before your presentation.

Deliver the Speech

Wear clothes that make you feel comfortable, but not out of place. Remember to smile and make eye contact with members of the audience. Take a few deep breaths if you are nervous. You will probably be less nervous once you begin. If you make a mistake, keep your sense of humor. I recall the famous chef Julia Child doing a live television production on how to cook a turkey. As she took the turkey out of the oven, it slipped and landed on the floor right in front of the television cameras. She calmly picked it up and said, "And remember that you are the only one that really knows what goes on in the kitchen." It was one of the shows that made her famous.

Writing and Speaking

Test what you have learned by selecting the correct answers to the following questions.

1. To make sure to get your paper done on time,

   a. have someone remind you of the deadline.
   b. write the due date on your calendar and the date for completion of each step.
   c. write your paper just before the due date to increase motivation.

2. The thesis statement is the

   a. most important sentence in each paragraph.
   b. key idea in the paper.
   c. summary of the paper.

3. If you have writer's block, it is helpful to

   a. delay writing your paper until you feel relaxed.
   b. make sure that your writing is perfect from the beginning.
   c. begin with brainstorming or free writing.

4. No college paper is complete without

   a. the references.
   b. a professional-looking cover.
   c. printing on quality paper.

5. You can deal with most of your anxiety about public speaking by

   a. striving for perfection.
   b. visualizing your anxiety.
   c. being well prepared.

How did you do on the quiz? Check your answers: 1. b, 2. b, 3. c, 4. a, 5. c

Journal Entry #4

Write one paragraph giving advice to a new college student on how to make a speech. Use any of these questions to guide your thinking:

- What are some ways to deal with anxiety about public speaking?
- How can you make your speech interesting?
- What are some steps in preparing a speech?
- What are some ideas that don't work?

KEYS TO SUCCESS

Be Selective

Psychologist and philosopher William James said, "The essence of genius is knowing what to overlook."[5] This saying has a variety of meanings. In reading, note taking, marking a college textbook, and writing, it is important to be able to pick out the main points first and then identify the supporting details. Imagine you are trying to put together a jigsaw puzzle. You bought the puzzle at a garage sale and all the pieces are there, but the lid to the box with the picture of the puzzle is missing. It will be very difficult, if not impossible, to put this puzzle together. Reading, note taking, marking, and writing are very much like putting a puzzle together. First you will need an understanding of the main ideas (the big picture) and then you can focus on the details.

How can you get the overall picture? When reading, you can get the overall picture by skimming the text. As you skim the text, you get a general outline of what the chapter contains and what you will learn. In note taking, actively listen for the main ideas and write them down in your notes. In marking your text, try to pick out about 20 percent of the most important material and underline or highlight it. In writing, think about what is most important, write your thesis statement, and then provide the supporting details.

To select what is most important, be courageous, think, and analyze.

Does this mean that you should forget about the details? No, you will need to know some details too. The supporting details help you to understand and assess the value of the main idea. They help you to understand the relationship between ideas. Being selective means getting the general idea first, and then the details will make sense to you and you will be able to remember them. The main ideas are like scaffolding or a net that holds the details in some kind of framework so you can remember them. If you focus on the details first, you will have no framework or point of reference for remembering them.

Experiment with the idea of being selective in your personal life. If your schedule is impossibly busy, be selective and choose to do the most important or most valuable activities. This takes some thinking and courage too. If your desk drawer is stuffed with odds and ends and you can never find what you are looking for, take everything out and only put back what you need. Recycle, give away, or throw away surplus items around the house. You can take steps toward being a genius by being selective and taking steps to simplify and organize your life and your work.

How can being selective help you achieve success in college and in life? Use any of these questions to guide your thinking:

- How can being selective help you to be a better note taker, writer, or speaker?
- How can being selective help you to manage your time and your life?
- What is the meaning of this quote by William James: "The essence of genius is knowing what to overlook?"

Stories from the Elders

In this chapter you have been introduced to various techniques that will improve your ability to take good notes and to write and speak effectively. You have explored methodologies for improving your ability to capture important information presented in lectures by taking notes and improving your listening skills. Good writing involves good planning and preparation. This will assist you in developing your ideas and writing a logical and cohesive piece. Remember, good writing will require several edits and revisions. And lastly, developing effective public speaking skills is critical to your college success. You will often be asked to present information individually and in small groups in your classes. If you choose to become involved in college leadership opportunities, again, public speaking will become an essential skill that will not only help you while in college, but throughout your professional and personal life.

How the Spider Symbol Came to the People

An Osage Story

The Osage people have clans that are Sky people and Earth people. This is an Earth people clan story and it goes like this.

A long time ago, one of the clans of the earth people lived far off, away from many of the other clans. The people always looked to their animal brothers to help them understand the world better and teach them about the natural ways of life. The chief of this clan felt that his people needed a little more guidance and that if he was to be a wise and strong leader, he should go off into the forest and look for a new symbol to help strengthen the people.

He thought, "I will go out and look for the strongest, most courageous symbol that I can find. One that will inspire

> "The one who tells the stories, rules the world."
> Hopi

strength, dedication, and valor for our clan is what I ask the creator to provide."

Out he went, and as he walked along he saw many of the creator's creatures along the way. He saw blue jays, hummingbirds, snakes, and beavers. And, although he gave thanks to the Creator for all the beauty of the creatures, he just knew he had to keep looking.

Eventually, he came across some hoof tracks in the moist earth by the riverbed. He thought, "Oh, the deer, so swift and regal, beautiful fur coat and yet, smart as they come. I will follow these tracks and find our symbol." With much excitement brewing in his heart, the chief followed the tracks, faster and faster, he moved through the forest. Running at full speed and sensing the great deer is just around the bend, when all of a sudden, he runs full force into an enormous spider web.

"What is this? I cannot see, I cannot open my eyes and yet I feel like I am cloaked in a net."

Spider says, "Why are you running through the forest with such speed? Is a wild cat chasing you?"

"No," the chief responds, "I am fast on the trail of a great deer's tracks, and now you and your silly web have detained me!"

"Why are you chasing the great deer? This is not the time of year to hunt the deer," replied spider.

"No, you silly spider, don't you see. I am looking for a great symbol to help teach my people the good ways and I know this deer is that symbol. I must hurry, or I will certainly loose his trail," the chief says with some impatience.

Spider says, "You look so silly, running through the forest without even looking where you are going. How are you going to catch the great deer, when you seem to have so little good sense?"

The chief looked down, wiping the web from his eyes, and then spider says, "Do not worry, I can be your symbol. I can teach you many lessons."

The chief is feeling a bit foolish now, but looks at the spider in disbelief. "How can you give my people strength? You are so small and so fragile."

"Oh, my son, look at me. I am watchful, and I know how to wait. I can be cunning and I am patient. I know that all things will come to me if I bide my time. I can teach your people to be strong, patient, and knowing that all good things will come."

Since that time, the spider has been the symbol for Osage people.

Notes

Osage Tribe

The Osage tribe was one of the tribes east of the Mississippi that traveled the Trail of Tears and was re-located to Kansas. By the time they negotiated the treaty of 1865, to purchase land in Oklahoma, the Osages had been reduced in population by 95%. Only 3,000 Osage People walked across the Kansas border into their new land. The Osage of today maintain their culture and traditions by clinging to the lessons of their ancestors. The modern day Osage is educated, diverse, and staunchly defends their Osage identity. They participate in dance, feasting, and naming ceremonies as a memorial to their past while celebrating their present culture. Members of the Osage tribe are proud of their identity and they return to their Osage reservation to commune with each other and be recognized each year during their ceremonies.

For more information contact: http://www.osagetribe.com/main_culture_overview.aspx

Reference

Bruchac, Joseph and Michael J. Caduto. *Native American Animal Stories.* Golden, Colorado: Fulcrum Publishing.

Talking Circle

Use these questions for discussion in a talking circle or consider at least one of these questions as you respond in a journal entry:

1. In this story, the chief had a plan for finding the new symbol, but was surprised by how his plan actually ended. Writing requires careful and thoughtful preparation and planning, but even with that you may find that what you start out to write changes as you go along. Can you talk about a piece you wrote and were surprised by the direction the writing took as you went along? Did you learn something about your own writing abilities through that experience?

2. The spider symbol in the story has traits that most students would find helpful along the way. Learning not to give up as you face challenges will carry you far toward reaching your educational goals. Persistence and patience can lead to good writing, good speaking, and college success. Can you share an experience you had when you were pleased with the results of your hard work, even when the task or assignment seemed too difficult to accomplish?

3. The chief had to rethink his definition of strength. He had no clue that a spider could teach his people anything, but in the end he saw the value of the spider's virtues. Public speaking is a skill that you will need to develop and, perhaps, rethink your ability to do so. Depending upon your personal characteristics, you may find this a difficult challenge. If in your culture, you have learned to watch, listen, and keep your thoughts to yourself, you will have to stretch out of your comfort zone to develop public speaking skills. How do you feel about speaking up in public? Have you ever delivered a speech in public?

© Lyudmyla Kharlamova/
Shutterstock.com

College Success 1

The College Success 1 website is continually updated with supplementary material for each chapter including Word documents of the journal entries, classroom activities, handouts, videos, links to related materials, and much more. See http://www.collegesuccess1.com/.

Notes

1. Pat Wyman, "Science-Backed Links on Why Handwritten Notes Improve Your Memory," March 10, 2020, https://www.howtolearn.com/2020/03/science-backed-links-on-why-handwritten-notes-improve-your-memory/

2. Paul Nolting, *Winning at Math*, (Bradenton, FL: Academic Success Press, 2014), 139.

3. T. Allesandra and P. Hunsaker, *Communicating at Work* (New York: Fireside, 1993), 169.

4. Lilly Walters, *Secrets of Successful Speakers: How You Can Motivate, Captivate, and Persuade* (New York: McGraw-Hill, 1993), 203.

5. Quoted in Rob Gilbert, ed., *Bits and Pieces,* August 12, 1999, 15.

Note-Taking Checklist

Name _____ Date _____

Place a checkmark next to the note-taking skills you have now.

_____ I attend every (or almost every) lecture in all my classes.

_____ I check the syllabus to find out what is being covered before I go to class.

_____ I read or at least skim through the reading assignment before attending the lecture.

_____ I attend lectures with a positive attitude about learning as much as possible.

_____ I am well rested so that I can focus on the lecture.

_____ I eat a light, nutritious meal before going to class.

_____ I sit in a location where I can see and hear easily.

_____ I have a laptop or a three-ring binder, looseleaf paper, and a pen for taking notes.

_____ I avoid external distractions (friends, sitting by the door).

_____ I am alert and able to concentrate on the lecture.

_____ I have a system for taking notes that works for me.

_____ I am able to determine the key ideas of the lecture and write them down in my notes.

_____ I can identify signal words that help to understand key points and organize my notes.

_____ I can write quickly using telegraphic sentences, abbreviations, and symbols.

_____ If I don't understand something in the lecture, I ask a question and get help.

_____ I write down everything written on the board or on visual materials used in the class.

_____ I review my notes immediately after class.

_____ I have intermediate review sessions to review previous notes.

_____ I use my notes to predict questions for the exam.

_____ I have clear and complete notes that help me to prepare adequately for exams.

Evaluate Your Note-Taking Skills

Name _____ Date _____

Use the note-taking checklist on the previous page to answer these questions.

1. Look at the items that you checked. What are your strengths in note taking?

2. What are some areas that you need to improve?

3. Write at least three intention statements about improving your listening and note-taking skills.

Assess Your College Writing Skills

Name _____ Date _____

Read the following statements and rate how true they are for you at the present time. Use the following scale:

5 Definitely true
4 Mostly true
3 Somewhat true
2 Seldom true
1 Never true

_____ I am generally confident in my writing skills.

_____ I have a system for reminding myself of due dates for writing projects.

_____ I start writing projects early so that I am not stressed by finishing them at the last minute.

_____ I have the proper materials and a space to write comfortably.

_____ I know how to use the library and the Internet to gather information for a term paper.

_____ I can write a thesis statement for a term paper.

_____ I know how to organize a term paper.

_____ I know how to write the introduction, body, and conclusion of a paper.

_____ I can cite references in the appropriate style for my subject.

_____ I know where to find information about citing material in APA, MLA, or Chicago style.

_____ I know what plagiarism is and know how to avoid it.

_____ I can deal with "writer's block" and get started on my writing project.

_____ I know how to edit and revise a paper.

_____ I know where I can get help with my writing.

_____ **Total**

60–70   You have excellent writing skills, but can always learn new ideas.

50–59   You have good writing skills, but there is room for improvement.

Below 50   You need to improve writing skills. The skills presented in this chapter will help. Consider taking a writing class early in your college studies.

Thinking about Writing

Name _____ Date _____

List 10 suggestions from this chapter that could help you improve your writing skills.

1.

2.

3.

4.

5.

6.

7.

8.

9.

10.

CHAPTER 8

Walk with Bare Feet on the Earth: Test Taking

Learning Objectives

Read to answer these key questions:

- What are some test preparation techniques?

- How should I review the material?

- How can I predict the test questions?

- What are some emergency test preparation techniques?

- How can I deal with test anxiety?

- How can I overcome math anxiety and be successful on math tests?

- What are some tips for taking math tests?

- What are some tips for taking objective tests?

- How can I write a good essay?

From *College & Career Success* Concise Version, Ninth Edition by Marsha Fralick. Copyright © 2021 by Kendall Hunt Publishing Company. Reprinted by permission. Text between ⌊half brackets⌋ was written by Marsha Fralick, Beatrice Zamora, and Larry Gauthier.

An important skill for survival in college is the ability to take tests. Passing tests is also important in careers that require licenses, certificates, or continuing education. Knowing how to prepare for and take tests with confidence will help you to accomplish your educational and career goals while maintaining your good mental health. Once you have learned some basic test-taking and relaxation techniques, you can turn your test anxiety into motivation and good test results.

Many traditional people believe that the earth is our mother and that we should never do her harm. Remembering to walk barefoot and feel her energy is soothing and healing to many. Gardening and planting can also bring great peace to those who touch the earth. This grounding to the earth can help you to build strength and balance that will help you to deal with anxiety and improve test-taking skills.

© Pinkasevich/Shutterstock.com

Begin Your Journey with Smudging

Co-author Larry Gauthier shares the Cree smudging tradition which is consistent among Native cultures, although some details of the ceremony may vary by region. Smudging is a way to increase awareness and cleanse the body, mind, emotions, and spirit which must be kept in balance. It rids humans of negativity and brings forth positive emotions. It is commonly used before ceremonies and sweat lodges. The smudging ceremony can also be used when starting something new, such as beginning a new day or beginning an educational journey. It can be used to prepare for exams or begin the learning process.

Understanding the smudging ceremony begins with an understanding of the Native world view. The world view is based on belief in a higher power, The Great Spirit. This world view is based on the idea that the galaxy gave life to the universe, the solar system, and to Mother Earth. Humans are born of Mother Earth; she is our mother. Our Mother Earth gave all life forms everything needed to survive. Humans were given the additional gift of the ability to reason so that they could find shelter and food, look after one another, and form the laws needed for a good society. In exchange for that gift came the responsibility to look after Mother Earth.

Mother Earth also gave us medicines to keep ourselves healthy. These medicines are used to cleanse mental, physical, emotional, and spiritual aspects of the human being. In the West, the cedar is often used as a medicine for smudging. It provides shelter and clothing, and is resistant to rot. In the plains, sage and sweet grass are commonly used for smudging. There are protocols for using these medicines. They cannot just be ripped from the ground; these medicines must be picked with a good mind and heart. Prayer is often used while picking the medicines.

Native beliefs are related to science and astronomy. It is believed that life forces have energies that vibrate on different levels. An example is photosynthesis, in which energy from the sun is used to create life. Smudging is used to bring our energy level to vibrate on the same level as Mother Earth. If someone leaves home and is lonely, their vibrations are out of synch with the vibrations of Mother Earth. Smudging is a way to bring the vibrations back in harmony.

Smudging consists of four stages of prayer: introductions, giving thanks, praying for others, and then petitioning for ourselves. Introductions are done by placing hands over the smoke. When the smoke dissipates into the air, it takes our petitions out to the universe.

We smudge our:

- minds to think positive thoughts.
- eyes so we only look for good.
- mouths so we use our words to be kind and encouraging.
- hearts to provide us guidance in how we interpret the world.
- spirits to connect with the universe.

Larry Gauthier uses the talking circle and smudging on Mondays to begin each week in his course, resulting in increased student success. Incorporating Native traditions helps traditional students relate to education. For students who are not so traditional, it is helpful to understand where you have come from to understand where you are going.⌋

Preparing for Tests

Attend Every Class

The most significant factor in poor performance in college is lack of attendance. Students who attend the lectures and complete their assignments have the best chance for success in college. Attending the lectures helps you to be involved in learning and to know what to expect on the test. College professors know that students who miss three classes in a row are not likely to return, and some professors drop students after three absences. After three absences, students can fall behind in their schoolwork and become overwhelmed with makeup work.

"Eighty percent of success is showing up."
Woody Allen

Photo courtesy of William Bright of Connors State College.

Distribute the Practice

The key to successful test preparation is to begin early and do a little at a time. Test preparation begins the first day of class. During the first class, the professor gives an overview of the course content, requirements, tests, and grading. These items are described in writing in the class calendar and syllabus. It is very important to attend the first class to obtain this essential information. If you have to miss the first class, make sure to ask the professor for the syllabus and calendar and read it carefully.

Early test preparation helps you to take advantage of the powerful memory technique called distributed practice. In distributed practice, the material learned is broken up into small parts and reviewed frequently. Using this method can enable you to learn a large quantity of material without becoming overwhelmed. Here are some examples of using distributed practice:

- If you have a test on 50 Spanish vocabulary words in two weeks, don't wait until the day before the test to try to learn all 50 words. Waiting until the day before the test will result in difficulty remembering the words, test anxiety, and a dislike of studying Spanish. If you have 50 Spanish vocabulary words to learn in two weeks, learn five words each day and quickly review the words you learned previously. For example, on Monday you would learn five words, and on Tuesday, you would learn five new words and review the ones learned on Monday. Give yourself the weekends off as a reward for planning ahead.

- If you have to read a history book with 400 pages, divide that number by the number of days in the semester or quarter. If there are 80 days in the semester, you will only have to read five pages per day or 10 pages every other day. This is a much easier and more efficient way to master a long assignment.

- Don't wait until the last minute to study for a midterm or final exam. Keep up with the class each week. As you read each chapter, quickly review a previous chapter. In this way you can comfortably master the material. Just before a major test, you can review the material that you already know and feel confident about your ability to get a good grade on the test.

Schedule a Time and a Place for Studying

To take advantage of distributed practice, you will need to develop a study schedule. Write down your work time and school time and other scheduled activities. Identify times that can be used for studying each day. Get in the habit of using these available times for studying each week. As a general rule, you need two hours of study time for each hour spent in a college classroom. If you cannot find enough time for studying, consider either reducing your course load or reducing work hours.

Use your study schedule or calendar to note the due dates of major projects and all test dates. Schedule enough time to complete projects and to finish major reviews for exams. Look at each due date and write in reminders to begin work or review well in advance of the due date. Give yourself plenty of time to meet the deadlines. It seems that around exam time, students are often ill or have problems that prevent them from being successful. Having some extra time scheduled will help you to cope with the many unexpected events that happen in everyday life.

Find a place to study. This can be an area of your home where you have a desk, computer, and all the necessary supplies for studying. As a general rule, do not study at the kitchen table, in front of the television, or in your bed. These places provide powerful cues for eating, watching television, or sleeping instead of studying. If you cannot find an appropriate place at home, use the college library as a place to study. The library is usually quiet and others are studying, so there are not too many distractions. Studying in different places can aid in recall.

Photo courtesy of First Nations University, of Canada.

Test Review Tools

There are a variety of tools you can use to review for tests. Choose the tools according to personal preference and the type of test for which you are preparing.

- **Flash cards.** Flash cards are an effective way to learn facts and details for objective tests such as true-false, multiple-choice, matching, and fill-in-the-blank. For example, if you have 100 vocabulary words to learn in biology, put each word on one side of a card and the definition on the other side. First, look at each definition and see if you can recall the word. It is helpful to visualize the word and even say it out loud. Carry the cards with you and briefly look at them as you are going about your daily activities. Make a game of studying by sorting the cards into stacks of information you know and those you still have to practice. Work with the flash cards frequently and review them quickly. Don't worry about learning all the items at once. Each day that you practice, you will recall the items more easily. You can also use online tools such as Quizlet (https://quizlet.com/) for making flashcards.

- **Summary sheets.** Summary sheets are used to record the key ideas from your lecture notes or textbook. It is important to be selective; write only the most important ideas on the summary sheets. At the end of the semester, you might have approximately 10 pages of summary sheets from the text and 10 pages from your notes.

- **Mind maps.** A mind map is a visual picture of the items you wish to remember. Start in the center of the page with a key idea and then surround it with related topics. You can use drawings, lines, circles, or colors to link and group the ideas. A mind map will help you to learn material in an organized way that will be useful when writing essay exams.

- **Study groups.** A study group is helpful in motivating yourself to learn through discussions of the material with other people. For the study group, select three to seven people who are motivated to be successful in class and can coordinate schedules. Study groups are often used in math and science classes. Groups of students work problems together and help each other understand the material. The study group is also useful in studying for exams. Give each member a part of the material to be studied. Have each person predict test questions and quiz the study group. Teaching the material to the study group can be the best way to learn it.

Reviewing Effectively

Begin your review early and break it into small parts. Remember that repetition is one of the effective ways to store information in long-term memory. Here are some types of review that help you to store information in long-term memory:

> **Review Tools**
>
> - Flash cards
> - Summary sheets
> - Mind maps
> - Study groups

> "I can accept failure. Everyone fails at something. But I can't accept not trying."
> Michael Jordan

- **Immediate review.** This type of review is fast and powerful and helps to minimize forgetting. It is the first step in storing information in long-term memory. Begin the process by turning each bold-faced heading in the text into a question. Read each section to answer the question you have asked. Read your college texts with a highlighter in hand so that you can mark the key ideas for review. Some students use a variety of colors to distinguish main ideas, supporting points, and key examples, for instance. When you are finished using the highlighter, quickly review the items you have marked. As you complete each section, quickly review the main points. When you finish the chapter, immediately review the key points in the entire chapter again. As soon as you finish taking your lecture notes, take a few minutes to review them. To be most effective, immediate review needs to occur as soon as possible or at least within the first 20 minutes of learning something.

Photo courtesy of First Nations University of Canada.

- **Intermediate review.** After you have finished reading and reviewing a new chapter in your textbook, spend a few minutes reviewing an earlier one. This step will help you to master the material and to recall it easily for the midterm or final exam. Another way to do intermediate review is to set up time periodically in your study schedule for reviewing previous chapters and classroom notes. Doing intermediate reviews helps to access the materials you have stored in long-term memory.

- **Final review.** Before a major exam, organize your notes, materials, and assignments. Estimate how long it will take you to review the material. Break the material into manageable chunks. For an essay exam, use mind maps or summary sheets to write down the main points that you need to remember and recite these ideas frequently. For objective tests, use flash cards or lists to remember details and concepts that you expect to be on the test. Here is a sample seven-day plan for reviewing 10 chapters for a final exam:

Day 1 Gather materials and study Chapters 1 and 2 by writing key points on summary sheets or mind maps. Make flash cards of details you need to remember. Review and highlight lecture notes and handouts on these chapters.

Day 2 Review Chapters 1 and 2. Study Chapters 3 and 4 and the corresponding lecture notes.

Day 3 Review Chapters 1 to 4. Study Chapters 5 and 6 and the corresponding lecture notes.

Day 4 Review Chapters 1 to 6. Study Chapters 7 and 8 along with the corresponding lecture notes.

Day 5 Review Chapters 1 to 8. Study Chapters 9 and 10 along with corresponding lecture notes.

Day 6 Review notes, summary sheets, mind maps, and flash cards for Chapters 1 to 10. Relax and get a good night's sleep. You are well prepared.

Day 7 Do one last quick review of Chapters 1 to 10 and walk into the test with the confidence that you will be successful on the exam.

Predicting Test Questions

There are many ways to predict the questions that will be on the test. Here are some ideas that might be helpful:

- Look for clues from the professor about what will be on the test. Many times professors put information about the tests on the course syllabus. During lectures, they often give hints about what will be important to know. If a professor repeats something more than once, make note of it as a possible test question. Anything written on the board is likely to be on the test. Sometimes the professor will even say, "This will be on the test." Write these important points in your notes and review them.

- College textbooks are usually written in short sections with bold headings. Turn each bold-faced heading into a question and read to answer the question. Understand and review the main idea in each section. The test questions will generally address the main ideas in the text.

- Don't forget to study and review the handouts that the professor distributes to the class. If the professor has taken the time and effort to provide extra material, it is probably important and may be on the test.

- Form a study group and divide up the material to be reviewed. Have each member of the group write some test questions based on the important points in each main section of the text. When the study group meets, take turns asking likely test questions and providing the answers.

- When the professor announces the test, make sure to ask what material is to be covered on the test and what kind of test it is. If necessary, ask the professor which concepts are most important. Know what kinds of test questions will be asked (essay, true-false, multiple-choice, matching, or short-answer). Some professors may provide sample exams or math problems.

- Use the first test to understand what is expected and how to study for future tests.

> "The will to win is not nearly as important as the will to prepare to win."
> Bobby Knight

Journal Entry # 1

Make a list of five good ideas for exam preparation.

Preparing for an Open-Book Test

In college, you may have some open-book tests. Open-book tests are often used in very technical subjects where specific material from the book is needed to answer questions. For example, in an engineering course, tables and formulas in the book may be needed to solve engineering problems on an exam. To study for an open-book test, focus on understanding the material and being able to locate key information for the exam. Consider making index tabs for your book so that you can locate needed information quickly. Be sure to bring your book, calculator, and other needed material to the exam.

Emergency Procedures

If it is a day or two before the test and you have not followed the above procedures, it is time for the college practice known as "cramming." There are two main problems that result from this practice. First, you cannot take advantage of distributed practice, so it will be difficult to remember large amounts of material. Within a week, you are likely to forget 75% of the material you learned while cramming.[1] It requires much effort and results in little benefit. Second, it is not fun and, if done often, will result in anxiety and a dislike of education. Because of these problems, some students who rely on cramming wrongly conclude that they are not capable of finishing their education.

© eldar nurkovic/Shutterstock.com

If you must cram for a test, here are some emergency procedures that may be helpful in getting the best grade possible under difficult circumstances:

- When cramming, **it is most important to be selective.** Try to identify the main points and recite and review them.
- Focus on reviewing and reciting the lecture notes. In this way, you will cover the main ideas the professor thinks are important.
- If you have not read the text, skim and search each chapter looking for the main points. Highlight and review these main points. Read the chapter summaries. In a math textbook, practice sample problems.
- Make summary sheets containing the main ideas from the notes and the text. Recite and review the summary sheets.
- For objective tests, focus on learning new terms and vocabulary related to the subject. These terms are likely to be on the test. Flash cards are helpful.
- For essay tests, develop an outline of major topics and review the outline so you can write an essay.
- Get enough rest. Staying up all night to review for the test can result in confusion, reduced mental ability, and test anxiety.
- Hope for the best.
- Plan ahead next time so that you can get a better grade.

If you have very little time to review for a test, you will probably experience information overload. One strategy for dealing with this problem is based on the work of George Miller of Harvard University. He found that the optimum number of chunks of information we can remember is seven plus or minus two (or five to nine chunks of information).[2] This is also known as the Magical Number Seven Theory. For this last-minute review technique, start with five sheets of paper. Next, identify five key concepts that are likely to be on the test. Write one concept on the top of each sheet of paper. Then check your notes and text to write an explanation, definition, or answer for each of these topics. If you have more time, find two to four more concepts and research them, writing the information on additional sheets. You should have no more than nine sheets of paper. Arrange the sheets in order of importance. Review and recite the key ideas on these sheets. Get a regular night's sleep before the test and do some relaxation exercises right before the test.

© YanLev/Shutterstock.com

Ideas That Don't Work

Some students do poorly on tests for the following reasons.

- Attending a party or social event the evening before a major test rather than doing the final review will adversely affect your test score. Study in advance and reward yourself with the party after the test.
- Skipping the major review before the test may cause you to forget some important material.
- Taking drugs or drinking alcohol before a test may give you the impression that you are relaxed and doing well on the test, but the results are disastrous to your success on the exam and your good health.
- Not knowing the date of the test can cause you to get a low grade because you are not prepared.
- Not checking or knowing about the final exam schedule can cause you to miss the final.
- Missing the final exam can result in a lower grade or failing the class.
- Arriving late for the exam puts you at a disadvantage if you don't have time to finish or have to rush through the test.
- Deciding not to buy or read the textbook will cause low performance or failure.
- Having a fight, disagreement, or argument with parents, friends, or significant others before the test will make it difficult to focus on the exam.
- Sacrificing sleep, exercise, or food to prepare for the exam makes it difficult to do your best.
- Cheating on an exam can cause embarrassment, a lower grade, or failure. It can even lead to expulsion from college.
- Missing the exam because you are not prepared and asking the professor to let you make up the exam later is a tactic that many students try. Most professors will not permit you to take an exam late.

"Failure is simply the opportunity to begin again more intelligently."
Henry Ford

- Inventing a creative excuse for missing an exam is so common that some professors have a collection of these stories that they share with colleagues. Creative excuses don't work with most professors.
- Arriving at the exam without the proper materials such as a pencil, Scantron, paper, calculator, or book (for open-book exams) can cause you to miss the exam or start the exam late.

QUIZ

Test Preparation

Test what you have learned by selecting the correct answers to the following questions.

1. In test preparation, it is important to use this memory technique:

   a. Distribute the practice.
   b. Read every chapter just before the test.
   c. Do most of the review right before the test to minimize forgetting.

2. To take advantage of distributed practice, it is important to develop a:

   a. summary sheet.
   b. study schedule.
   c. mind map.

3. Effective tools to learn facts and details are

   a. mind maps.
   b. summary sheets.
   c. flash cards.

4. The best way to review is

   a. to start early and break it into small parts.
   b. immediately before the test.
   c. in large blocks of time.

5. If you have to cram for an exam, it is most important to

   a. stay up all night studying for the exam
   b. focus on the lecture notes and forget about reading the text
   c. be selective and review and recite the main points

How did you do on the quiz? Check your answers: 1. a, 2. b, 3. c, 4. a, 5. c

Ten Rules for Success

Here are 10 rules for success on any test. Are there any new ideas you can put into practice?

1. **Make sure to set your alarm,** and consider having a backup in case your alarm doesn't go off. Set a second alarm or have someone call to make sure you are awake on time.

2. **Arrive a little early for your exam.** If you are taking a standardized test like the Scholastic Aptitude Test (SAT) or Graduate Record Exam (GRE), familiarize yourself with the location of the exam. If you arrive early, you can take a quick walk around the building to relax or spend a few minutes doing a review so that your brain will be tuned up and ready.

3. **Eat a light breakfast including some carbohydrates and protein.** Be careful about eating sugar and caffeine before a test, because this can contribute to greater anxiety and low blood sugar by the time you take the test. The worst breakfast would be something like a doughnut and coffee or a soda and candy bar. Examples of good breakfasts are eggs, toast, and juice or cereal with milk and fruit.

4. **Think positively about the exam.** Tell yourself that you are well prepared and the exam is an opportunity to show what you know.

5. **Make sure you have the proper materials:** Scantrons, paper, pencil or pen, calculator, books and notes (for open-book exams).

6. **Manage your time.** Know how long you have for the test and then scan the test to make a time management plan. For example, if you have one hour and there are 50 objective questions, you have about a minute for each question. Halfway through the time, you should have completed 25 questions. If there are three essay questions in an hour, you have less than 20 minutes for each question. Save some time to look over the test and make corrections.

7. **Neatness is important.** If your paper looks neat, the professor is more likely to have a positive attitude about the paper before it is even read. If the paper is hard to read, the professor will start reading your paper with a negative attitude, possibly resulting in a lower grade.

8. **Read the test directions carefully.** On essay exams, it is common for the professor to give you a choice of questions to answer. If you do not read the directions, you may try to answer all of the questions and then run out of time or give incomplete answers to them.

9. **If you get stuck on a difficult question, don't worry about it.** Just mark it and find an easier question. You may find clues on the rest of the test that will aid your recall, or you may be more relaxed later on and think of the answer.

10. **Be careful not to give any impression that you might be cheating.** Keep your eyes on your own paper. If you have memory aids or outlines memorized, write them directly on the test paper rather than a separate sheet so that you are not suspected of using cheat notes.

Journal Entry #2

Make a list of five common mistakes students make when getting ready for an exam.

Dealing with Test Anxiety

Some anxiety is a good thing. It can provide motivation to study and prepare for exams. However, it is common for college students to suffer from test anxiety. Too much anxiety can lower your performance on tests. Some symptoms of test anxiety include:

- Fear of failing a test even though you are well prepared
- Physical symptoms such as perspiring, increased heart rate, shortness of breath, upset stomach, tense muscles, or headache
- Negative thoughts about the test and your grade
- Mental blocking of material you know and remembering it once you leave the exam

© Stuart Miles/Shutterstock.com

You can minimize your test anxiety by being well prepared and by applying the memory strategies described in earlier chapters. Prepare for your exams by attending every class, keeping up with your reading assignments, and reviewing during the semester. These steps will help increase your self-confidence and reduce anxiety. Apply the principles of memory improvement to your studying. As you are reading, find the important points and highlight them. Review these points so that they are stored in your long-term memory. Use distributed practice and spread out learning over time rather than trying to learn it all at once. Visualize and organize what you need to remember. Trust in your abilities and intend to remember what you have studied.

If you find that you are anxious, here are some ideas you can try to cope with the anxiety. Experiment with these techniques to see which ones work best for you.

Tips to Minimize Anxiety

- Exercise
- Sleep
- Take deep breaths
- Visualize success
- Acknowledge anxiety
- Easy questions first
- Yell, "Stop!"
- Daydream
- Practice perspective
- Give yourself time
- Get help

- **Do some physical exercise.** Physical exercise helps to use up stress hormones. Make physical activity a part of your daily routine. Arrive for your test a little early and walk briskly around campus for about 20 minutes. This exercise will help you to feel relaxed and energized.

- **Get a good night's sleep before the test.** Lack of sleep can interfere with memory and cause irritability, anxiety, and confusion.

- **Take deep breaths.** Immediately before the test, take a few deep breaths; hold them for three to five seconds and let them out slowly. These deep breaths will help you to relax and keep a sufficient supply of oxygen in your blood. Oxygen is needed for proper brain function.

- **Visualize and rehearse your success.** Begin by getting as comfortable and relaxed as possible in your favorite chair or lying down in bed. Visualize yourself walking into the exam room. Try to imagine the room in as much detail as possible. If possible, visit the exam room before the test so that you can get a good picture of it. See yourself taking the exam calmly and confidently. You know most of the answers. If you find a question you do not know, see yourself circling it and coming back to it later. Imagine that you find a clue on the test that triggers your recall of the answers to the difficult questions. Picture yourself handing in the exam with a good feeling about doing well on the test. Then imagine you are getting the test back and you get a good grade on the test. You congratulate yourself for a job well done. If you suffer from test anxiety, you may need to rehearse this scene several times. When you enter the exam room, the visual picture that you have rehearsed will help you to relax.

- **Acknowledge your anxiety.** The first step in dealing with anxiety is to admit that you are anxious rather than trying to fight it or deny it. Say to yourself, "I am feeling anxious." Take a few deep breaths and then focus your attention on the test.

- **Do the easy questions first and mark the ones that may be difficult.** This will help you to relax. Once you are relaxed, the difficult questions become more manageable.

- **Yell, "Stop!"** Negative and frightening thoughts can cause anxiety. Here are some examples of negative thoughts:

  I'm going to fail this test.

  I don't know the answer to number 10!

  I never do well on tests.

  Essays! I have a hard time with those.

  I'll never make it through college.

  I was never any good in math!

These types of thoughts don't help you do better on the test, so stop saying them. They cause you to become anxious and to freeze up during the test. If you find yourself with similar thoughts, yell, "Stop!" to yourself. This will cause you to interrupt your train of thought so that you can think about the task at hand rather than becoming more anxious. Replace negative thoughts with more positive ones such as these:

  I'm doing the best I can.

  I am well prepared and know most of the answers.

  I don't know the answer to number 10, so I'll just circle it and come back to it later.

  I'll make an outline in the margin for the essay question.

  College is difficult, but I'll make it!

  Math is a challenge, but I can do it!

- **Daydream.** Think about being in your favorite place. Take time to think about the details. Allow yourself to be there for a while until you feel more relaxed.
- **Practice perspective.** Remember, one poor grade is not the end of the world. It does not define who you are. If you do not do well, think about how you can improve your preparation and performance the next time.
- **Give yourself time.** Test anxiety develops over a period of time. It will take some time to get over it. Learn the best ways to prepare for the exam and practice saying positive thoughts to yourself.
- **Get help.** If these techniques do not work for you, seek help from your college health or counseling center.

Journal Entry #3

You have a friend who prepares for exams, but suffers from text anxiety. Make a list of five ideas for dealing with text anxiety that you could share with your friend. Consider both physical and mental preparation as well as some relaxation techniques that can be helpful.

Dealing with Math Anxiety

Math anxiety is a negative physical and/or emotional reaction toward math. It can lead to avoidance of math and procrastination in doing your math homework. It is often caused by negative experiences with math in elementary school or at home with parents helping with homework. Often students were embarrassed by being asked to solve a problem on the board and not being successful. Perhaps teachers, parents, siblings, or friends made negative comments about your math ability. It is important to think about the source of your math anxiety and then move on to new possibilities.

© Creativa Images/Shutterstock.com

Math anxiety is often related to low confidence in math. To build self-confidence, begin with positive thinking. You may have had difficulty with math in the past, but with a positive attitude and the proper study techniques, you can meet the challenge. The first step to success in math is to put in the effort required. Attend class, do your homework, and get help if needed. It is important to experience success, even in small steps, and build on your success. If you put in the effort and hard work, you will gain experience in math. If you gain experience with math, you will become more confident in your ability to do math. If you have confidence, you will gain satisfaction in doing math. You may even learn to like it! If you like the subject, you can gain competence. The process looks like this:

Hard work → Experience → Confidence → Satisfaction → Competence

If you suffer from math anxiety, you can make an appointment to talk with your instructor, advisor, or counselor to find out what resources may be available to you. Although you may have had difficulty with math in the past, you can become successful by following these steps. Your reward is self-satisfaction and increased opportunity in technical, scientific, and professional careers. Math is required for graduation too.

Math Tests

Taking a math test involves some different strategies:

1. Some instructors will let you write down formulas on an index card or a small crib sheet. Prepare these notes carefully, writing down the key formulas you will need for the exam.

2. If you have to memorize formulas, review them right before the test and write them on the test immediately.

3. As a first step, quickly look over the test. Find a problem you can solve easily and do this problem first.

4. Manage your time. Find out how many problems you have to solve and how much time is available for each problem. Do the problems worth the most points first. Stay on track.

5. Try this four-step process:

   a. Understand the problem.

   b. Devise a plan to solve the problem. Write down the information that is given. Think about the skills and techniques you have learned in class that can help you to solve the problem.

   c. Carry out the plan.

   d. Look back to see if your answer is reasonable.

6. If you cannot work a problem, go on to the next question. Come back later when you are more relaxed. If you spend too much time on a problem you cannot work, you will not have time for the problems that you can work.

7. Even if you think an answer is wrong, turn it in. You may get partial credit.

8. Show all the steps in your work and label your answer. On long and complex problems, it is helpful to use short sentences to explain your steps in solving the problem.

9. Estimate your answer and see if it makes sense or is logical.

10. Write your numbers as neatly as possible to avoid mistakes and to make them legible for the professor.

11. Leave space between your answers in case you need to add to them later.

12. Check for careless errors. Forgetting a plus or a minus sign or adding or subtracting incorrectly can have a big impact on your grade. Be sure to use all the time allowed for the test. Save at least five minutes at the end of your test to read over your test.

13. Build your confidence and reinforce your memory by doing a final review of the most important concepts and formulas right before you go to sleep. Do not learn new material right before sleeping since this could cause math anxiety.

14. Get enough sleep before the math test. Remember that you are missing 30% of your IQ points if you miss sleeping the night before the test. If you are mentally sharp, the test will be easier.

Tips for Avoiding Common Math Errors[2]

- Any quantity multiplied by zero is zero
- Any quantity raised to the zero power is one·
- Any fraction multiplied by its reciprocal is one
- Only like algebraic terms may be combined
- Break down to the simplest form in algebra
- In algebra, multiply and divide before adding and subtracting
- If an algebraic expression has more than one set of parentheses, get rid of the inner parenthesis first and work outward
- Any operation performed on one side of the equation must be performed on the other side

Journal Entry #4

You are enrolled in a math course that is required for graduation and want to make sure that you are successful in this course. List and briefly explain five ideas that will help you to be successful in this math course.

© Ivelin Radkov/Shutterstock.com

Taking Tests

True-False Tests

Many professors use objective tests such as true-false and multiple-choice because they are easy to grade. The best way to prepare for these types of tests is to study the key points in the textbook, lecture notes, and class handouts. In the textbook, take each bold-faced topic and turn it into a question. If you can answer the questions, you will be successful on objective tests.

In addition to studying for the test, it is helpful to understand some basic test-taking techniques that will help you to determine the correct answer. Many of the techniques used to determine whether a statement is true or false can also be used to eliminate wrong answers on multiple-choice tests.

To develop strategies for success on true-false exams, it is important to understand how a teacher writes the questions. For a true-false question, the teacher identifies a key point in the book or lecture notes. Then he or she has two choices. For a true statement, the key idea is often written exactly as it appears in the text or notes. For a false statement, the key idea is changed in some way to make it false.

One way to make a statement false is to add a **qualifier** to the statement. **Absolute** qualifiers often make a statement false. **General** qualifiers are often found in true statements.

Absolute Qualifiers (false)		General Qualifiers (true)	
all	none	usually	frequently
always	never	often	sometimes
only	nobody	some	seldom
invariably	no one	many	much
best	worst	most	generally
everybody	everyone	few	ordinarily
absolutely	absolutely not	probably	a majority
certainly	certainly not	might	a few
no	every	may	apt to

Seven Tips for Success on True-False Tests

1. **Identify the key ideas in the text and class notes and review them.**

2. **Accept the question at face value.** Don't overanalyze or create wild exceptions in your mind.

3. **If you don't know the answer, assume it is true.** There are generally more true statements because we all like the truth (especially teachers) and true questions are easier to write. However, some teachers like to test students by writing all false statements.

4. **If any part of a true-false statement is false, the whole statement is false.** Carefully read each statement to determine if any part of it is false. Students sometimes assume a statement is true if most of it is true. This is not correct.

   Example: Good relaxation techniques include deep breathing, exercise, and visualizing your failure on the exam.

   This statement is false because visualizing failure can lead to test anxiety and failure.

5. **Notice any absolute or general qualifiers.** Remember that absolute qualifiers often make a statement false. General qualifiers often make a statement true.

   Example: The student who crams **always** does poorly on the exam.

   This statement is false because **some** students are successful at cramming for an exam.

   Be careful with this rule. Sometimes the answer can be absolute.

   Example: The grade point average is always calculated by dividing the number of units attempted by the grade points. (true)

6. **Notice words such as *because, therefore, consequently,* and *as a result*.** They may connect two things that are true but result in a false statement.

   Example: Martha does not have test anxiety. (true)

   Martha makes good grades on tests. (true)

   Martha does not have test anxiety and therefore makes good grades on tests.

   This statement is false because she also has to prepare for the exam. Not having test anxiety could even cause her to lack motivation to study and do poorly on a test.

7. **Watch for double negatives.** Two nos equal a yes. If you see two negatives in a sentence, read them as a positive. Be careful with negative prefixes such as un-, im-, mis-, dis-, il-, and ir-. For example, the phrase "not uncommon" actually means "common." Notice that the word "not" and the prefix "un-" when used together form a double negative that equals a positive.

   Example: Not being **un**prepared for the test is the best way to earn good grades.

   The above sentence is confusing. To make it clearer, change both of the negatives into a positive:

   Being prepared for the test is the best way to earn good grades.

Practice True-False Test

Answer the following questions by applying the tips for success in the previous section. Place a T or an F in the blanks.

_____ 1. If a statement has an absolute qualifier, it is always false.

_____ 2. Statements with general qualifiers are frequently true.

_____ 3. If you don't know the answer, you should guess true.

_____ 4. Studying the key points for true-false tests is not unimportant.

_____ 5. Good test-taking strategies include eating a light breakfast that includes carbohydrates and protein and drinking plenty of coffee to stay alert.

_____ 6. Ryan attended every class this semester and therefore earned an A in the class.

How did you do on the test? Answers: 1. F, 2. T, 3. T, 4. T, 5. F, 6. F

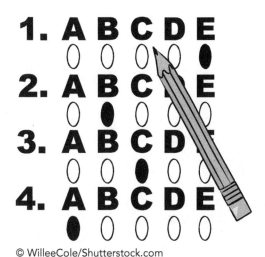

© WilleeCole/Shutterstock.com

Multiple-Choice Tests

College exams often include multiple-choice questions rather than true-false questions because it is more difficult to guess the correct answer. On a true-false question, the student has a 50 percent chance of guessing the correct answer, while on a multiple-choice question, the odds of guessing correctly are only 25 percent. You can think of a multiple-choice question as four true-false questions in a row. First, read the question and try to answer it without looking at the options. This will help you to focus on the question and determine the correct answer. Look at each option and determine if it is true or false. Then choose the **best** answer.

To choose the best option, it is helpful to understand how a teacher writes a multiple-choice question. Here are the steps a teacher uses to write a multiple-choice exam:

1. Find an important point in the lecture notes, text, or handouts.

2. Write a **stem**. This is an incomplete statement or a question.

3. Write the correct answer as one of the options.

4. Write three or four plausible but incorrect options that might be chosen by students who are not prepared. These incorrect options are called **decoys**. Here is an example:

   Stem: If you are anxious about taking math tests, it is helpful to:

   a. Stay up the night before the test to review thoroughly. (**decoy**)

   b. Visualize yourself doing poorly on the test so you will be motivated to study. (**decoy**)

   c. Practice math problems regularly during the semester. (**correct answer**)

   d. Do the most difficult problem first. (**decoy**)

Being well prepared for the test is the most reliable way of recognizing the correct answer and the decoys. In addition, becoming familiar with the following rules for recognizing decoys can help you determine the correct answer or improve your chances of guessing the correct answer on an exam. If you can at least eliminate some of the wrong answers, you will improve your odds of selecting the correct answer.

Rules for recognizing a decoy or wrong answer:

1. **The decoys are all true or all false statements.** Read each option and determine which options are false and which statements are true. This will help you to find the correct answer.

   Example: To manage your time on a test, it is important to:

   a. Skip the directions and work as quickly as possible. (false)

   b. Skim through the test to see how much time you have for each section. (true)

   c. Do the most difficult sections first. (false)

   d. Just start writing as quickly as possible. (false)

   Read the stem carefully, because sometimes you will be asked to identify one false statement in a group of true statements.

2. **The decoy may contain an absolute qualifier.** The option with the absolute qualifier (e.g., always, only, every) is likely to be false because few things in life are absolute. There are generally exceptions to any rule.

3. **The decoy can be partly true.** However, if one part of the statement is false, the whole statement is false and an incorrect answer.

   Example: Memory techniques include visualization, organization, and telling yourself you won't remember.

   In this example, the first two techniques are true and the last part is false, which makes the whole statement false.

4. **The decoy may have a conjunction or other linking words that makes it false.** Watch for words and phrases such as *because, consequently, therefore,* and *as a result.*

5. **The decoy may have a double negative.** Having two negatives in a sentence makes it difficult to understand. Read the two negatives as a positive.

6. **The decoy may be a foolish option.** Writing multiple decoys is difficult, so test writers sometimes throw in foolish or humorous options.

   Example: In a multiple-choice test, a decoy is:

   a. a type of duck.

   b. an incorrect answer.

c. a type of missile used in air defense.

d. a type of fish.

The correct answer is b. Sometimes students are tempted by the foolish answers.

7. **The decoy is often a low or high number.** If you have a multiple-choice question with numbers, and you are not sure of the correct answer, choose the number in the middle range. It is often more likely to be correct.

Example: George Miller of Harvard University theorized that the optimum number of chunks of material that we can remember is:

a. 1–2 (This low number is a decoy.)

b. 5–9 (This is the correct answer.)

c. 10–12 (This is close to the correct answer.)

d. 20–25 (This high number is a decoy.)

There is an exception to this rule when the number is much higher or lower than the average person thinks is possible.

8. **The decoy may look like the correct answer.** When two options look alike, one is incorrect and the other may be the correct answer. Test writers often use words that look alike as decoys.

Example: In false statements, the qualifier is often:

a. absolute.

b. resolute.

c. general.

d. exaggerated.

The correct answer is a. Answer b is an incorrect look-alike option.

9. **Decoys are often shorter than the correct answer.** Longer answers are more likely to be correct because they are more complete. Avoid choosing the first answer that seems to be correct. There may be a better and more complete answer.

Example: Good test preparation involves:

a. doing the proper review for the test.

b. good time management.

c. a positive attitude.

d. having good attendance, studying and reviewing regularly, being able to deal with test anxiety, and having a positive mental attitude.

Option d is correct because it is the most complete and thus the best answer.

10. **Decoys may be grammatically incorrect.** The correct answer will fit the grammar of the stem. A stem ending with "a" will match an answer beginning with a consonant; stems ending with "an" will match a word beginning with a vowel. The answer will agree in gender, number, and person with the stem.

Example: In test taking, a decoy is an:

a. incorrect answer.

b. correct answer.

c. false answer.

d. true answer.

The correct answer is A. It is also the only answer that grammatically fits with the stem. Also note that decoys can be all true or all false. In standardized tests, the grammar is usually correct. On teacher-made tests, the grammar can be a clue to the correct answer.

11. **A decoy is sometimes an opposite.** When two options are opposites, one is incorrect and the other is sometimes, but not always, correct.

Example: A decoy is:

a. a right answer.

b. a wrong answer.

c. a general qualifier.

d. a true statement.

The two opposites are answers a and b. The correct answer is b.

12. **A decoy may be the same as another answer.** If two answers say the same thing in different ways, they are both decoys and incorrect.

Example: A true statement is likely to have this type of qualifier:

a. extreme

b. absolute

c. general

d. factual

Notice that answers a and b are the same and are incorrect. The correct answer is c.

Example: How much does a gallon of water weigh?

a. 8.34 pounds

b. 5.5 pounds

c. 5 pounds 8 ounces

d. 20 pounds

B and c are the same and are therefore incorrect answers. Answer d is a high number. The correct answer is a.

If you are unable to identify any decoys, these suggestions may be helpful:

- Mark the question and come back to it later. You may find the answer elsewhere on the test, or some words that help you remember the answer. After answering some easier questions, you may be able to relax and remember the answer.

- Trust your intuition and choose something that sounds familiar.

- Do not change your first answer unless you have misread the question or are sure that the answer is incorrect. Sometimes students overanalyze a question and then choose the wrong answer.

- The option "All of the above" is often correct because it is easier to write true statements rather than false ones. Options like A and B, B and D, or other combinations are also likely to be correct for the same reason.

- If you have no idea about the correct answer, guess option B or C. Most correct answers are in the middle.

© Peter Gyure/Shutterstock.com

Practice Multiple-Choice Test

Circle the letters of the correct answers. Then check your answers using the key at the end of this section.

1. The correct answer in a multiple-choice question is likely to be
    a. the shortest answer.
    b. the longest and most complete answer.
    c. the answer with an absolute qualifier.
    d. the answer that has some truth in it.

2. When guessing on a question involving numbers, it is generally best to
    a. choose the highest number.
    b. choose the lowest number.
    c. choose the mid-range number.
    d. always choose the first option.

3. If you have test anxiety, what questions should you answer first on the test?
    a. The most difficult questions
    b. The easiest questions
    c. The questions at the beginning
    d. The questions worth the least number of points

4. When taking a multiple-choice test, you should
    a. pick the first choice that is true.
    b. read all the choices and select the best one.
    c. pick the first choice that is false.
    d. choose the extreme answer.

5. A good method for guessing is to
    a. identify which choices are true and false.
    b. use the process of elimination.
    c. notice absolute qualifiers and conjunctions.
    d. all of the above.

6. The key to success when taking a multiple-choice test is
    a. cheating.
    b. good preparation.
    c. knowing how to guess.
    d. being able to recognize a qualifier.

7. The following rule about decoys is correct:

    a. A decoy is always absolute.

    b. A decoy can be partly true.

    c. Every decoy has a qualifier.

    d. Decoys are invariably false statements.

8. An example of an absolute qualifier is

    a. generally.

    b. never.

    c. sometimes.

    d. frequently.

9. Statements with absolute qualifiers are generally

    a. true.

    b. false.

    c. irrelevant.

    d. confusing.

10. If two multiple-choice options are the same or very similar, they are most likely

    a. a decoy and a correct answer.

    b. a correct answer.

    c. a true answer.

    d. a mistake on the test.

11. It is generally not a good idea to change your answer unless

    a. you are very anxious about the test.

    b. you do not have good intuition.

    c. you notice that your intelligent friend has a different answer.

    d. you have misread the question and you are sure that the answer is incorrect.

How did you do on the quiz? Check your answers: 1. b, 2. c, 3. b, 4. b, 5. d, 6. b, 7. b (Notice the absolute qualifiers in the decoys), 8. b, 9. b (Notice the opposites), 10. a (Notice the grammar), 11. d

Matching Tests

A matching test involves two lists of facts or definitions that must be matched together. Here are some tips to help you successfully complete a matching exam:

1. Read through both lists to discover the pattern or relationship between the lists. The lists might give words and definitions, people and accomplishments, or other paired facts.

2. Count the items on the list of answers to see if there is only one match for each item or if there are some extra answer choices.

3. Start with one list and match the items that you know. In this way, you have a better chance of guessing on the items that you do not know.

4. If you have difficulty with some of the items, leave them blank and return later. You may find the answers or clues on the rest of the test.

Practice Matching Test

Match the items in the first column with the items in the second column. Write the letter of the matching item in the blank at the left.

_____ **1.** Meaningful organization

_____ **2.** Visualization

_____ **3.** Recitation

_____ **4.** Develop an interest

_____ **5.** See the big picture

_____ **6.** Intend to remember

_____ **7.** Distribute the practice

_____ **8.** Create a basic background

A. Learn small amounts and review frequently.

B. The more you know, the easier it is to remember.

C. Tell yourself you will remember.

D. Pretend you like it.

E. Make a mental picture.

F. Rehearse and review.

G. Focus on the main points first.

H. Personal organization.

Answers: 1. H,   2. E,   3. F,   4. D,   5. G,   6. C,   7. A,   8. B

Sentence-Completion or Fill-in-the-Blank Tests

Fill-in-the-blank and sentence-completion tests are more difficult than true-false or multiple-choice tests because they require the **recall** of specific information rather than the **recognition** of the correct answer. To prepare for this type of test, focus on facts such as definitions, names, dates, and places. Using flash cards to prepare can be helpful. For example, to memorize names, place each name on one side of a card and some identifying words on the other side. Practice looking at the names on one side of the card and then recalling the identifying words on the other side of the card. Then turn the cards over and look at the identifying words to recall the names.

Sometimes the test has clues that will help you to fill in the blank. Clues can include the length of the blanks and the number of blanks. Find an answer that makes sense in the sentence and matches the grammar of the sentence. If you cannot think of an answer, write a general description and you may get partial credit. Look for clues on the rest of the test that may trigger your recall.

Practice Fill-in-the-Blank Test

Complete each sentence with the appropriate word or words.

1. Fill-in-the-blank tests are more difficult because they depend on the _____ of specific information.

2. On a true-false test, a statement is likely to be false if it contains an _____ qualifier.

3. Test review tools include _____, _____, and _____.

4. When studying for tests, visualize your _____.

Answers: 1. recall, 2. absolute, 3. flash cards, summary sheets, and mind maps (also study groups and highlighters), 4. success

Essay Tests

Many professors choose essay questions because they are the best way to show what you have learned in the class. Essay questions can be challenging because you not only have to know the material, but must be able to organize it and use good writing techniques in your answer.

© Lucky Business/Shutterstock.com

Essay questions contain key words that will guide you in writing your answer. One of the keys to success in writing answers to essay questions is to note these key words and then structure your essay accordingly. As you read through an essay question, look for these words:

Analyze	Break into separate parts and discuss, examine, or interpret each part.
Argue	State an opinion and give reasons for the opinion.
Comment	Give your opinion.
Compare	Identify two or more ideas and identify similarities and differences.
Contrast	Show how the components are the same or different.
Criticize	Give your opinion and make judgments.
Defend	State reasons.
Define	Give the meaning of the word or concept as used within the course of study.
Describe	Give a detailed account or provide information.
Demonstrate	Provide evidence.
Diagram	Make a drawing, chart, graph, sketch, or plan.
Differentiate	Tell how the ideas are the same and how they are different.
Describe	Make a picture with words. List the characteristics, qualities, and parts.
Discuss	Describe the pros and cons of the issues. Compare and contrast.
Enumerate	Make a list of ideas, events, qualities, reasons, and so on.
Explain	Make an idea clear. Show how and why.
Evaluate	Describe it and give your opinion about something.
Illustrate	Give concrete examples and explain them. Draw a diagram.
Interpret	Say what something means. Describe and then evaluate.
Justify	Prove a point. Give the reasons why.
Outline	Describe the main ideas.
Prove	Support with facts. Give evidence or reasons.
Relate	Show the connections between ideas or events.
State	Explain precisely. Provide the main points.
Summarize	Give a brief, condensed account. Draw a conclusion.
Trace	Show the order of events.

Here are some tips on writing essays:

1. To prepare for an essay test, use a mind map or summary sheet to summarize the main ideas. Organize the material in the form of an outline or mental pictures that you can use in writing.

2. The first step in writing an essay is to quickly survey the test and read the directions carefully. Many times you are offered a choice of which and how many questions to answer.

3. Manage your time. Note how many questions need to be answered and how many points each question is worth. For example, if you have three questions to answer in one hour, you will have less than 20 minutes for each question. Save some time to check over your work.

   If the questions are worth different numbers of points, divide up your time proportionately. In the above example with three questions, if one question is worth 50 points and the other two are worth 25 points, spend half the time on the 50-point question (less than 30 minutes) and divide the remaining time between the 25-point questions (less than 15 minutes each).

4. If you are anxious about the test, start with an easy question in order to relax and build your confidence. If you are confident in your test-taking abilities, start with the question that is worth the most points.

5. Get organized. Write a brief outline in the margin of your test paper. Do not write your outline on a separate sheet of paper because you may be accused of using cheat notes.

6. In the first sentence of your essay, rephrase the question and provide a direct answer. Rephrasing the question keeps you on track and a direct answer becomes the thesis statement or main idea of the essay.

   Example: (Question:) Describe a system for reading a college textbook.
   (Answer:) A system for reading a college textbook is Survey, Question, Read, Review, Recite, and Reflect (SQ4R). (Then you would go on to expand on each part of the topic.)

7. Use the principles of good composition. Start with a thesis statement or main idea. Provide supporting ideas and examples to support your thesis. Provide a brief summary at the end.

8. Write your answer clearly and neatly so it is easy to grade. Grading an essay involves an element of subjectivity. If your paper looks neat and is easy to read, the professor is likely to read your essay with a positive attitude. If your paper is difficult to read, the professor will probably read your paper with a negative attitude.

9. Determine the length of your essay by the number of points it is worth. For example, a five-point essay might be a paragraph with five key points. A 25-point essay would probably be a five-paragraph essay with at least 25 key points.

10. Save some time at the end to read over your essays. Make corrections, make sure your answers make sense, and add any key information you may have forgotten to include.

What to Do When Your Test Is Returned

When your test is returned, use it as feedback for future test preparation in the course. Look at your errors and try to determine how to prevent these errors in the future.

- Did you study correctly?
- Did you study the proper materials?
- Did you use the proper test-taking techniques?
- Was the test more difficult than you expected?
- Did you run out of time to take the test?
- Was the test focused on details and facts or on general ideas and principles?
- Did you have problems with test anxiety?

Analyzing your test performance can help you to do better in the future.

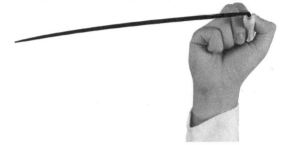

SUCCESS NEEDS
PREPARATION

© airdone/Shutterstock.com

Journal Entry #5

Of course it is a good idea to be well prepared for exams, but there are times when you will have to figure out the answer or even make a guess on the correct answer. Review the section on "Taking Tests" and list five ideas for guessing that you can try in the future.

KEYS TO SUCCESS

Be Prepared

The key idea in this chapter is to be prepared. Good preparation is essential for success in test taking as well as in many other areas of life. Being successful begins with having a vision of the future and then taking steps to achieve your dream.

Sometimes people think of success in terms of good luck. Thomas Jefferson said, "I'm a great believer in luck, and I find the harder I work, the more I have of it." Don't depend on good luck. Work to create your success.

You can reach your dream of attaining a college education through preparation and hard work. Use the ideas in this chapter to ensure your success. Remember that preparation begins on the first day of class; it does not begin when the professor announces a test. On the first day of class, the professor provides an overview, or outline, of what you will learn. Attend every class. The main points covered in the class will be on the test. Read your assignments a little at a time starting from the first day. If you distribute your practice, you will find it easier to learn and to remember.

When it comes time to review for the test, you will already know what to expect on the test, and you will have learned the material by attending the lectures and reading your text. Reviewing for the test is just review; it is not original learning. It is a chance to strengthen what you have learned so that you can relax and do your best on the test. Review is one of the final steps in learning. With review, you will gain a sense of confidence and satisfaction in your studies.

If you are not prepared, you will need to cram for the test and you may not be as successful on the test as you could be. If you are not successful, you may get the mistaken idea that you cannot be successful in college. Cramming for the test produces stress, since you will need to learn a great deal of information in a short time. Stress can interfere with memory and cause you to freeze up on exams. It is also difficult to remember if you have to cram. The memory works best if you do a small amount of learning regularly over a period of time. Cramming is hard work and no fun. The worst problem with cramming is that it causes you to dislike education. It is difficult to continue to do something that you have learned to dislike.

Good preparation is the key to success in many areas of life. Whether you are taking a college course, playing a basketball game, going on vacation, planning a wedding, or building a house, good preparation will help to guarantee your success. Begin with your vision of the future and boldly take the first steps. The best preparation for the future is the good use of your time today.

"The secret of getting ahead is getting started. The secret of getting started is breaking your complex, overwhelming tasks into small manageable tasks, and then starting on the first one."

Mark Twain

"The future starts today, not tomorrow."
Pope John Paul II

Interview from the Elder: Ms. Elaine St. John

In this chapter you have been introduced to test-taking strategies to assist you not only with improving college success, but also lifelong success, as you may find the need to take tests throughout your career. You have discovered new techniques for preparing wisely and calmly for tests; explored tips for dealing with test anxiety by using smudging and becoming physically and mentally prepared; explored a methodology for learning to develop a positive attitude toward difficult subjects like math; and you have explored specific success factors for successfully taking various types of tests.

The following interview is from Lakota elder Ms. Elaine St. John. As you read through the comments she has made on her life, think about how she has led a fulfilling, successful, and healthy life that bridges both traditional and modern times. She successfully faced many challenges in earning a college education.

Interviews from the Elders
As told to Beatrice Zamora, March 2021

© Sterling St. John

Ms. Elaine Lefthand St. John, age 92, lives on the Standing Rock Lakota Indian Reservation in South Dakota.

Meet Ms. Elaine St. John

I live in South Dakota in the Standing Rock Reservation in the community of Kenel. I was born there, and we lived a country life. We used to get our water from the Missouri River. Later, they had running water, but back then we didn't, and Papa would go to the river and put the water in barrels and bring it home. Sometimes, my sister and I would help dip the water and put it in the barrels.

I will always be Lakota. I'm proud because that's what my grandparents and parents did. My dad was full blooded Sioux/Lakota, and my mom one half Chipewa from the Turtle Mountain Reservation in North Dakota. They met at a dance. They just fell in love! They were eighteen years old when they got married. Mama, she hung in there, it was kind of a rough life living with the Sioux. My Chipewa grandparents always wanted her to come home with all of us, but Papa, he would never leave home. There were eight girls and three brothers in our family. They are all gone except three of us.

Today I see a lot of things are way different. I tell my children about how and what we had to do to survive. We had a log cabin out in the country that Papa built. My dad cut the logs and laid them for us. There was timber growing by the river, so we could cut the logs, and before that everybody lived in tents and teepees. I always lived in a log cabin when I was growing up. And at one point we stayed in a teepee for a while—it was really crazy.

Making Friends in College; Forming an Educational Family Can Help You Through the Process

In my culture, we call Grandpa, Lala, and Grandma, Unci. It's the Sioux/Lakota name for grandparents. You can make relatives if you want to. It's the Lakota way. You meet someone, an elder, and you like them, you can call them Lala or Unci, that's our way. (hunka lowanpi…. the making of relatives ceremony)

Honoring Our Ancestors, Our Traditional Teachers

As I'm sitting here talking to you this morning, I was looking for some documents to talk to you about some stuff you might ask me. I ran into my paternal grandma and grandpa's pictures, dressed, in their Indian regalia. I'm looking at it right now, just thinking my grandma made those outfits they wore when they danced. I used to stay with them, and I learned a lot of good things from them.

My Lala got his name, Lefthand, because when he was about two years old, his parents noticed he was left-handed, so they gave him his Indian name, Left Hand. When the Bureau of Indian Affairs (BIA) got a hold of it, our name was supposed to be Catch-the-Bear, but the BIA recorded it Left Hand. Then they corrected it to Left Hand, Catch the Bear. Lala never went by that name, Catch the Bear, and we didn't go by that name until the BIA added it.

Papa had a drum group and he played the old-time fiddle for the square dances. I used to dance the square dance. It was fun. The people who lived across the river, the White people, when the rivers froze, they would come over for our dances. It was all right to meet them and make friends, they weren't scared. **Indians are supposed to be fierce, but we weren't**. They would come across in their little boats to our little store in Kenel. Kenel was named after a Catholic priest. I guess this one priest was so good to the Natives and he learned to speak Lakota. He lived with them and ate with them, and they liked him so much they named their community after Father Martin Kenel.

Respect

I was married in Deep Bend, where the river bends. People just lived out there. It was not a town. These old people would come to visit my mother-in-law, and they would stay for a couple of days. The three families would come and visit, and they found out that one of the boys got married, Al, my husband. They spoke Lakota. They asked my mother-in-law, in the Lakota way, you don't say your daughter-in-law, your mother or father-in-law, you don't say their names, you have to have respect, so the old-timers gave me an Indian name. They called me the Woman from the North because I lived north of where I was married. I lived a few miles from North Dakota. They give you a name that honors you. You **never say your in-laws' name, you don't even talk to them, you have to have respect. Don't walk in front of them, that's the Lakota way. In my day, I still honor that. If it was absolutely necessary, you would talk to them. I would talk to my mother-in-law a couple of times when necessary. When she wanted to talk to me, she talks to my little girl, she wants me to hear that. You have to have respect. You are not loud, have respect.**

Appreciation and Giving Thanks (No One Is Entitled) and Doing Things in a Nice Way

In the summertime there was a lot of food growing out there on the prairie. The Great Spirit (wakan tanka) put it there for us to use. We used to dig up turnips and pick cherries, and things like that out in the prairie. There were a lot of berries. We didn't have refrigerators or freezers, so we had to dry all that food that we brought from the prairie and save it for winter. All summer we were getting ready for winter.

Digging turnips and picking berries was a work of art. We had to do it at a certain time of year, the summer, and how you dig, how you pick—you had to do it a certain way. You had to do it nicely and appreciate what our Great Spirit put there for us on the land where all these things grow. We didn't just dig a turnip and chew it and throw the peelings on the ground. We never did that. We appreciated the good earth, so that's how I grew up.

The wild turnips grow by themselves. You dig out there with the grandmothers. As kids, we went in a wagon, and we would stay out all day and dig the turnips and then we would break the tops off the turnip, the stem, and put it back in the hole where we dug it out and cover it. In this way, it will make flowers and those seeds from the flowers will be blown by the wind and then next year we will have more turnips. The turnips were also dried for winter. They tasted really good. The medium size is kind of sweet. When you peel the turnips, you put all the peels in a pile and dry them and then you can burn them like wood. You have to appreciate what the Great Spirit put there for you. Don't waste anything!

When you do something, do it right, do it nicely. I tell my kids, the Great Spirit gave us knowledge about the right way to pick the cherries and harvest the turnips. We knew what time it was because you can tell by the sun. When the sun is straight up, it's 12 noon. Unci could even tell when it was around 4 p.m. and then we would head home. When the sun comes up, they appreciate that. I was just a little kid, and we were living in teepees, and I saw this old grandpa and he was coming out of this teepee and he was singing, and the sun was coming up. He walked over away from the tent and he had his hands up and he was singing and praying. He was greeting the sun, greeting a new day, and they were happy that they could see a new day, and that is why they were thanking the Great Spirit; they used to do that. I still do that sometimes.

Old Ways Teach Healthy Ways

I learned how to use what the Great Spirit put there for you, turnips, berries and hunting. My dad was a hunter. We didn't go to the store to buy it, the men hunted. We dried the meat in the summertime, so we could save it for the winter. **We had hot windy summers, and the Great Spirit gave us that weather so we could dry our food.** Cherries, the grandmothers pounded them and made little patties, and put them out to dry and we would save that for the pudding we would make in the winter. **Woshapee, sweet pudding, was made with dried cherries. They didn't use sugar because those cherries were so sweet; we didn't use sugar or salt, like today. I'm 92 years old and I'm not diabetic. I can eat anything I want to eat.**

Grandpa liked to hunt deer. We had deer meat and cottontails, and what I really liked was Prairie Chicken. Unci made a soup with the Prairie Chicken. It's like a wild chicken.

I like to eat meat. That's what we ate when I was growing up, but it was dried meat, and sometimes we made soup. I never questioned. Whatever they cooked for me, I ate it and was happy to get it. So, all that dried food I ate growing up, did me some good. I'm thankful that today I can still eat all those foods. I like my Lakota ways of eating and cooking.

Rabbits, you have to cook and make soup right away, but you don't dry them. You can fry or roast cottontails which are the right kind of rabbits. You have to set a small trap to catch the cottontails; they are really small. They had all sizes of traps and they had to use the right one.

At the end of the day when the sun is going down now, Papa came to Unci and he told her, "You can hear the coyotes out in the west. It's going to be stormy tomorrow," or "It's going to be nice tomorrow." They could tell the weather by the way the coyotes were yelping. The clouds above the sun, they could read the sky. They could tell you about the weather. How did they learn that? Somebody had to teach them that; they learned from one another. But from the very beginning, who taught them that? I don't know, I just wonder.

The Love of Learning and the Anticipation of Growing

I wasn't old enough to go to school, but when I was five, I got up to go to school because I really liked that schoolhouse. I would get up while everyone was still sleeping and get ready and I would go to that school. The teacher would be there because she lived downstairs in the schoolhouse. It was a nice and warm school and it was new. I just loved it! When Mama and Papa got up and they were getting ready they knew where to find me. They would come up and find me and the teacher told them I wasn't old enough to go to school. I had to be six. I had to wait till the next year, and I dreaded that. It was Christmas and the school had a little party, and all the kids had to say a speech, so the teacher made a little poem for me to say. So, they called me up and Mama and Papa and Grandpa were there. I still remember that poem even today because the teacher made it for me. It went like this:

"My teacher said I was too young to speak a piece tonight, but I said I wasn't, now which one of us is right?"

I grew up with the Catholic religion. I went away to a Catholic boarding school when I was in third to eighth grade. The priest in church introduced us to those schools, and the bus came for us, and we went from September through May. We stayed for nine months and then we came home for summer, and in the fall they sent us again. It was strict, and not like home, but I learned a lot of good things from the Sisters. They teach you to go to church, have manners, talk outside of the church. They kept a lot of silence, but that's Catholic school.

There's nobody here in this town who speaks Lakota; they speak English. But in some places, you can hear it, or on the radio station you can hear Lakota from some of the other districts, but here in Kenel nobody cares to speak it. I do, but there is no one to speak to. I wish I had someone to talk to in Lakota. Unci and Lala never spoke English, only Lakota. I listened to them and I learned. **Listen and learn. You listen and you learned it right the first time.**

I would tell kids today, the reason why you are going to school is because you want to learn, so sit there and pay attention, and you learn. You listen and you learn. If you're not paying attention or listening, then you are not learning.

I was born on the reservation, and the only time I left was for the boarding schools, then in high school I went to Fort Yates, just a few miles from here. Then I went to college in Rapid City and I took my husband and eight kids. My husband got sick and couldn't work anymore, so I went to school and got a job. I studied secretarial. I went to a studio college. The instructor worked with us individually. **Sometimes my class started at 5 a.m., and I would get ready and my husband would stay home and watch the kids, and some went to school. I had to walk nine blocks downtown. I did it. I made up my mind I was going to do it and I did it.** After I finished college, we came back, and the BIA hired me. That's where I worked. Then I moved to work for the tribe.

Why Standing Rock?

There is an incredible legend and history about the rock located in front of the Standing Rock Sioux tribal office. Years ago, a Dakota man took a second wife therefore bruising the ego of his first. As camp was breaking up and the tribe was moving on, the first wife pouted and refused to move, and stayed behind with her baby. The tribe moved on and the husband repented, sending his brothers to collect her. They returned to find that she and her child had turned to stone. From that point on the stone was thought to be holy and was moved with the tribe and always given a place of honor at the center of camp. It now rests upon a brick pedestal. It is from this stone the agency derived its name, Standing Rock.

COVID-19 Pandemic

My granddaughter was bringing me provisions, and I could not talk to her because of the pandemic. It is hard to understand COVID-19. Sometimes they say it is getting worse, and sometimes it is getting better. Some people are not taking care, not careful, not wearing the masks and washing their hands. It's hard to understand why someone would not do what they are supposed to do. You need to pray, pray a lot; everybody has got to pray. I believe in prayer; I pray a lot. I'm not extra special, but I pray. When it's cold outside, I just stay home, and I pray at home with the spiritual mass. Yes, you can pray any place.

Talking Circle

Use these questions for discussion in a talking circle or consider at least one of these questions as you respond in a journal entry.

1. Ms. Elaine talks about respecting the elders. Why is this important? How is this demonstrated in your hometown or village?

2. How was digging up turnips or picking berries an art? How did it demonstrate caring for the earth? What are some ways you have learned to respect the earth?

3. How did a love of learning contribute to Miss Elaine's success?

4. How did Ms. Elaine show persistence and grit in completing her college degree?

5. Ms. Elaine has enjoyed good health throughout life. How did the foods she ate contribute to her good health? Do you think you have a healthy diet? Are there ways you can improve?

6. How did Standing Rock get its name? What is the moral lesson from the story of Standing Rock?

7. What challenges have Native Americans faced resulting from the pandemic of 2020–21? What lessons can be learned from this experience? What changes should be made to deal with future pandemics?

College Success 1

The College Success 1 website is continually updated with supplementary material for each chapter including Word documents of the journal entries, classroom activities, handouts, videos, links to related materials, and much more. See http://www.collegesuccess1.com/.

© Lyudmyla Kharlamova/
Shutterstock.com

Notes

1. Terry Doyle and Todd Zakrajsek. The New Science of Learning (Sterling, Virginia: Stylus) 2013, 75.

2. G. A. Miller, "The Magical Number Seven, Plus or Minus Two: Some Limits on Our Capacity for Processing Information," *Psychological Review* 63 (March 1956): 81–97.

Test-Taking Checklist

Name _____ Date _____

Place checkmarks next to the test-taking skills you have now.

_____ Attend every class (or almost every class)

_____ Have a copy of the course syllabus with test dates

_____ Start test preparation early and study a little at a time

_____ Do not generally cram for exams

_____ Have a place to study (not the kitchen, TV room, or bedroom)

_____ Participate in a study group

_____ Review immediately after learning something

_____ Review previous notes and reading assignments on a regular basis

_____ Schedule a major review before the exam

_____ Know how to predict the test questions

_____ Get enough rest before a test

_____ Visualize my success on the exam

_____ Eat a light but nutritious meal before the exam

_____ Maintain a regular exercise program

_____ Read all my textbook assignments before the exam

_____ Review my classroom notes before the exam

_____ Skim through the test and read all directions carefully before starting the test

_____ Answer the easy questions first and return later to answer the difficult questions

_____ Check over my test before handing it in

_____ Write an outline before beginning my essay answer

_____ Manage my study time to adequately prepare for the test

_____ Review my returned tests to improve future test preparation

_____ Write the test neatly and make sure my writing is legible

_____ Avoid test anxiety by being well prepared and practicing relaxation techniques

_____ Prepare adequately for tests

Analyze Your Test-Taking Skills

Name _____ Date _____

Use the test-taking checklist on the previous page to answer the following questions.

1. My strengths in test-taking skills are

2. Some areas I need to improve are

3. Write three intention statements about improving your test-taking skills.

Math Success Checklist

Name _____ Date _____

Highlight or place a checkmark next to the items you regularly do in your math course.

_____ I spend about 10 hours a week or more studying for my math course.

_____ My goal is to make an A or a B on my first math test.

_____ I have confidence that I can succeed in my math course.

_____ If I don't understand something in my math course, I ask questions or get help.

_____ I take notes in my math course and review them as soon as possible after class.

_____ I write as neatly as possible in my math homework and exams.

_____ I make note cards on important information and review them frequently.

_____ I learn the definition of math terms in my class.

_____ I preview the chapter in my math text before the lecture.

_____ I practice math problems until I feel comfortable with them.

_____ I study math and do my math homework when I am most alert during the day.

_____ I make it a priority to attend all my math classes.

_____ I have a weekly study schedule for studying math.

_____ I know about some relaxation techniques I can use if I become anxious during the exam.

_____ I use practice tests to prepare for math exams.

_____ The night before math exams, I do a quick review and then get a good night's sleep.

_____ On math exams, I quickly survey the test and do the easy questions first.

_____ On math exams, I estimate the answer and see if it makes sense and is logical.

To improve my success in math, I intend to:

Practice with Short Essays

Name _____   Date _____

Your professor may ask you to do this as a classroom exercise. Review the section in the text on how to write a short essay. Answer the following short essay question worth five points.

1. Explain how you can improve your chances of success when preparing for exams. Include the physical, mental, and emotional preparation necessary for success.

2. Rate your essay. Did you do the following?

   _____   I read the directions and the essay question thoroughly before I began.

   _____   I organized my thoughts or made a brief outline before starting.

   _____   The first sentence was a direct answer and rephrased the question.

   _____   My thesis statement or main idea was clear.

   _____   The remaining sentences in the essay supported my main idea.

   _____   Since this is a five-point essay, I made at least five key points in the essay.

   _____   My answer was written clearly and neatly. My handwriting was legible.

   _____   I spelled the words correctly and used good grammar.

   _____   I read over my essay to make sure it made sense.

3. For essay exams, I need to work on

CHAPTER 9

Walking in Beauty and Harmony: Thinking Positively about the Future

Learning Objectives

Read to answer these key questions:

- How can I use positive thinking to increase my success?

- What are some strategies for positive thinking?

- What are some beliefs of successful people?

- What are some secrets to achieving happiness?

- How can I make positive changes in my life?

College students begin their college education with the dream of having a better future and achieving happiness in life. This chapter includes some tools for thinking positively about your future, analyzing what happiness means, and taking the steps to achieve happiness in your life.

Walking in Beauty is to acknowledge your inner spirit and learning to connect with all of nature and the universe, remembering to never do harm to them. When you feel capable in life and like someone who can contribute to your community, your nation, you will find balance and harmony in your world. May you walk in beauty always!

Thinking Positively about Your Career

You have assessed your personal strengths, interests, and values and are on your way to choosing a major and career that will achieve your goals and make you happy in life. It is interesting to note that thoughts about work often determine whether it is just a job, a career, or a calling that makes life interesting and fulfilling. For example, consider the parable of the bricklayers:

> Three bricklayers are asked: "What are you doing?"
> The first says, "I am laying bricks."
> The second says, "I am building a church."
> The third says, "I am building the house of God."[1]

The first bricklayer has a job, the second one has a career, and the third one approaches his job with a sense of purpose and optimism; he has a calling. Depending on your thoughts, any career can be a job, a career, or a calling. You can find your calling by thinking about your purpose and how your job makes the world a better place. Although purposes are unique, you can analyze your beliefs about any job in this way and look for greater satisfaction in what you are doing. If your current work is not a calling, find ways to change or improve it to match your personal strengths and purpose. People who have found their calling are consistently happier than those who have a job or even a career.

Photo courtesy of Navajo Technical University.

Optimism, Hope, and Future-Mindedness

You can increase your chances of success by using three powerful tools: optimism, hope, and future-mindedness. These character traits lead to achievement in athletics, academics, careers, and even politics. They also have positive mental and physical effects. They reduce anxiety and depression as well as contributing to physical well-being. In addition, they aid in problem solving and searching out resources to solve problems. A simple definition of optimism is expecting good events to happen in the future and working to make them happen. Optimism leads to continued efforts to accomplish goals, whereas pessimism leads to giving up on accomplishing goals. A person who sets no goals for the future cannot be optimistic or hopeful.

Being hopeful is another way of thinking positively about the future. Hope is the expectation that tomorrow will be better than today.[2] When you face challenges, you learn from mistakes, expect a positive outcome, and work to overcome the challenge. It is the opposite of accepting failure, expecting the worst, and giving up. In this way hope is related to the growth mindset and perseverance, or grit. One research study showed for entering college freshmen, level of hope was a better predictor of college grades than standardized tests or high school grade point average.[3] Students who have a high level of hope set higher goals and work to attain them. If they are not successful, they think about what went wrong and learn from it, or change goals and move in a new direction with a renewed sense of hope for a positive future.

Future-mindedness is thinking about the future, expecting that desired events and outcomes will occur, and then acting in a way that makes the positive outcomes come true. It involves setting goals for the future and taking action to accomplish these goals as well as being confident in accomplishing these goals. Individuals with future-mindedness are conscientious and hardworking and can delay gratification. They make to-do lists and use schedules and day planners. Individuals who are future-minded would agree with these statements:[4]

- Despite challenges, I always remain hopeful about the future.
- I always look on the bright side.
- I believe that good will always triumph over evil.
- I expect the best.
- I have a clear picture in mind about what I want to happen in the future.
- I have a plan for what I want to be doing five years from now.
- If I get a bad grade or evaluation, I focus on the next opportunity and plan to do better.

Photo courtesy of Navajo Technical University.

Believe in Yourself

Anthony Robbins defines belief as "any guiding principle, dictum, faith, or passion that can provide meaning and direction in life . . . Beliefs are the compass and maps that guide us toward our goals and give us the surety to know we'll get there."[5] The beliefs that we have about ourselves determine how much of our potential we will use and how successful we will be in the future. If we have positive beliefs about ourselves, we will feel confident and accomplish our goals in life. Negative beliefs get in the way of our success. Robbins reminds us that we can change our beliefs and choose new ones if necessary.

"Attitude is the librarian of our past, the speaker of our present and the prophet of our future."
John Maxwell

"¡Sí, se puede!" (Yes, you can!)
César Chavez

"The birth of excellence begins with our awareness that our beliefs are a choice. We usually do not think of it that way, but belief can be a conscious choice. You can choose beliefs that limit you, or you can choose beliefs that support you. The trick is to choose the beliefs that are conducive to success and the results you want and to discard the ones that hold you back."[6]

The Self-Fulfilling Prophecy

The first step in thinking positively is to examine your beliefs about yourself, your life, and the world around you. Personal beliefs are influenced by our environment, significant events that have happened in life, what we have learned in the past, and our picture of the future. Beliefs cause us to have certain expectations about the world and ourselves. These expectations are such a powerful influence on behavior that psychologists use the term "self-fulfilling prophecy" to describe what happens when our expectations come true.

For example, if I believe that I am not good in math (my expectation), I may not try to do the assignment or may avoid taking a math class (my behavior). As a result, I am not good in math. My expectations have been fulfilled. Expectations can also have a positive effect. If I believe that I am a good student, I will take steps to enroll in college and complete my assignments. I will then become a good student. The prophecy will again come true.

To think positively, it is necessary to recognize your negative beliefs and turn them into positive beliefs. Some negative beliefs commonly heard from college students include the following:

> I don't have the money for college.
> English was never my best subject.
> I was never any good at math.

When you hear yourself saying these negative thoughts, remember that these thoughts can become self-fulfilling prophecies. First of all, notice the thought. Then see if you can change the statement into a positive statement such as:

> I can find the money for college.
> English has been a challenge for me in the past, but I will do better this time.
> I can learn to be good at math.

If you believe that you can find money for college, you can go to the financial aid office and the scholarship office to begin your search for money to attend school. You can look for a better job or improve your money management. If you believe that you will do better in English, you will keep up with your assignments and go to the tutoring center or ask the professor for help. If you believe that you can learn to be good at math, you will attend every math class and seek tutoring when you do not understand. Your positive thoughts will help you to be successful.

> "If I believe I cannot do something, it makes me incapable of doing it. But when I believe I can, then I acquire the ability to do it, even if I did not have the ability in the beginning."
> Mahatma Gandhi

> "Human beings can alter their lives by altering their attitude of mind."
> William James

Photo courtesy of Navajo Technical University.

Positive Self-Talk and Affirmations

Self-talk refers to the silent inner voice in our heads. This voice is often negative, especially when we are frustrated or trying to learn something new. Have you ever had thoughts about yourself that are similar to these:

> How could you be so stupid!
> That was dumb!
> You idiot!

What do you say to yourself when you are angry or frustrated? Write several examples of your negative self-talk.

Negative thoughts can actually be toxic to your body. They can cause biochemical changes that can lead to depression and negatively affect the immune system.[7] Negative self-talk causes anxiety and poor performance and is damaging to self-esteem. It can also lead to a negative self-fulfilling prophecy. Positive thoughts can help us build self-esteem, become confident in our abilities, and achieve our goals. These positive thoughts are called affirmations.

If we make the world with our thoughts, it is important to become aware of the thoughts about ourselves that are continuously running through our heads. Are your thoughts positive or negative? Negative thoughts lead to failure. What we hear over and over again shapes our beliefs. If you say over and over to yourself such things as, "I am stupid," "I am ugly," or "I am fat," you will start to believe these things and act in a way that supports your beliefs. Positive thoughts help to build success. If you say to yourself, "I'm a good person," "I'm doing my best," or "I'm doing fine," you will begin to believe these things about yourself and act in a way that supports these beliefs. Here are some guidelines for increasing your positive self-talk and making affirmations:

> "We are what we think. All that we are arises With our thoughts. With our thoughts we make the world."
>
> Buddha

1. Monitor your thoughts about yourself and become aware of them. Are they positive or negative?

2. When you notice a negative thought about yourself, imagine creating a new video with a positive message.

3. Start the positive message with "I" and use the present tense. Using an "I" statement shows you are in charge. Using the present tense shows you are ready for action now.

> "The most common way people give up their power is by thinking they don't have any."
>
> Alice Walker

4. Focus on the positive. Think about what you want to achieve and what you can do rather than what you do not want to do. For example, instead of saying, "I will not eat junk food," say, "I will eat a healthy diet."

5. Make your affirmation stronger by adding an emotion to it.

6. Form a mental picture of what it is that you want to achieve. See yourself doing it successfully.

7. You may need to say the positive thoughts over and over again until you believe them and they become a habit. You can also write them down and put them in a place where you will see them often.

Here are some examples of negative self-talk and contrasting positive affirmations:

Negative: I'm always broke.

Affirmation: I feel really good when I manage my finances. See yourself taking steps to manage finances. For example, a budget or savings plan.

Negative: I'm too fat. It just runs in the family.

Affirmation: I feel good about myself when I exercise and eat a healthy diet. See yourself exercising and eating a healthy diet.

Negative:	I can't do this. I must be stupid.
Affirmation:	I can do this. I am capable. I feel a sense of accomplishment when I accomplish something challenging. See yourself making your best attempt and taking the first step to accomplish the project.

ACTIVITY

Select one example of negative self-talk that you wrote earlier. Use the examples above to turn your negative message into a positive one and write it here.

Journal Entry #1

Write five positive statements about your future.

© Sergey Nivens/Shutterstock.com

Visualize Your Success

Visualization is a powerful tool for using your brain to improve memory, deal with stress, and think positively. Coaches and athletes study sports psychology to learn how to use visualization along with physical practice to improve athletic performance. College students can use the same techniques to enhance college success.

If you are familiar with sports or are an athlete, you can probably think of times when your coach asked you to use visualization to improve your performance. In baseball, the coach reminds players to keep their eye on the ball and visualize hitting it. In swimming, the coach asks swimmers to visualize reaching their arms out to touch the edge of the pool at the end of the race. Pole-vaulters visualize clearing the pole and sometimes even go through the motions before making the jump. Using imagery lets you practice for future events and pre-experience achieving your goals. Athletes imagine winning the race or completing the perfect jump in figure skating. In this way they prepare mentally and physically and develop confidence in their abilities. It still takes practice to excel.

"The future first exists in imagination, then planning, then reality."
R.A. Wilson

Just as the athlete visualizes and then performs, the college student can do the same. It is said that we create all things twice. First we make a mental picture, and then we create the physical reality by taking action. For example, if we are building a house, first we get the idea; then we begin to design the house we want. We start with a blueprint and then build the house. The blueprint determines what kind of house we construct. The same thing happens in any project we undertake. First we have a mental picture, and then we complete the project. Visualize what you would like to accomplish in your life as if you were creating a blueprint. Then take the steps to accomplish what you want.

As a college student, you might visualize yourself in your graduation robe walking across the stage to receive your diploma. You might visualize yourself in the exam room confidently taking the exam. You might see yourself on the job enjoying your future career. You can make a mental picture of what you would like your life to be and then work toward accomplishing your goal.

Successful Beliefs

Stephen Covey's book *The 7 Habits of Highly Effective People* has been described as one of the most influential books of the 20th century.[8] In 2004, he released a new book called *The 8th Habit: From Effectiveness to Greatness.*[9] These habits are based on beliefs that lead to success.

1. **Be proactive.** Being proactive means accepting responsibility for your life. Covey uses the word "response-ability" for the ability to choose responses. The quality of your life is based on the decisions and responses that you make. Proactive people make things happen through responsibility and initiative. They do not blame circumstances or conditions for their behavior.

2. **Begin with the end in mind.** Know what is important and what you wish to accomplish in your life. To be able to do this, you will need to know your values and goals in life. You will need a clear vision of what you want your life to be and where you are headed.

3. **Put first things first.** Once you have established your goals and vision for the future, you will need to manage yourself to do what is important first. Set priorities so that you can accomplish the tasks that are important to you.

4. **Think win-win.** In human interactions, seek solutions that benefit everyone. Focus on cooperation rather than competition. If everyone feels good about the decision, there is cooperation and harmony. If one person wins and the other loses, the loser becomes angry and resentful and sabotages the outcome.

5. **First seek to understand, then to be understood.** Too often in our personal communications, we try to talk first and listen later. Often we don't really listen: we use this time to think of our reply. It is best to listen and understand before speaking. Effective communication is one of the most important skills in life.

6. **Synergize.** A simple definition of synergy is that the whole is greater than the sum of its parts. If people can cooperate and have good communication, they can work together as a team to accomplish more than each individual could do separately. Synergy is also part of the creative process.

7. **Sharpen the saw.** Covey shares the story of a man who was trying to cut down a tree with a dull saw. As he struggled to cut the tree, someone suggested that he stop and sharpen the saw. The man said that he did not have time to sharpen the saw, so he continued to struggle. Covey suggests that we need to take time to stop and sharpen the saw. We need to stop working and invest some time in ourselves by staying healthy physically, mentally, spiritually, and socially. We need to take time for self-renewal.

8. **Find your voice, and inspire others to find theirs.** Believe that you can make a positive difference in the world and inspire others to do the same. Covey says that leaders "deal with people in a way that will communicate to them their worth and potential so clearly that they will come to see it in themselves." Accomplishing this ideal begins with developing one's own voice or "unique personal significance."[10]

Successful Beliefs

- Be proactive
- Begin with the end in mind
- Put first things first
- Think win-win
- First seek to understand, then to be understood
- Synergize
- Sharpen the saw
- Find your voice, and inspire others to find theirs

Journal Entry #2

List five beliefs that will help you to be successful in the future.

Positive Thinking

Test what you have learned by selecting the correct answers to the following questions.

1. The self-fulfilling prophecy refers to

   a. the power of belief in determining your future.
   b. good fortune in the future.
   c. being able to foretell the future.

2. Positive self-talk results in

   a. lower self-esteem.
   b. overconfidence.
   c. higher self-esteem.

3. The statement "We create all things twice" refers to

   a. doing the task twice to make sure it is done right.
   b. creating and refining.
   c. first making a mental picture and then taking action.

4. A win-win solution means

   a. winning at any cost.
   b. seeking a solution that benefits everyone.
   c. focusing on competition.

5. The statement by Stephen Covey, "Sharpen the saw," refers to

   a. proper tool maintenance.
   b. studying hard to sharpen thinking skills.
   c. investing time to maintain physical and mental health.

How did you do on the quiz? Check your answers: 1. a, 2. c, 3. c, 4. b, 5. c

Secrets to Happiness

"Most folks are about as happy as they make up their minds to be."
Abraham Lincoln

Checklist for Achieving Happiness

- Express gratitude.
- Be an optimist.
- Think positively.
- Use your personal strengths.
- Practice kindness.
- Increase flow activities.
- Savor life's joys.
- Accomplish your goals.
- Take care of your body.

Many of you probably have happiness on your list of lifetime goals. It sounds easy, right? But what is happiness, anyway?

Psychologist Martin Seligman says that real happiness comes from identifying, cultivating, and using your personal strengths in work, love, play, and parenting.[11] You have identified these strengths by learning about your personality type, multiple intelligences, interests, and values.

It means living the good life in the present and increasing your longevity. These factors are associated with happiness: expressing gratitude, being optimistic, being employed, having positive self-esteem, enjoying leisure activity, having good health, and enjoying friendships.[12] Happy individuals have better marriages, friendships, and mental health. They have better work performance, and higher levels of employment and income.

Seligman contrasts authentic happiness with hedonism. He states that a hedonist "wants as many good moments and as few bad moments as possible in life."[13] Hedonism is a shortcut to happiness that leaves us feeling empty. For example, we often assume that more material possessions will make us happy. However, the more material possessions we have, the greater the expectations, and we no longer appreciate what we have.

Most people assume that happiness is increased by having more money to buy that new car or HDTV. However, a process called hedonistic adaptation occurs that makes this type of happiness short-lived. Once you have purchased the new car or TV, you get used to it quickly. Soon you will start to think about a better car and a bigger TV to continue to feel happy. Seligman provides a formula for happiness:[14]

$$Happiness = S + C + V$$

In the formula *S* stands for set range. Psychologists believe that 50 percent of happiness is determined by heredity. In other words, half of your level of happiness is determined by the genes inherited from your ancestors. In good times or bad times, people generally return to their set range of happiness. Six months after receiving a piece of good fortune such as a raise or promotion or winning the lottery, unhappy people are still unhappy. Six months after a tragedy, naturally happy people return to being happy.

The letter *C* in the equation stands for circumstances such as money, marriage, social life, health, education, climate, race, gender, and religion. These circumstances account for 8 to 15 percent of happiness. Here is what psychologists know about how these circumstances affect happiness:

- Once basic needs are met, greater wealth does not increase happiness.
- Having a good marriage is related to increased happiness.
- Happy people are more social.
- Moderate ill health does not bring unhappiness, but severe illness does.
- Educated people are slightly happier.
- Climate, race, and gender do not affect level of happiness.
- Religious people are somewhat happier than nonreligious people.

The letter *V* in the equation stands for factors under your voluntary control. These factors account for approximately 40 percent of happiness. Factors under voluntary control include positive emotions and optimism about the future. Positive emotions include hope, faith, trust, joy, ecstasy, calm, zest, ebullience, pleasure, flow, satisfaction, contentment, fulfillment, pride, and serenity. Seligman suggests the following ideas to increase your positive emotions:

- Realize that the past does not determine your future. The future is open to new possibilities.
- Be grateful for the good events of the past and place less emphasis on the bad events.
- Build positive emotions through forgiving and forgetting.
- Work on increasing optimism and hope for the future.
- Find out what activities make you happy and engage in them. Spread these activities out over time so that you will not get tired of them.
- Take the time to savor the happy times. Make mental photographs of happy times so that you can think of them later.

"Success is getting what you want; happiness is wanting what you get."
Dale Carnegie

"Happiness is not something ready made. It comes from your own actions."
Dalai Lama

- Take time to enjoy the present moment.
- Build more flow into your life. Flow is the state of gratification we feel when totally absorbed in an activity that matches our strengths.

Are you interested in taking steps to increase your happiness? Here are some activities proposed by Sonya Lyubomirsky, a leading researcher on happiness and author of *The How of Happiness*.[15] Choose the ones that seem like a natural fit for you and vary them so that they do not become routine or boring. After putting in some effort to practice these activities, they can become a habit.

1. **Express gratitude.** Expressing gratitude is a way of thinking positively and appreciating good circumstances rather than focusing on the bad ones. It is about appreciating and thanking the people who have made positive contributions to your life. It is feeling grateful for the good things you have in life. Create a gratitude journal and at the end of each day write down things for which you are grateful or thankful. Regularly tell those around you how grateful you are to have them in your life. You can do this in person, by phone, in a letter, or by email. Being grateful helps us to savor positive life experiences.

2. **Cultivate optimism.** Make a habit of looking at the bright side of life. If you think positively about the future, you are more likely to take the effort to reach your goals in life. Spend some time thinking or writing about your best possible future. Make a mental picture of your future goals as a first step toward achieving them. Thinking positively boosts your mood and promotes high morale. Most importantly, thinking positively can become a self-fulfilling prophecy. If you see your positive goals as attainable, you are more likely to work toward accomplishing them and invest the energy needed to deal with obstacles and setbacks along the way.

3. **Avoid overthinking and social comparison.** Overthinking is focusing on yourself and your problems endlessly, needlessly, and excessively. Examples of overthinking include "Why am I so unhappy?" "Why is life so unfair?" and "Why did he/she say that?" Overthinking increases sadness, fosters biased thinking, decreases motivation, and makes it difficult to solve problems and take action to make life better.

   Social comparison is a type of overthinking. In our daily lives, we encounter people who are more intelligent, beautiful, richer, healthier, or happier. The media fosters images of people with impossibly perfect lives. Making social comparisons can lead to feelings of inferiority and loss of self-esteem.

   Notice when your are overthinking or making comparisons with others and stop doing it. Use the "Yell, 'Stop!'" technique to refocus your attention. This technique involves yelling, "Stop!" to yourself or out loud to change your thinking. Another way to stop overthinking is to distract yourself with more positive thoughts or activities. Watch a funny movie, listen to music, or arrange a social activity with a friend. If these activities are not effective, try writing down your worries in a journal. Writing helps to organize thoughts and to make sense of them. Begin to take some small steps to resolve your worries and problems.

4. **Practice acts of kindness.** Doing something kind for others increases your own personal happiness and satisfies your basic need for human connection. Opportunities for helping others surround us each day. How about being courteous on the freeway, helping a child with homework, or helping your elderly neighbor with yard work? A simple act of kindness makes you feel good and often sets off a chain of events in which the person who receives the kindness does something kind for someone else.

5. **Increase flow activities.** Flow is defined as intense involvement in an activity so that you do not notice the passage of time. Musicians are in the flow when they are totally involved in their music. Athletes are in the flow when they are totally focused on their sport. Writers are in the flow when they are totally absorbed in writing down their

"Finish each day and be done with it. You have done what you could; some blunders and absurdities have crept in; forget them as soon as you can. Tomorrow is a new day; you shall begin it serenely and with too high a spirit to be encumbered with your old nonsense."
Ralph Waldo Emerson

ideas. The key to achieving flow is balancing skills and challenges. If your skills are not sufficient for the activity, you will become frustrated. If your skills are greater than what is demanded for the activity, you will become bored. Work often provides an opportunity to experience flow if you are in a situation in which your work activities are matched to your skills and talents.

As our skills increase, it becomes more difficult to maintain flow. We must be continually testing ourselves in ever more challenging activities to maintain flow. You can take some action to increase the flow in your life by learning to fully focus your attention on the activity you are doing. It is important to be open to new and different experiences. To maintain the flow in your life, make a commitment to lifelong learning.

6. **Savor life's joys.** Savoring is the repetitive replaying of the positive experiences in life and is one of the most important ingredients of happiness. Savoring happens in the past, present, and future. Think often about the good things that have happened in the past. Savor the present by relishing the present moment. Savor the future by anticipating and visualizing positive events or outcomes in the future.

There are many ways to savor life's joys. Replay in your mind happy days or events from the past. Create a photo album of your favorite people, places, and events and look at it often. This prolongs the happiness. Take a few minutes each day to appreciate ordinary activities such as taking a shower or walking to work. Engage the senses to notice your environment. Is it a sunny day? Take some time to look at the sky, the trees, and the plants. Landscape architects incorporate artwork, trees, and flowers along the freeways to help drivers to relax on the road. Notice art and objects of beauty. Be attentive to the present moment and be aware of your surroundings. Picture in your mind positive events you anticipate in the future. All of these activities will increase your "psychological bank account" of happy times and will help deal with times that are not so happy.

> "Happiness consists more in small conveniences or pleasures that occur every day, than in great pieces of good fortune that happen but seldom."
> Benjamin Franklin

7. **Commit to accomplishing your goals.** Working toward a meaningful life goal is one of the most important things that you can do to have a happy life. Goals provide structure and meaning to our lives and improve self-esteem. Working on goals provides something to look forward to in the future.

The types of goals that you pursue have an impact on your happiness. The goals that have the most potential for long-term happiness involve changing your activities rather than changing your circumstances. Examples of goals that change your circumstances are moving to the beach or buying a new stereo. These goals make you happy for a short time. Then you get used to your new circumstances and no longer feel as happy as when you made the initial change. Examples of goals that change your activities are returning to school or taking up a new sport or hobby. These activities allow you to take on new challenges that keep life interesting for a longer period of time. Choose intrinsic goals that help you to develop your competence and autonomy. These goals should match your most important values and interests.

> "An aim in life is the only fortune worth finding."
> Robert Louis Stevenson

8. **Take care of your body.** Engaging in physical activity provides many opportunities for increasing happiness. Physical activity helps to:
   * Increase longevity and improve the quality of life.
   * Improve sleep and protect the body from disease.
   * Keep brains healthy and avoid cognitive impairments.
   * Increase self-esteem.
   * Increase the opportunity to engage in flow.
   * Provide a distraction from worries and overthinking.

© Efired/Shutterstock.com

9. Take the time to think about the good things in your life. As an exercise, at the end of each day, pause to think about the good things that happened.

Journal Entry #3

Psychologists Martin Seligman and Sonya Lyubomirsky write about the secrets to happiness. List five of their ideas and tell whether you agree or disagree with them.

Just as you have made a decision to get a college degree, make a decision to be happy. Make a decision to be happy by altering your internal outlook and choosing to change your behavior. Here are some suggestions for consciously choosing happiness.

1. Find small things that make you happy and sprinkle your life with them. A glorious sunset, a pat on the back, a well-manicured yard, an unexpected gift, a round of tennis, a favorite sandwich, a fishing line cast on a quiet lake, the wagging tail of the family dog, or your child finally taking some responsibility—these are things that will help to create a continual climate of happiness.

2. Smile and stand up straight; unhappy people tend to slouch as they walk.[16]

3. Learn to think like an optimist. "Pessimists tend to complain; optimists focus on solving their problems."[17] Never use the word "try"; this word is for pessimists. Assume you will succeed.

4. Replace negative thoughts with positive ones.

5. Fill your life with things you like to do.

6. Get enough rest. If you do not get enough sleep, you will feel tired and gloomy. Sleep deprivation can lead to depression.

7. Learn from your elders. Psychologist Daniel Mroczek says that "people in their sixties and seventies who are in good health are among the happiest people in our society. . . . They may be better able to regulate their emotions, they've developed perspective, they don't get so worried about little things, and they've often achieved their goals and aren't trying to prove themselves."[18]

8. Reduce stress.

9. Take charge of your time by doing first things first.

10. Close relationships are important. Myers and Mroczek report higher levels of happiness among married men and women.[19]

11. Keep things in perspective. Will it matter in six months to a year?

12. Laugh more. Laughter produces a relaxation response.

Journal Entry #4

Write five intention statements about increasing your future happiness.
I intend to . . .

QUIZ

Secrets to Happiness

Test what you have learned by selecting the correct answers to the following questions.

1. Psychologist Martin Seligman says that real happiness comes from:

   a. having enough money to buy the things you want.
   b. identifying, cultivating, and using your personal strengths in work, love, play, and parenting.
   c. your circumstances in life.

2. You can increase happiness by:

   a. expressing gratitude.
   b. being realistic.
   c. comparing yourself with other successful people.

3. Psychologists have found that this factor increases happiness:

   a. great wealth.
   b. living in a good climate.
   c. being educated.

4. About 40% of happiness is due to:

   a. factors under your voluntary control such as positive emotions and optimism.
   b. your circumstances in life such as money, marriage, and climate.
   c. the career you choose.

5. The key to intense involvement or "flow" are activities that:

   a. exceed your skills.
   b. are easy.
   c. balance skills and challenges.

How did you do on the quiz: Check your answers: 1. b, 2. a, 3. c, 4. a, 5. c

---

Making Positive Changes in Your Life

You are probably aware of the importance of implementing many of the ideas in this textbook. However, actually making some positive changes is difficult. Dr. James Prochaska has studied the process of change and identifies the six stages of change.[20]

1. **Precontemplation**

   In this stage, a person denies that there is a problem and is not ready to change. If the habit causes difficulties, the person may blame the problems on others, especially those who are pressuring them to change. There are two ways to move out of this stage. One way is through increasing awareness or knowledge about the problem. Another way to move past this stage is through emotional arousal. For example, although friends and family have noticed that you spend too much time online, you deny it. You see a video on Internet addiction and begin to wonder if time spent online is interfering with the accomplishment of personal goals.

2. **Contemplation**

   In this stage, a person begins to become aware of a problem and begins to think seriously about taking some action. In this stage, people weigh the pros and cons and the benefits and sacrifices. They think about the difficulty of change. People can only move to the next stage when they develop the self-confidence to believe that they can make a change. Continuing our example of Internet addiction, at this stage, a person would begin to look at the negative consequences of spending too much time online but would consider change difficult.

3. **Preparation**

   During this stage, individuals develop a strategy for change. They realize that change is necessary, and they desire to make the change. They discuss the change with friends and find the needed resources to make the change. They set an actual date to take action. In our Internet example, a person would begin talking with friends and family about the issue and would make a plan for spending a reasonable amount of time online.

4. **Action**

   This is the "just do it" stage. Without action, the goal cannot be accomplished. This stage requires some commitment. A person would take steps to reduce time spent online, such as putting the phone away, turning off notifications, and limiting time online.

5. **Maintenance**

   Once you have reached your goal, maintenance is the next step. This stage is the most difficult one, in which people struggle with returning to old patterns. Once a person has limited the time spent online, the real test is maintaining the behavior.

6. **Termination**

   This is permanent change. It is a time when temptations stop. Many people will find it difficult to reach this stage, and temptations will always exist. Limiting the time spent online becomes a habit, although temptations can reoccur.

What is important to realize about Prochaska's model is that change is a process and that there will be slip-ups along the way. His research shows that successful changers will experience some failures along the way. However, he suggests that action that fails is better than no action at all. His research showed that those who tried to act and failed were more likely to succeed in the future. In one study of two hundred people who made New Year's resolutions and were still keeping them two years later, they had an average of fourteen lapses before they were successful in keeping their resolutions.

Setbacks in the process of change are natural, and it is important not to give up. The process of change is difficult but rewarding when you can follow through. When you are successful, you gain confidence in your ability to make additional positive changes.

Journal Entry #5

What is one behavior you would like to change to increase success and happiness in your life? Using the model just outlined, what are some beginning steps to making this change?

KEYS TO SUCCESS

You Are What You Think

"Whether you think you can, or think you can't . . . you're right." Henry Ford

© iQoncept/Shutterstock.com

Sometimes students enter college with the fear of failure. This belief leads to anxiety and behavior that leads to failure. If you have doubts about your ability to succeed in college, you might not go to class or attempt the challenging work required in college. It is difficult to make the effort if you cannot see positive results ahead. Unfortunately, failure in college can lead to a loss of confidence and lack of success in other areas of life as well.

Henry Ford said, "What we believe is true, comes true. What we believe is possible, becomes possible." If you believe that you will succeed, you will be more likely to take actions that lead to your success. Once you have experienced some small part of success, you will have confidence in your abilities and will continue on the road to success. Success leads to more success. It becomes a habit. You will be motivated to make the effort necessary to accomplish your goals. You might even become excited and energized along the way. You will use your gifts and talents to reach your potential and achieve happiness. It all begins with the thoughts you choose.

"Watch your thoughts; they become words.
Watch your words; they become actions.
Watch your actions; they become habits.
Watch your habits; they become character.
Watch your character; it becomes your destiny."[21]

—*Frank Outlaw*

To help you choose positive beliefs, picture in your mind how you want your life to be. Imagine it is here now. See all the details and experience the feelings associated with this picture. Pretend it is true until you believe it. Then take action to make your dreams come true.

Stories from the Elders

We are now at the end of the book and at the gateway to your future college and career success. This chapter has provided you with a foundation for choosing happiness and creating positivity in your life. As the chapter states, "You are what you think."

One of the main goals of this course and this book is to help you understand the demands and responsibilities placed upon college students. If you are one of the first in your family to attend college, or if you have lived a rural life and are now attending college in a city, you will have to develop a strategy for your own personal success. We talked to some of the experts and asked them for suggestions to help you be successful in college.

Ms. Carmen Moffett, Director of Indian Education for the Gallup-McKinley County Schools recently said that most Native American college students need to build English and math skills for college success. She added, "Native American students need support programs that will help them develop skills such as writing and building a social support network at the college." Ms. Moffet explains that the world of higher education can create "culture shock" for students who are living far from home, off the reservation, and interfacing with students from different tribes and cultures. Ms. Moffet also stated, "In most tribal communities, education and health offer the highest number of employment and highest paying positions. Generally, these high paying positions are held by non-Native Americans. We need more Native Americans to hold these positions, which often require education beyond a bachelor's degree. If Native American communities had more Native Americans is these positions, Native American communities would benefit." Ms. Moffet went on to quote Navajo Chief Manuelito, "go my son, go and climb the ladder…Get an education."

Dr. Mario Aguilar, Assistant Director of the Early Academic Outreach Program at UCSD and a San Diego State University lecturer in the College of Education states that "Native American students face great challenges that students from other communities never have to think about. An example is the Hollywood and mass media stereotypical portrayal that we are either "noble savages" living in peace and harmony with nature (and thus incapable of being engineers, doctors, lawyers, or state governors,) or we are "wild savages" who cannot escape alcoholism, drugs, or violence (and therefore cannot possibly be successful in college)." Dr. Aguilar goes on to state, "We are all part of a historic chain of experience that goes back thousands of generations. We know where we come from, we know where our ancestors are buried, and we need to know where our future generations will come from. We cannot become the weakest link in this chain; we need to be that strong and educated link, so that in the future there will be those to speak for our tribes."

Larry Gauthier, Director of Student Success Services at the First Nations University in Regina, Canada, also offered some suggestions. As part of their culture, Native Americans are taught not to ask questions. Students need to develop the skills of critical thinking and asking questions to be successful in college. If students lack confidence in their educational skills, they should attend a tribal college first to gain the skills needed for success and then transfer to a mainstream college to complete their degree. Larry likes to use the phrase, "education is our buffalo." In the past, the buffalo gave us everything we needed to exist. Now that the buffalo is gone, education has taken its place. It will give you the tools you need to be good providers for your families and also help with self-determination and self-government.

We have exposed you to many ideas in this book that we believe will help you be a successful college student and a contributing member of our world. Through the great tradition of storytelling, we have tried to connect Native-American history, spirituality, and philosophies to fundamental concepts related to college success. Read this story with intentionality about your college and life success.

Coyote Creates the Earth

This story was written by Larry Gauthier based on story from his great grandfather, Kem ma soom bun, an elder of the Woodland Cree.

© J Hindman/Shutterstock.com

Long ago there was no earth, only water. Coyote was floating around on a small raft when he met the ducks. They were the only other creatures. "My brothers," he said, "There is no one else around. It is no good to be alone like this. You must get me some earth so I can make things right."

He turned to the red-headed mallard. "Dive beneath this water and try to bring up some earth. We'll use it as a means of living."

The red-headed mallard dove into the water. He remained down for a long time but came up without bringing any earth.

Coyote turned to the pinto duck, "I sent the older one, but he was not able to get any earth. Now I will let you try."

The pinto duck came up after a long time and said, "My brother, I was not able to get any."

"How is that? I thought surely you would bring some."

Then Coyote asked a smaller, blue-feathered duck to dive. "If you do not bring up any, we will have no land to live on."

He dived down, but he came up with no earth. Coyote did not know what to do.

Then the grebe spoke up. "My older brother, you should have asked me to go before you asked these others. They are my superiors, but they are helpless." He took his turn diving and stayed down a long time. When he came up, Coyote asked, "What sort of luck did you have?"

"I have brought some." He had a little dirt between his webbed feet.

Coyote said, "To every undertaking there are always four trials. You have achieved it." Then he took the mud and said, "I will make this into the earth. You will live in the ponds and streams and multiply there where you can build your nests. Now, I am going to make this earth."

Coyote took the mud in his hand and he started in the east. "I will make it large so we have plenty of room." As he traveled along he spread the mud around and made the earth. He traveled like this for a long time going toward the west. When he had finished he said, "Now that we have this earth, there are some things that want to be here."

They heard a wolf howling.

"Already there is one howling," said Coyote.

He pointed toward the Sun, which was going down, and said, "Listen, there is another one out there now." It was a coyote. "That coyote has attained life by his own powers," said Coyote. "He is great."

Then they all went for a walk. Out on the plains they saw some shining objects. When they got up close they saw that these were medicine stones.

"This is part of the earth," said Coyote, picking up one of the stones which looked like a buffalo, "the oldest part. There shall be stones like this everywhere. They are separate beings."

When they had gone on some ways, they saw a person standing near a hill.

"Look," said Coyote, "there is a human being. He is one of the Stars, but now he is down here standing on the ground. Let's go look at him."

When they got up close, the star-person changed himself into a plant. It was the tobacco plant. There were no other plants around at the time. It was the first. Coyote said, "From now on all people will have this plant. Take it in the spring and raise it. It is the Stars up above that have come down like this. They will take care of the people. Take care of this plant. It will be the means of your living. Use it in dancing."

After that, Coyote found there was no grass. "This is no good." He made it. "Let us make some mountains, hills, and trees." He made them all.

He saw there were no fish in the creeks, so he put some there. This is the way he started the whole thing.

> "Like the Thunderbird of old I shall rise again out of the sea; I shall grab the instruments of the white man's success, his education, his skills, and with these new tools I shall build my race into the proudest segment of your society."
>
> Chief Dan George

Talking Circle

Use these questions for discussion in a talking circle or consider at least one of these questions as you respond in a journal entry:

1. Coyote created the world. He saw what was needed and he made it. What do you see that is needed in your world? How will you create that which you need in your life?

2. The story talks about the interconnectedness of all things, living and nonliving. But all things are important and have a place and a contribution to the earth and to the universe. Even the small grebe, who saw himself as inferior to the others, was able to make a huge contribution to the creation of the world. Sometimes, we all have felt like a small grebe, but we go on and with perseverance and commitment, we accomplish things. Have you thought about the contributions you wish to make to the world? What are your top three contributions you would like to accomplish?

3. Coyote asked several creatures for help in bringing up some earth with no results. Just when he was wondering what to do, the grebe, his older brother, offered to help and was successful. Is there someone who can help you if you feel like giving up?

4. In the story, the human being was once a Star in the universe, then came to earth as a human, and changed himself into a tobacco plant to be used in ceremonies and in dancing. The human intentionally transformed himself into a useful medicine. How will you intentionally change yourself while you are in college? How will your college education transform your life and your tribal or community world?

5. The concept of four is large in many Native American cultures. The four directions, four colors, four rounds of songs, four years of commitment to a sun dance ceremony, and so on. In this story, Coyote talks about four trials for every undertaking. Can you name four trials or obstacles you have had to overcome since you entered college? How does the concept of perseverance relate to the four trials for every undertaking?

"You become what you believe."
Oprah Winfrey

© Lyudmyla Kharlamova/ Shutterstock.com

College Success 1

The College Success 1 website is continually updated with supplementary material for each chapter including Word documents of the journal entries, classroom activities, handouts, videos, links to related materials, and much more. See http://www.collegesuccess1.com/.

Notes

1. Angela Duckworth, Grit: The Power of Passion and Perseverance (New York: Scribner, 2016), 149.

2. Ibid., 169.

3. Daniel Goleman, "Hope Emerges as a Key to Success in Life," *New York Times*, December 24, 1991.

4. Peterson and Seligman, *Character Strengths and Virtues*, 570. Goleman "Hope Emerges as a Key to Success in Life."

5. Anthony Robbins, Unlimited Power (New York:Fawcett Columbine, 1986), 54–55.

6. Ibid., 54–55.

7. Joan Smith, "Nineteen Habits of Happy Women," *Redbook Magazine*, August 1999, 68.

8. Stephen R. Covey, *The 7 Habits of Highly Effective People* (New York: Simon and Schuster, 1989).

9. Stephen R. Covey, *The 8th Habit: From Effectiveness to Greatness* (New York: Free Press, 2004).

10. Ibid.

11. Christopher Peterson, A Primer in Positive Psychology (Oxford: University Press, 2006), 92.

12. Martin Seligman, Authentic Happiness: Using the New Positive Psychology to Realize Your Potential for Lasting Fulfillment (New York: The Penguin Press, 2008).

13. Ibid., 6.

14. Ibid., 45.

15. Sonya Lyubomirsky, *The How of Happiness* (New York: The Penguin Press, 2008).

16. Ibid.

17. Ibid.

18. Ibid.

19. Ibid.

20. "Prochaska and DiClemente's Transtheoretical Model of Change," Exploring Your Mind, April 21, 2018, https://exploringyourmind.com/prochaska-diclementes-transtheoretical-model-of-change/.

21. Rob Gilbert, ed., *Bits and Pieces* (Fairfield, NJ: The Economics Press), Vol. R, No. 40, p. 7, copyright 1998.

Measure Your Success

Name _____ Date _____

Now that you have finished the text, complete the following assessment to measure your improvement. Compare your results to the assessment taken at the beginning of class.

Read the following statements and rate how true they are for you at the present time.

5 Definitely true
4 Mostly true
3 Somewhat true
2 Seldom true
1 Never true

© Kenishirotie/Shutterstock.com

_____ I am motivated to be successful in college.

_____ I know the value of a college education.

_____ I know how to establish successful patterns of behavior.

_____ I avoid multi-tasking while studying.

_____ I am attending college to accomplish my own personal goals.

_____ I believe to a great extent that my actions determine my future.

_____ I am persistent in achieving my goals.

_____ **Total points for Motivation**

_____ I understand the steps in making a good decision about a major and career.

_____ I can describe my personality type and matching careers.

_____ I can describe my personal strengths and matching careers.

_____ I can list my vocational interests and matching careers.

_____ I can list my five most important values and tell how they are useful in deciding on a career

_____ I understand career outlook and what careers will be in demand in the future.

_____ **Total Points for Choosing a Major**

_____ I have a list or mental picture of my lifetime goals.

_____ I know what I would like to accomplish in the next four years.

_____ I spend my time on activities that help me accomplish my lifetime goals.

_____ I effectively use priorities in managing my time.

_____ I can balance study, work, recreation, and time spent on technology.

_____ I generally avoid procrastination on important tasks.

_____ I am good at managing my money.

_____ **Total points for Managing Time and Money**

_____ I understand the difference between short-term and long-term memory.

_____ I use effective study techniques for storing information in long-term memory.

_____ I can apply memory techniques to remember what I am studying.

_____ I know how to minimize forgetting.

_____ I know how to use mnemonics and other memory tricks.

_____ I know how to keep my brain healthy throughout life.

_____ I use positive thinking to be successful in my studies.

_____ **Total points for Brain Science and Memory**

_____ I understand the latest findings in brain science and can apply them to studying.

_____ I use a reading study system based on memory strategies.

_____ I am familiar with e-learning strategies for reading and learning online.

_____ I know how to effectively mark my textbook.

_____ I understand how math is different from studying other subjects.

_____ I have the math study skills needed to be successful in my math courses.

_____ I take responsibility for my own success in college and in life.

_____ **Total points for Brain Science and Study Skills**

_____ I know how to listen for the main points in a college lecture.

_____ I am familiar with note-taking systems for college lectures.

_____ I know how to review my lecture notes.

_____ I feel comfortable with writing.

_____ I know the steps in writing a college term paper.

_____ I know how to prepare a speech.

_____ I am comfortable with public speaking.

_____ **Total points for Taking Notes, Writing, and Speaking**

_____ I know how to adequately prepare for a test.

_____ I can predict the questions that are likely to be on the test.

_____ I know how to deal with test anxiety.

_____ I am successful on math exams.

_____ I know how to make a reasonable guess if I am uncertain about the answer.

_____ I am confident of my ability to take objective tests.

_____ I can write a good essay answer.

_____ **Total points for Test Taking**

_____ I expect good things to happen in the future and work to make them happen.

_____ Despite challenges, I always remain hopeful about the future.

_____ I have self-confidence.

_____ I use positive self-talk and affirmations.

_____ I have a visual picture of my future success.

_____ I have a clear idea of what happiness means to me.

_____ I usually practice positive thinking.

_____ **Total points for Future**

_____ I am confident of my ability to succeed in college.

_____ I am confident of my ability to succeed in my career.

_____ **Total additional points**

Total your points:

_____ Motivation

_____ Personality and Major

_____ Managing Time and Money

_____ Brain Science and Memory

_____ Brain Science and Study Skills

_____ Taking Notes, Writing, and Speaking

_____ Test Taking

_____ Future

_____ Additional Points

_____ **Grand total points**

If you scored

290–261   You are very confident of your skills for success in college and your career.

260–232   You have good skills for success in college. You can always improve.

231–203   You have average skills for success in college.

Below 202   You need some help to survive in college. Visit your college counselor for further assistance or re-read some of the chapters in this text.

Use these scores to complete the exercise "Chart Your Success" as in Chapter 2. Note that the additional points are not used in the chart.

Success Wheel

Name _____ Date _____

Use your scores from "Measure Your Success" to complete the following success wheel. Use different colored markers to shade in each section of the wheel.

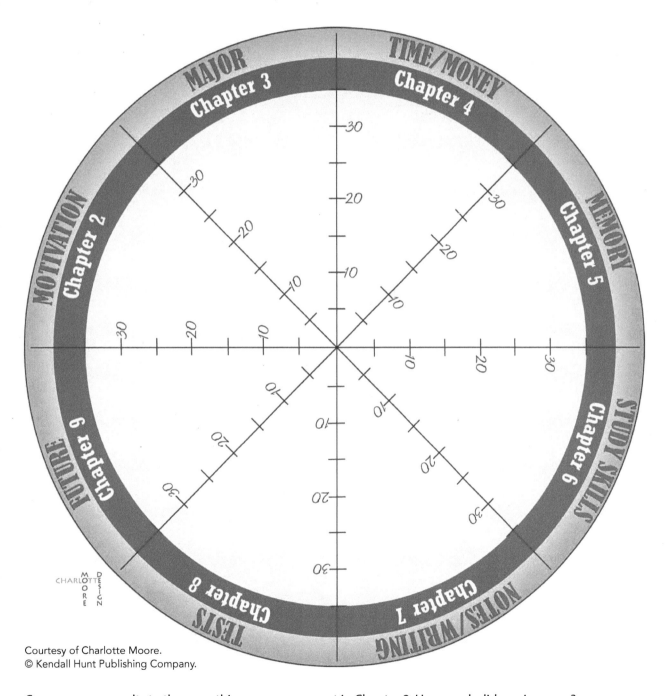

Courtesy of Charlotte Moore.
© Kendall Hunt Publishing Company.

Compare your results to those on this same assessment in Chapter 2. How much did you improve?

Visualize Your Success

Name _____ Date _____

To be successful, you will need a clear mental picture of what success means to you. Take a few minutes to create a mental picture of what success means to you. Include your education, career, family life, lifestyle, finances, and anything else that is important to you. Make your picture as specific and detailed as possible. Write about this picture or draw it in the space below. You may wish to use a mind map, list, outline, or sentences to describe your picture of success.

Happiness Is . . .

Name _____ Date _____

Think of small things and big things that make you happy. List or draw them in the space below.

Intentions for the Future

Name _____ Date _____

Look over the table of contents of this book and think about what you have learned and how you will put it into practice. Write 10 intention statements about how you will use the material you have learned in this class to be successful in the future.

1.

2.

3.

4.

5.

6.

7.

8.

9.

10.

Stories from the Elders

The story you are about to read is one that is shared with us from the Maidu Tribe located in Northern California. The story of "To'lowim Woman and Butterfly Man" has as its main intention to teach about self-control and to be faithful and dedicated to the family. Within this story are several ideas that correlate to the subject of motivation as discussed in this chapter.

To'lowim Woman and Butterfly Man

Based on a Maidu story

In the old days, during the time of the Deer Drive, To'lowim Man was fishing and hunting with his tribal brothers and when they returned home they would begin ceremonies to give thanks. To'lowim Woman was a good wife and mother, but she was bored during these days when women were to keep their distance from the men.

On a bright and sunny day, To'lowim Woman decided to take a walk with her baby. She carried her baby in a cradleboard, strapped to her back, and walked out to see the beautiful flowers that were in bloom. Along the way, she looked for berries and roots, and eventually saw various brightly colored flowers. After awhile, she sat beside a shady bush to rest, while her baby laid safely asleep in his cradleboard. Soon a large and brightly colored butterfly flew by her.

To'lowim Woman was amazed by the butterfly's beauty. She had never seen a butterfly so large, so strong, and with such vibrant colors like blues as deep as turquoise, yellows like the golden poppies, and greens like the iridescence of the abalone shell. To'lowim Woman was mesmerized by its beauty. She reached out to touch the butterfly and it stroked her hand as it flew by, sending a shiver through her body.

Without thinking much about her baby and knowing that the baby would sleep safely under the shady bush, To'lowim Woman ran after the butterfly. She hadn't felt the ticklish feel of passion for some time and she knew she had to catch this butterfly for her own. She ran this way and that way following the fluttering butterfly. Each time she stretched to catch the butterfly, it flittered further away and To'lowim Woman lost all sense of time and distance.

As the day turned to dusk, To'lowim Woman found herself in a valley she had never seen before and she dropped to the ground with exhaustion. Soon the butterfly landed next to To'lowim Woman to keep her safe through the dark night. When she awoke as the morning sun warmed her face, she found a handsome and strong man holding her in his arms. He said, "I am Butterfly Man and you have followed me to this Butterfly Valley. Come with me and we will have a happy and safe life together." To'lowim Woman could not resist the passion she felt for Butterfly Man, so she agreed to follow him. He warned her to hold on to his belt. He told her she would be enchanted by other butterflies along the way, but if she held on tightly and stayed the course, they would reach his home before sunset.

As they traveled through the beautiful valley, filled with flowers that To'lowim Woman had never gazed upon before, she became very excited about her new life. She knew she would be happy with her Butterfly Man and that she would never feel the boredom of the past. They wove through the valley swiftly, and butterflies approached. Many of vibrant virile colors like red, purple, and orange flew close to To'lowim Woman, taunting her to reach out for just one touch. She tried to stay the course, but could no longer restrain herself and reached out with one hand to touch a huge butterfly. She lost her hold of Butterfly Man and soon found herself in a whirlwind of thousands of butterflies leading her in every direction.

Humankind has not woven the web of life. We are but one thread within it. Whatever we do to the web, we do to ourselves. All things are bound together. All things connect. We are a part of the earth and it is part of us."

Chief Seattle, Suquamis

Everything a power does, does in a circle."

Lakota

Butterfly Man continued on his journey and To'lowim Woman could not reach him, even though she tried. The butterflies clouded her vision and eventually, she lost all sight of Butterfly Man. To'lowim Woman kept chasing her butterfly dreams, but could never catch one. Her clothes became tattered and torn as she brushed against thorny bushes and trees, and eventually To'lowim Woman found herself nearly naked. The people say To'lowim Woman lost her way in the valley and never returned home.

Notes

For more information about the Maidu Tribe of California, visit their website at www.maidu.com.

References

Kroeber, Theodora. 1959. *The Inland Whale.* California: University of California Press.

Woodhead, Henry, and Jane Edwin. 1994. *The American Indians: The Indians of California.* Richmond, Virginia: Time Life Books series.

"Every fire is the same size when it starts."

Seneca

Talking Circle

Use these questions for discussion in a talking circle or consider at least one of these questions as you respond in a journal entry. For the talking circle, students sit in a circle and one student speaks at a time. The professor asks a question and the first student on the left responds. Then move to the next student on the left to continue the discussion. Students may pass if they do not wish to speak. It is important to listen carefully and respect the contributions of each student.

1. What are some of the possible challenges you will encounter with self-control as you begin to focus more time and energy toward your study?

2. How will your family, friends, or community respond to your time away from them?

3. How can you help your family, friends, and community to better understand and appreciate the educational/career goals you have set for yourself?

4. What characteristics do you share with To'lowim Woman?

5. To'lowim Woman struggles with creating balance in her life and she lets passion take control. How is passion related to your life's goals on a personal and educational level?

6. What will it mean to you if you are pulled in other directions by the butterflies? Can this be a positive reaction?

The story you are about to read is one that comes to us from the Hopi Nation and it is the story of The Youth Who Brought the Corn. The Hopi live a very traditional life even in today's modern world. They live primarily on reservation land and even though they have all the modern conveniences of city life, they practice a strict ceremonial social structure that, often times, revolves around the sustenance of life.

In this story you will meet a young character who must endure several challenging tests as he prepares to take a courageous journey to help his people. As you read this story, think about the correlations that may exist for you as a college student taking your courageous journey through higher education. College is challenging because you are learning about a new culture of higher education, new expectations for behavior and for improving your ability to learn. This can be a foreign experience for those who come from communities where few have attended college, or from communities that are group focused. College, in many ways, asks you to think and act as an individual, even though you may be a part of a close-knit community. As you build your confidence with test taking, you will be able to demonstrate your learning through an individual challenge—the exam. This takes courage, persistence, and belief in one's own ability to be successful.

The Youth Who Brought the Corn

Based on a Hopi story

Long ago the ancient people lived in a wonderful land where there was an abundance of rain and the corn grew plentiful. Their gods had sent them a message to travel to new lands and eventually they came upon a land that was drier, but their gods advised them to make this their new home. It seemed the gods had forsaken them, but being a peaceful and obedient people, they built their new village.

The days passed and skies stayed clear with no rain in sight. The people began to worry and were filled with doubt about this new home. A wise old man came to them. His presence seemed to bring a peacefulness to their hearts and he said to them, "Do not despair because your sadness gives Masauwuh strength. Masauwuh will feed upon your fears and bring evil days and hunt for spirits. My sisters are wives to the great Calako; pray to them and they will help you."

With this the people built two altars to offer prayer sticks to Calako and ask for his help. They knew that when Calako appeared, his feet would set upon the earth and create a deep gorge. They brought big rocks for Calako to stand upon. After much labor, the men began to swing their rattles, but they did not know the magic song. As they stood quietly, afraid to go on, a youth stepped forward and took the largest rattle. He shook the rattle and sang a loud and melodic song.

Soon they heard loud gushing waters, but saw no water. Then they heard the sound of whirling winds, but not even the feathers on the altars moved. As they looked at the largest rock on the altar they noticed a deep hole had been pierced through, and from there the sounds emerged.

The people were terror-stricken and retreated, as they had never witnessed such an occurrence before. The youth stayed strong and a voice spoke to him, "I have heard your good song. Let the one with courage among you come down and greet the Germ God." The young man responded, "I am strong, and I will help my people. Tell me how to enter the Underworld?" "Touch the rock and close your eyes," said the voice.

With that, the boy touched the rock and the hole enlarged and seemed to pull him through. As he emerged from the rock he saw a beautiful room adorned with abalone shells, sky blue turquoise, and deep red coral. Standing there was a divine being holding a shining shield in one hand and a yucca whip in the other. By his side sat his two wives who were exceedingly beautiful and arrayed with fine garments. They wore great headdresses of clouds and every kind of corn which they were to give to the Hopi to plant for food. These were white, red, yellow, blue, black, blue and white speckled, and red and yellow speckled corn, and a seeded grass (kwapi).

Calako said to the boy, "You will have to endure pain and suffering while you are here. But, if you survive and are strong of will, you can carry back to your people gifts of the highest value."

The boy replied, "I am ready to take this challenge, my people are depending upon me."

"Bow down before me, and we will see," said Calako.

The god raised the Yucca whip and began to whip the boy's back. Each searing stroke left a red welt across his young flesh. With his back bruised and swollen, the beatings finally stopped and through it all the boy never let a squeal or sob leave his lips.

Finally, Calako said, "You have proven yourself worthy, come with me to the altar." There he gave the boy a plumed and beaded prayer stick and told him that each year the stick should be planted at the altar the people had built and in return, he would send good crops. Calako also gave the boy a pouch of corn seeds to plant and directed him to put his hands upon the rock. It opened and the boy crawled through to find his family and friends on the other side. The people were saddened to see his wounds, but the boy said, "Do not worry. The great Calako will provide for us. I will heal and I have survived the test of suffering that Calako presented me, and now I have these seedlings and this prayer stick for you, my people. Calako has appointed me to be the chief of his altar. We will have food for many seasons."

The boy went on to lead his people as a chief and to teach others. After many other challenges, Calako eventually returned to them his blessings, and since that time the Hopi make a feast to Calako every year called Powamu. It is said that Calako challenges the Hopi youth to test their bravery to this day.

> "I shall see our young braves and our chiefs sitting in the houses of law and government, ruling and being ruled by the knowledge and freedom of our great land. So shall we shatter the barriers of our isolation. So shall the next hundred years be the greatest and proudest in the proud history of our tribes and nations."
>
> Chief Dan George, Salish

Notes

For more information about the Hopi Tribe of Arizona, visit their official tribal website at: http://www.hopi-nsn.gov/

References

Harper Fussell, Betty. 1992. *The Story of Corn.* New York: Alfred Knoph.

Mullett, G.M. 1979. *Spider Woman Stories.* Tucson, Arizona: University of Arizona Press.

Talking Circle

Use these questions for discussion in a talking circle or consider at least one of these questions as you respond in a journal entry:

1. The young boy in this story had to call upon an inner strength to be able to meet the challenge that Calako placed before him. Describe the source of your inner strength. What is it that you call upon when the going gets rough?

2. The young boy was asked to act independently as he took the challenge of visiting the underworld and bringing back the corn and the prayer stick. In the end, the boy received many gifts. What were some of those gifts? What gifts do you think you will receive as you learn to be a successful test taker? Who will benefit from your educational success?

3. Masauwuh is a god that threatens famine and takes weak spirits in this story. Some believe we all have challengers in our lives. These can be people that we know, circumstances we have experienced, or inner thoughts. What are some of your "Masauwuh" obstacles? How can you overcome these as they relate to test-taking and college success?

4. What characteristics do you share with the young boy?

You have just explored techniques that can improve your ability to learn. You have explored your personality and you now know that we are all a compilation of multiple intelligences. We can learn to develop areas of weakness and to expand the breadth of our strengths. Through college and life, you will be exposed to different environments and given varying tasks, some work well with your strengths and others will not. Our hope is that you will practice strategies that will help you to have success in most everything you do. Some successes will be greater, but the point is to always complete the task at hand as best as you can. The story you are about to read comes to us from the Karuk peoples of Northern California.

How Coyote Got His Cunning

When Kareya first created the world, he created every living creature as equals. He soon realized that this would not work for the world, so he went to the first man and said, "Since I have made you wiser with the intelligence to think with your brain and speak with your mouth, to walk about on two legs, and to sense the aroma and beauty around you; I will trust you with an important task. Go out and make all the bows and arrows you can. Be sure to use strong materials so that you can be proud of your work. Make them of all sizes and so plenty that there will be one for every animal I have created on this earth."

The man went out to the woods to find the best wood for making the bows and arrows and after nine long days of labor, he had created them all. He went back to Kareya and said, "I have used my wit of mind, my skill of hand and tool, and I have created for you many bows and arrows of all sizes for your animal creatures. Some are of fancy colors with feathers I have collected in the forest."

Kareya responded, "You have done good work and you will see the benefit of this labor for all time. Now, go out and gather all of my animal creatures."

When all were assembled, Kareya told his creatures, "As you can see before you, many, many bows and arrows have been created. Some are large, some are small, some are long, and some are wide, but the one who takes the longest bow will be the strongest among you all. Go now and rest, for the dawn will come soon and we will know who will be the strongest."

The animal creatures all stayed nearby, planning and scheming about how to get the longest bow. Coyote thought, "If I stay awake all through the dark night, I will be the first to see Kareya as the sun begins to peak its rays of light, and I will get that longest bow."

So coyote stayed awake, as one by one he saw the beaver, the otter, the owl, and all the others drift off to sleep. As coyote thought about the morning and that longest bow he had seen, the one with two red stripes and two eagle feathers as adornments, his eyes became heavy, and heavier, so coyote stood up. "No," he thought, "I cannot fall asleep now." He walked around being careful not to wake the others and tried to sing a song in his head to keep himself awake.

As the sun began to shine its first rays of light, there lay poor coyote asleep to the world. Kareya and the man greeted all the creatures and gave out the bows, the longest going to cougar and bear, and all down the line. Meanwhile, coyote slept through it all.

When he awoke, there beside him lay the shortest of all the bows and arrows. All the other animals thought it so funny that coyote, the boastful one, had slept through it all. Coyote was embarrassed and began to pray for Kareya's help. Kareya helped coyote by giving him more cunning than all other animals, "You may be foolish of heart, but I hear your prayers and I know you tried to stay awake all night long. I will give you the gift of cunning and you can outsmart even those with the largest bows!"

> "Knowledge was inherent in all things. The world was a library and its books were the stones, leaves, grass, brooks and the birds and animals that shared, alike with us, the storms and blessings of the earth. We learn to do what only the student of nature ever learns, and that is to feel beauty."
>
> Chief Luther Standing Bear, Oglala Sioux

The Karuk Tribe

The Karuk Tribe of California, a federally recognized Indian Tribe, occupies some 1.4 million acres of land located in Siskiyou and Humboldt Counties of northern California. The ancestors of the current Karuk people were among the earliest inhabitants of north-western California and are close neighbors to the Yurok and Hupa. Their land is heavily forested and mountainous country where the Klamath and Salmon Rivers flow. Historically, the tribe had great salmon fishermen, hunters, and gatherers. They are known for the great connection and care of the land and use of fire as a land management tool. They lived at one with the land and created sustainable environments without degrading the land base. For more information about the tribe visit: http://www.karuk.us

Reference

Erodes, Richard, and Alfonso Ortiz. 1984. *American Indian Myths and Legends.* New York: Pantheon Books.

Talking Circle

Use these questions for discussion in a talking circle or consider at least one of these questions as you respond in a journal entry:

1. Coyote gets his cunning almost by accident. He planned to be the winner of the largest bow, but instead he gets the shortest, but still comes out a winner. Can you relate this to a time when your results were not in accordance with your plan? Or a time when you were pleased the results differed?

2. When considering your own personality type, with which creature do you relate the most? The story mentions the coyote and his cunning, but what personality traits and intelligence strengths would you associate with cougar, bear, and owl? Which is more closely aligned with your own traits? Which has traits you would like to emulate or strengthen?

3. How will you learn to utilize your skills and minimize the weaknesses as coyote has done? In the end the boastful coyote gets the small bow, but gets the skill of keen cunning. This skill has, most likely, saved his breed from extinction. How will you learn to capitalize on your strengths?

The Gifts of Gluscap

Four brothers were unhappy with their place in life and felt that if Gluscap, the creator of so many things, would listen to their plea, life would be so much better for them. So they set out to find the great giant Gluscap and beg him to help. Off they went into the forest in search of the great Gluscap. After some time, they sat by a spring to rest, when all of a sudden Gluscap, the all-knowing, appeared to them.

"What do you four brothers want of me? I have heard your voices carried to me by the North winds that you seek my help?" asked Gluscap.

The first brother stood and said, "Many have said you have created the animals and all the trees in the forest, and that sometimes you do good deeds for the people. I am but an angry man with a disagreeable disposition. I find fault with everyone and carry a frown upon my face. I ask you to help me become a gentle and kind spirit."

The second brother stood and said, "As you can see by my attire, I am but a poor man. I spend most of my days begging others to share their bounty with me. Most people look the other way when they see me nearby. I want to be a rich man, with a beautiful home filled with many friends to care for."

The third brother knelt in homage to Gluskap, and said humbly, "Great One, you do not know what it is to live among your people, who laugh when you are near. They think me foolish and simple-minded. I want to walk among my tribe as an ordinary man and be looked upon with respect, if you will, oh great one?"

The fourth brother jumped out in front of the others and said, "Gluscap, my request is a simple one. As you can see, I am of keen intelligence and a handsome man of good build and height, but I want to be the best of all. I want to be the tallest of all my tribe, the most handsome of all men, and I know that I deserve this gift."

Gluskap responded to the four brothers, "I see you have traveled a long way to find me and that you have thought about these requests for some time. I will give you each a gift of a medicine pouch, but go now and open your pouch when you arrive home."

The brothers headed home eagerly awaiting the gifts they carried in their pouches. Upon arriving home the first three brothers opened their pouches and poured the contents into their hands. The fragrance of the medicine was so enticing they began to rub the medicine on their chests and arms and all about. Soon the angry discontented brother had a smile on his face and his heart was filled with peacefulness. The poor beggar soon became wealthy and loved by all his people. The simple-minded brother was soon worthy of respect and began to lead his people.

Now, the fourth brother, filled with conceit, could not wait to arrive home to open his pouch. He stopped along the way and tore the pouch open. No sooner had he done so, he grew tall and stately and he smiled with pride. He spread his arms out wide and said, "Oh, I will be the tallest and most handsome of all." Suddenly, more arms appeared, more and more, and soon he became the tallest of all the pine trees in the forest, each arm a prickly branch of pine needles.

> "Everyone who is successful must have dreamed of something."
>
> Maricopa

Notes

The Algonquian of the East Coast are comprised of several tribes including the Wabanaki, the Ojibwa, and the Anishinabe as well as several others. The Algonquians of the East Coast regard themselves as the original people. Many believe in a giant character known as Gluscap (Glooskap, Gluscab) who is said to have come to the earth in a stone canoe when there were no people living on the land. Gluscap is credited with creating the constellations and stars, all the animals of the earth, and the people.

References

Burland, Cottie, and (revised by) Marion Wood. 1996. *Library of the World's Myths and Legend: North American Indian Mythology.* London: Chancellor Press (imprint of Reed International Books Limited, Michelin House).

Gill, Sam D., and Irene F. Sullivan. 1992. *Dictionary of Native American Mythology.* New York: Oxford University Press.

Talking Circle

Use these questions for discussion in a talking circle or consider at least one of these questions as you respond in a journal entry:

1. Careful planning will result in many rewards or gifts. In this story of the four brothers receiving gifts from Gluscap, which gift is more closely aligned with your own desires for the future?

2. Researching career options is an important step in your future success. Some majors or careers may appear to be different than they actually are. Can you draw parallels with the fourth brother's request and what he received?

3. The brothers had planned their request and they were clear on their desired needs, and the payoff worked for three, but not the fourth. Why do you think this is so?

4. Has there been a time in your life that you attained a goal or received a specific gift that you had desired, and in the end were disappointed? Why is it that the accomplishment or the gift was not all you had expected it to be? How will you avoid this type of pitfall when it comes to planning your career and education?

Communication styles and relationship building are key to success in life. Understanding your personality and communication style will serve you well as you learn to navigate different environments. Developing listening skills and taking responsibility for your words contribute to your ability to communicate effectively. Friendships, significant others, family members, and community are all part of your inner circle and can play a major role in your success in college and in life. Learning to deal with loss is another part of maturing and coping with the complexity of relationships and life itself. Learning to interrelate in your home and community may require certain skills that often collide with the communication skills needed in the college world. Often times, we are asked to learn several different modes of communication, those that work best based on the setting in which we find ourselves. This can be a challenge, but if you can identify those skills needed in each of the settings you live and work, you will find greater success.

The story you are about to read comes to us from the Iroquois people and it focuses upon the relationship of a family unit and loss.

The Wooden Doll, Iroquois, Northeast

A man lived alone with his wife far from the village. They had no children, but they loved and cared for one another. He always said to her, "You are the love of my life and when you go with me to the hunt, I am always successful. I am proud to be your husband and to take care of you."

When his wife stayed at home, she cleaned their lodge and tended to the garden. She seemed to be growing thin and the husband worried about her well-being. "I must make a good catch today, my wife needs to eat some good meat," he thought.

One day, when he arrived home he found his wife lying in the garden, burning with fever. He quickly went out to pick some healing herbs and made a tea for her. He burnt some sage and blessed her and prayed to the creator, "Please heal my good wife. She is all I have and I don't know what I will do if you take her to the spirit world now."

By the morning, his wife had died. The man was filled with sorrow and great pain. He moped around and did not go out to hunt for many, many days. Finally, one day he realized he needed food, the clothes needed to be washed, the garden was ready to be harvested, so he went about his work. He did all his own work and that of his wife's, and went to bed at night so very, very tired. But still, he missed her so.

The next day as he headed out to hunt, he came across a tree that had tumbled over. He sat on the log for a while and felt a certain message coming through the log. He said to himself, "I will drag this tree home, and use it to carve a likeness of my wife. At least that way I will remember what

she looks like since her beautiful face is starting to fade in my memory."

When he was all done, he dressed the wooden doll in his wife's favorite buckskin fringed dress. He adorned the doll with earrings, beads, and soft moccasins. She was beautiful. He began to talk to her as if she were his wife. He felt a little better and went out to hunt again and life began to feel normal.

One day, when he arrived home, the fire was already lit, but his wooden doll wife was still sitting in the same place she was when he left in the morning. "That is strange. I wonder who lit that fire?" he said. This went on for several days, the fire was always lit, food was cooking in the kettle, but his wooden wife was still seated in her chair.

He decided he would sneak home early one day to see what was going on. When he arrived, he found his wooden wife had become alive again. He couldn't believe his eyes and he was overjoyed with happiness. She quickly warned him, "I am here because creator felt so sorry for your sadness, but you cannot touch me. If you do, I will turn to wood again. Take me to the

"You must speak straight so that your words may go as sunlight into our hearts.
Cochise, Chiracahua Apache

"May the stars carry your sadness away,
May the flowers fill your heart with beauty,
May hope forever wipe away your tears,
And, above all, may silence make you strong."
Chief Dan George, Salish

village, and when the medicine man blesses me, then and only then can you touch me."

The man and wife headed toward the village. The man still couldn't believe his eyes, and soon he could no longer control his urge. He reached out and pulled her close to his heart and as he did, she became stiff and cold and was wood again. He screamed with rage and threw her to the snow covered ground. The people in the village heard his wailing and came out to see what was going on. He cried to them, "Look at my wife, she has turned to wood. What am I to do?" They all looked at one another and thought this man is out of his mind. "That is a wooden doll, not his wife," they mumbled among one another. He stood up and said, "I know what you are thinking, but I am telling you the truth. Look, at the footprints, there are mine large and wide, and see another set small and thin!" The people looked and realized that the man was telling them the truth.

Notes

The Iroquois peoples live primarily in upstate New York and in Canada. Some of the original Iroquois Leagues were composed of the Mohawk, Oneida, Onondaga, Cayuga, and Seneca, and the Tuscarora nation. They became known as the Six Nations. The current day Six Nations is the largest First Nation in Canada with a total of 23,902 members. The Association of Iroquois and Allied Indians (AIAI) is a non-profit organization which advocates for the political interests of eight member Nations in Ontario. For more information on the Iroquois, the Six Nations, and the AIAI visit: http://www.aiai.on.ca

Reference

Ferguson, Diana. 2001. *Native American Myths.* London: Collins and Brown.

Talking Circle

Use these questions for discussion in a talking circle or consider at least one of these questions as you respond in a journal entry:

1. In this story, the man loses his wife to illness and is at a loss to continue his life. College students often find that when they have lost a significant person in their life due to illness, death, or separation, that focusing upon education can be a challenge. Have you ever experienced this type of loss? How did it affect your productivity? What can you do to overcome loss?

2. The man creates a wooden doll to fill the void of his lost wife and lost relationship. It seems to fill his need on a temporary basis and allows him to begin to function again in life. Has there ever been a time in your life when you have taken temporary measures to deal with a difficult obstacle? Was the "temporary fix" worthwhile, or did you regret those actions?

3. The man finds his happiness again when his wooden doll comes to life. Because of his impatience and lack of self-control, he loses that which is most important to him. College and life success requires a fair amount of patience and self-discipline. Can you share how you are learning to master these skills as they relate to college success and career success? What are the challenges you are encountering as you focus more and more upon your studies?

The story you are about to read tells us how the Lakota/Sioux believe the sacred bundle and pipe came to them through the beautiful White Buffalo Calf Woman. They believe that this sacred pipe provides guidance and keeps their tribe strong. As one elder stated, "When you smoke the pipe, only truth can be heard."

Becoming a successful college student helps you to develop skills that will improve your life in general. If your family is involved in ceremonial life, you may find that the traditions and spiritual practices help you to understand the cycle of life and give your life greater meaning. In moderation, many ceremonies include the use of alcohol and tobacco offerings. However, avoiding addictions to alcohol and tobacco can help you to maintain your good health. Read the story and see if you can draw some parallels to your own life and personal well-being.

White Buffalo Calf Woman

A Sioux/Lakota story

During a very difficult time for the people, when food was scarce and starvation nearby, the Chiefs decided to send out two young warriors who had proven themselves as courageous and upright to go out on the plain and look for food.

The two young men prepared one evening by listening to their elder's advice and counsel. "Go out and be observant of all that you see. Look for the special signs of the buffalo, listen to the birds, feel the wind's voice, and open your hearts to the sun for guidance. Come back to us when you can lead us to the buffalo. Remember all the teachings of your youth and stay pure of thought and faith."

In the early morning, just as the sun was rising, the two set out on their journey. They traveled for some time enjoying the peacefulness of the early morning calm. After some time, they came upon a ravine that had a cool stream of mountain water trickling through. They found a shady spot and took a rest to consider what they had seen. As they chatted about which direction to take next, one of young warriors saw movement up upon the crest of the mountain where the sun's rays were glistening through.

"Look, do my eyes deceive me? Is there a woman dressed in white up on the ridge?" he asked his brother.

"How strange, yes, what would a woman, all alone, be doing out here on the range? She must be a special sign, the one the elders told us to look for," he replied.

As the woman descended down toward the ravine, her beauty far surpassed any they had ever seen. She wore a white buffalo calf skin, so pure and smooth. The two boys looked at one another in awe, for neither had ever seen a pure white buffalo before.

The first youth gasped, without thinking about the counsel from his elders, "She is the most beautiful woman I have ever seen. I must feel the warmth of her body close to mine."

His brother warns him, "Take care, she must be a sacred one. Look at her beauty and the perfect pelt she wears. Discard those lustful thoughts and remember the teachings of our past."

They are drawn to her magnificent light and they approach the beautiful apparition. As the first youth reaches out to touch her, she says, "Come closer, I know you want to caress me."

As he does, an ominous cloud of mist surrounds the two. Suddenly a gust of wind blows the cloud away and the other youth sees that his brother has turned to dry bones.

The sacred one says, "You are the warrior with a pure spirit. Return to your people and tell them that I am coming. I will help them find the way to peace and sustenance."

The youth turns and hurries back to camp. Once there he tells his elders about all that he has seen and about the terrible fate that has come to his brother. He tells them to prepare because the great apparition is coming soon.

When White Buffalo Calf Woman arrives at camp, she is carrying a sacred bundle. She tells the chiefs, "You sent me two young men, one of honor and one with weakness. It is because of the honorable one that I come to teach you these sacred ways. This bundle, this red pipe, and this sacred tobacco will keep your people strong. Use it to pray for food and the buffalo will come to you. Use it to pray for peacefulness, and you will see

> "Love your life, perfect your life, beautify all things in your life. Seek to make your life long and its purpose in the service of your people."
>
> Tecumseh, Shawnee

the morning sun rise. Use it to pray for healings and you shall live a healthy life."

She opened the sacred bundle to offer to the four directions, and laid the bundle in front of the chief. It contained a pipe made of beautiful red stone with a carving of a bison calf on one side and 12 eagle feathers adorning the other.

With that, she turned and walked away. In silence the people watched her as she appeared to glide into the sunset. At first they see the beautiful woman and as she moves she transforms into a white buffalo.

Since that time, the people have honored her teachings and keep the pipe sacred.

Notes

Sioux/Lakota Tribe-Plains Region of the U.S.

The Sioux Nation is made up of seven original councils with Lakota, Dakota, and Nakota being three. Many tribes, especially those located in the Plains relied upon the buffalo for much of their sustenance and for that reason hold the buffalo in high esteem. The meat, the skin, and the bones were used as a source of food, clothing, shelter, tools, and for ceremonial adornments.

The story you just read is widely told with variations, but at the heart of the story is the teaching of living a spiritual life, observing ceremonies, and using the pipe to promote peace and prosperity for the tribe.

For more information about the Lakota/Sioux tribes of the Great Plains, visit http://www.oglalalakotanation.org/OLN/Home.html or http://www.rosebudsiouxtribe-nsn.gov

References

Gill, Sam D., and Irene F. Sullivan. 1992. *Dictionary of Native American Mythology.* New York: Oxford University Press.

Woodhead, Henry, and Jane Edwin. 1992. *The American Indians: The Spirit World.* Richmond, Virginia: Time Life Books series.

Woodhead, Henry, and Jane Edwin. 1993. *The American Indians: The Buffalo Hunters.* Richmond, Virginia: Time Life Books series.

Talking Circle

Use these questions for discussion in a talking circle or consider at least one of these questions as you respond in a journal entry:

1. The two young warriors had a reputation of being courageous and upright, yet their behavior told another story. When it comes to healthful living, are there times that your words do not support your actions?

2. The White Buffalo Calf Woman was seen as magnificently beautiful. What were the qualities of that beauty? How do you define beauty in your culture? Is beauty connected to health?

3. The second young warrior remembered his tribal teachings and that helped him to make good decisions. The elder told the warriors, "Go out and be observant of all that you see. Look for the special signs of the buffalo, listen to the birds, feel the wind's voice, and open your hearts to the sun for guidance. Come back to us when you can lead us to the buffalo. Remember all the teachings of your youth and stay pure of thought and faith." What are some of the teachings of your elders that can help you to maintain your peace of mind and take good care of your health?

4. The buffalo is a magnificent creation of nature and much revered by many Native peoples. Why do you believe this animal is so important to the people? What are some characteristics of the buffalo that make them strong and important? Do you share any common characteristics with the buffalo?

Aboriginal   This term refers to the people who first occupied a geographical area.

Acronym   Acronyms are short cuts in our language using the first letter of each word in the phrase to create a new word. For example, NASA stands for National Aeronautics and Space Administration.

Acrostic   This is a creative rhyme, song, poem or sentence that helps you to remember. For example, you can remember the oceans with the acrostic "I Am a Person" (Indian, Arctic, Atlantic, Pacific)

Affirmation   This is a true statement. Making positive statements increases success.

Assimilation   This is the process of acquiring the social characteristics and language of the dominant group.

Auditory learning strategies   This is learning through listening and talking.

Brain science   This is another word for neuroscience which is the branch of science dealing with how the brain works, including how we learn.

Chronotype   Chronotype in this textbook refers to your time preference and when you are most alert. It is your prime time for accomplishing challenging tasks.

Cornell format   This is a note taking system for taking organized notes consisting of a recall column and a section for taking notes.

Cramming   In college, this is the practice of waiting until the last minute to study for exams and then studying for a long period of time just before the test. This practice often leads to test anxiety and poor performance.

Critical thinking   One of the goals of higher education is learning critical thinking which includes questioning established ideas, creating new ideas, and using information to solve problems. It includes respect for the ideas of others.

Cultural traditionalism   This concept describes how closely one adheres to traditional culture.

Decoy   In this textbook, a decoy is an incorrect answer on a test. The text provides rules for recognizing a decoy, or incorrect answer.

Distribute the practice   This memory technique involves learning small amounts of material and reviewing it frequently.

Education is our buffalo   In the past buffalos provided everything we needed for survival, including tools. clothing, shelter, threads, and heat from the buffalo chips. Education is our new buffalo. It provides us with everything we need to be good providers for our families.

Elaboration   This is a memory technique that involves adding details and connections to enhance memory. For example, you can increase elaboration by writing the material in your own words, rewriting your notes, using flash cards or creating a mind map.

E-learning strategies   These are strategies for learning or studying online.

Empirical knowledge   This is scientific knowledge based on careful observation of living beings and their environment. In Native culture, this term is closely related to ecology and caring for the earth.

Euro-centric   When people focus on European history and culture and exclude a wider view of the world, they are called Euro-centric.

Existential intelligence   This is one of the multiple intelligences and is defined as the capacity to ask profound questions about the meaning of life and death.

Experiential learning   This type of learning is learning from experience and using all the senses in learning.

Extrinsic motivation   Extrinsic motivation comes as a result of a reward from someone else. For example, money is an extrinsic motivation for working.

Extrovert   This personality type is energized by social interaction and enjoys occupations with much social contact.

Fear of failure   This is a major reason for procrastination.

Fear of success   Fear of success is not taking the last step needed to be successful because success would require major life changes. It is another reason for procrastination.

Feeling type   This personality type makes decisions based on personal values and excels at occupations dealing with people.

First Nations   The descendants of the original inhabitants of Canada are referred to as First Nations peoples.

Future-mindedness   This is thinking about the future, expecting that desired events and outcomes will occur, and then acting in a way that makes the positive outcomes come true.

Gustatory learning strategies   This involves learning through taste.

Hedonist   This refers to a person who wants as many good moments and as few bad moments as possible in life.

Hedonistic adaptation   Some people assume that having more money or possessions leads to happiness, but the more you have, the more you want.

Holistic   This term means looking at all parts as interrelated. For example, Native ceremonies include fire, water, air, and land. Power comes from bringing these energies together.

Indigenous   This term includes all people who are native to the land which they inhabit.

Interpersonal intelligence   This is one of the multiple intelligences and is defined as understanding people.

Intrapersonal intelligence   This is one of the multiple intelligences and is defined as the ability to understand oneself and how to best use your natural talents and abilities.

Intrinsic motivation   This means that you do an activity because you enjoy it and it has personal meaning for you. College students are more likely to be successful if they use intrinsic motivation.

Introvert   This personality type prefers more limited social contacts. They are often described as quiet or reserved. Their personal strengths are helpful in complex occupations requiring quiet for concentration.

Inuit   This term refers to the Native people of Alaska, Northern Canada and Greenland. They are also known as Inupik.

Immediate review   This is a powerful memory technique that involves reviewing immediately after learning something to prevent forgetting.

Intermediate review   This is a short review done periodically to minimize forgetting.

Intuitive type   This personality type focuses on possibilities, meanings and implications and enjoys creative occupations.

Judging type   This personality type is orderly and organized and often excels in business. Note that it does not mean to judge other people, as the term implies.

Kinesthetic learning strategies   This involves learning through movement, as in learning to ride a bicycle.

Loci systems   This is a memory technique that uses familiar places to aid in memory. For example, in a speech, imagine the entryway of a building and associate it with the introduction to the speech.

Locus of control   The locus of control is where you place the responsibility for control over your life. In other words, "Who is in control?" Students using internal locus of control believe that they are in control of their lives and take the steps needed to be successful. Students with an external locus of control blame others and may not take action to be successful.

Long-term memory This type of memory involves storage of memories over a long period of time as contrasted with short-term memory which quickly disappears.

Magical Number 7 Theory George Miller of Harvard University found that the optimum number of chunks or bits of information we can hold in short-term memory is five to nine. It is frequently recommended to group information into 7 categories for the most efficient recall.

Math anxiety You have math anxiety when you have a negative physical or emotional reaction toward math.

Metis In Canada this term is used to describe a person of mixed Indigenous and European ancestry.

Mind map This is a system for taking notes that shows the relationship between ideas in a visual way.

Mindset A mindset is a mental attitude that influences a person's responses and attitudes. A growth mindset involves positive thinking that leads a person to put in the effort needed to be successful. A fixed mindset is based on negative thinking and can be an obstacle to success.

Mnemonic This word comes from the Greek word mneme which means to remember. Mnemonics include memory techniques such as acrostics, acronyms, and loci systems.

Modified three column note-taking method This note-taking method is suggested for taking notes in math and includes a column for key words, examples and explanations.

Multiple Intelligences This is the human ability to design or compose something valued in at least one culture. This definition broadens the scope of human intelligence.

Multisensory integration This means using all the senses to learn more efficiently.

Native American and First Nations College and Career Success.

Naturalist intelligence This is one of the multiple intellegences and is defined as the ability to recognize, classify and analyze plants, animals, and cultural artifacts.

Neuroscience This is the science that deals with the structure and function of the brain, including how we learn.

Olfactory learning strategies This involves learning by using the sense of smell.

Outline method This is a system for taking notes using an outline format.

Peg systems This is a memory device that uses words or numbers and associations to remember lists of words.

Perceptive type This personality type likes to live life in a spontaneous and flexible way and is good at dealing with change. This type may need to work on time management to be successful.

Positive self-talk This means using positive thoughts that influence behavior and increase personal success.

Power writing This system for writing a college term paper includes prepare, organize, write, edit and revise.

Prime time In this textbook, prime time is the time that you are most alert. Use this time to accomplish challenging academic tasks.

Procrastination When you habitually delay or postpone doing important tasks, you are procrastinating.

Resiliency This is the ability to recover from setbacks, adapt to change, and to keep going when faced with problems or challenges.

Revealed knowledge This knowledge comes through dreams, visions, and intuitions.

Self-determination This is the process by which people control their own lives.

Self-fulfilling prophecy   Beliefs that we have about ourselves have such a powerful influence on behavior that the expectations become true.

Sensing type   This personality type learns through experience and trusts information that is concrete and observable. They excel in careers that require detailed work.

Short-term memory   This is often called the working memory which is like a temporary space or desktop used to process information. Information stored in short-term memory quickly disappears.

Signal words   These words are clues to understanding the structure and content of a lecture. Some examples include: in addition, next, first, and most important.

Smart goal   Smart goals are specific, measurable, achievable, realistic and timely.

Smudging   This is a Native American prayer to increase awareness and cleanse the body, mind, emotions, and spirit. The ceremony involves burning cedar, sage, or sweet grass.

Spatial intelligence   This is one of the multiple intelligences. It is defined as the ability to manipulate objects in space.

SQ4R   This study system for reading a college textbook includes survey, question, read, recite, review and reflect.

STEM occupations   These occupations include science, technology, engineering, and math. They generally have higher incomes and good job outlooks.

Tactile learning strategies   This is learning through touching the material or using a "hands on" approach to learning.

Telegraphic sentences   These sentences are used in note taking and are shortened and abbreviated similar to text messages.

Test anxiety   This is the fear of failing a test which can cause students to have difficulty with recall when taking tests. It is often caused by lack of proper test preparation.

Time bandit   In this textbook, the term refers to the many things that keep us from spending time on important goals.

Thinking type   This personality type prefers logical thinking and excels in scientific, business and technical occupations.

Transculturation   When people are able to successfully navigate between two or more cultures or settings, this is referred to as transculturation.

Values   Values are defined as what we think is important and what we feel is right and good.

Visual clue   This is a memory device that involves using a memory jogger to improve memory. For example, place your keys on your books to remember to take your books to class.

Visual learning strategies   This involves learning through reading, observing or seeing things.

Wishful thinking   In this fallacy in reasoning, an extremely positive outcome is proposed to distract from logical thinking. It is often involved in "get rich quick" scams.

Writer's block   This happens when you cannot think of what to write or how to begin. It is often caused by anxiety about writing.